QUIET
DESPERATION

This book is dedicated to the late
Conrad Rice
and to Nick, Herb, and Patricia

QUIET DESPERATION

THE TRUTH ABOUT SUCCESSFUL MEN

ACKNOWLEDGMENTS

Without the men who shared their lives with me, this book would not be. To them I owe so much.

The late Dr. Carl Rogers planted the seed for this study. He was an exceptional human being and I am grateful for the influence he had on my professional development.

Gary Moore and John Lazar were my sounding boards throughout the project. In many respects this book is as much a reflection of their understanding of the conflicts men are experiencing as it is mine.

My agent, Kathy Robbins, believed in this book when others were incapable of comprehending the changes men were making. She stood by me for three long years before her involvement, commitment and efforts reaped any rewards. I am deeply grateful for her continued support and encouragement. Without her, these men's stories would not be told.

The people at Warner Books—Nancie Neiman, Larry Kirshbaum, Jamie Raab and Bernie Shir-cliff—understood this material when others were afraid of the truths it yielded.

Dr. Lynne O'Shea Thybony plays many roles in my life. She is my best friend, colleague, "adopted" sister, advisor, critic, confidante, and soulmate. Without her criticism of my writing, without her prodding and encouragement this book might have never come to be.

I am indebted to Dr. Nick Cummings, Dr. Herb Freudenberger, Dr. Chip Bell, Bill Ryan and Don Butler. They believed in my talents and abilities when I didn't believe in myself.

Dr. Warren Bennis and Dr. Edgar Mitchell are very special people. Each one, in his own way, has made a great contribution to the field of human relations. I am fortunate to have them as colleagues and friends. Whenever I felt no one understood my findings, I only needed to call them up. They always understood.

My business partners, Dr. Doug Wilson and Mr. Robert Gaynor, have offered thoughtful suggestions and criticism. I am proud to be associated with them.

Leslee Dart read and re-read the early drafts. Her comments helped shape the book into what it is today. I am deeply grateful.

Arlynn Whitaker, Chuck Rubey, Reagan Gray Dyer, Kathleen McDonough, Dick MacPherson, and Bill Ross took their valuable time to read the early drafts of this book.

Mary Powelson has given an enormous amount of time in proofreading the manuscript. Her valuable comments and criticisms have contributed greatly.

I owe a special thanks to Victor Friedman and Sara Ann Friedman for their generosity in opening their home to me and making me part of their family during my first year in business.

Susan Hahn Hilgren, Laurel Paris, Fred Suess, Rob Little, Russ Alley, Chris Kalabokes, Joseph Moore, Kathi Gallagher, Louise Bernikow, Beth Milwid, Mark Millan, Rita Gallagher, Ginger Mews, Charlene Battaglia, Christopher Caproni, Karen Myrland, Ruby Peterson, Stephanie Fine, Nancy and Charles Loewenberg, Terry Pettingill, and Bob Greber have listened to me describe this study for years. It is a true test of friendship that they listened with interest and continued to encourage me.

Pat Rice Prideaux was the best role model anyone could have.

Mom and Pop Messing, thanks for your love.

QUIET
DESPERATION

The mass of men lead lives of quiet desperation.

—Henry David Thoreau

INTRODUCTION:

A STUDY OF SUCCESSFUL MEN

It was never my intention to write a book. In May 1977, I started a market research project, surveying Fortune 500 executives and managers about the problems they faced in leading and developing their employees. My goal was to design a management training program that could conquer these problems.

Most of the managers and executives I spoke with were searching for more than a comfortable leadership style. Our conversations frequently began by exploring career or management problems. However, I noticed the focus would frequently change to broader issues: relationships, marriage, careers, success, dreams, failure, or change. These men would tell me about problems and conflicts held close to their chest. We explored the reasons they were reluctant to talk to peers, spouses, and friends, or what held them back from making the changes they desired. By revealing their inner secrets, these men forced me to look at them from a different perspective. I could no longer treat them simply as "executives."

As they lamented about the burden of their work and home life, they would often say to me, "I don't know how to change. I just know I want to get from *here* to *there*, wherever there is." I challenged them to face the dilemmas and overcome their fears, offering them skills to do so. As a result, I watched these men push

1

themselves to new emotional heights and discover aspects of themselves that had been stifled or suppressed.

Quiet Desperation is a culmination of ten years of fascination and concern about the changes men are currently experiencing. It is a book about the *process*; about the steps men encounter, run from, tackle, fear, challenge, and, finally, overcome. It is a compendium of experiences drawn from 4,126 interviews and an in-depth study of forty-three top-level executives, whose lives were followed for two years. Some of the country's most successful men speak out about power, risk-taking, security, change, competition, extramarital affairs, women, love, intimacy, and trust.

It is a book about and for men who have begun to look inside themselves for the answers that pave the way to true success, and for the women in their lives who want to understand what their men think and feel.

HOW THE STUDY BEGAN

I began my consulting business in 1976 after working as an advertising account executive, as a political appointee for New York Major John Lindsay, and as a manager for a computer manufacturer. Through these experiences, I became unhappy with the way companies treated their employees.

About a year before I started my business, I went through my own identity crisis. My father almost died of a massive coronary. It was the first time death had come so close to me. I remember asking myself, "If I died tomorrow could I say I lived today the happiest way possible?" The answer was, "No. I was living my life as I thought I should." In the past, I had never asked myself what I wanted. But I did then.

While I was "having my identity crisis," I went into psychotherapy with a well-known psychologist. During the course of my treatment, my therapist recognized my raw talent and encouraged me to consider becoming a psychotherapist. I went back to school and began my training.

Early on I knew I wasn't cut out to be in private practice. So I set up a consulting practice that would bring psychology to business, allowing me to blend the two worlds I loved, business and psychology, into a fulfilling profession. It seemed there was a great need for the services I decided to offer: management, communication, and sales training. Within a few years the business had grown to $1.3 million in billings with a training center in New York, a satellite office in San Francisco, and a staff of ten people. We provided training and consulting services to companies such as Bank of America, IBM, Xerox, Lucasfilm, Ralston Purina, American Airlines, International Harvester, Citibank, and various city and state government agencies. Since founding the company, I have personally trained over ten thousand executives and managers.

When I started my business, everyone was entering training and consulting, and I knew for us to survive we had to make it past the five-year mark. And to that end, we had to offer something different from everyone else. I felt my educational and professional training gave me a unique perspective on the business world. While few corporate psychologists have any managerial experience, I had over fifteen years. And few management consultants have experience in counseling and psychotherapy. I had practiced both these disciplines.

In 1978, I began training and subsequently working with Dr. Carl Rogers, the noted humanistic psychologist. I was blessed with the opportunity to share my findings with him and question the way management is taught. In 1981, he selected me to translate his theories for application to the business world. I took the best of the concepts of management theory and combined them with the best of psychological practices. I no longer assumed the role of expert. I did not provide five easy steps for giving a performance appraisal or for making a marriage work. My workshops and individual counseling sessions encouraged people to find their own solutions, to choose what would work for them. Emphasizing that there were many possible approaches to solving a problem, I strove to help managers search for their own leadership styles.

Thus, *Quiet Desperation* grew out of my work with executives and managers across the country. Initially I spoke with only three hundred men. Over eight months I went to Boston, Chicago, Dallas, New York, Seattle, San Francisco, Los Angeles, Tampa, and Phoenix, interviewing a broad sample of men from Fortune 500 companies, in management, sales, and sales management positions. Based on their responses, I felt I was on to ''something,'' but I didn't know what. So I continued talking to any man who would agree to be interviewed.

In the process, I was struck by the comments made by the men because they contradicted many of the myths we have come to believe about successful men, even men in general:

- Men can separate their personal and professional lives. *Rarely.*

- Men are natural-born leaders. *Not necessarily.*

- Men who repress their feelings are stronger than men who respond emotionally. *Not true.*

- Successful men are more secure than unsuccessful men. *Not always.*

- Men at the top are lonely. *Not all of them.*

Then I conducted another study to test my initial findings. I gathered four groups of twenty men, asking them to comment on the findings. When I said, "quiet desperation," men said, "I relate." When I said, "Without my job, I feel like nobody," men said, "I've been there before." When I said, "I've dreamed my wife would run away with someone else or get killed in a plane crash," men said, "My version is slightly different, but I've had the same thought." When I explained my findings, many men said, "I identify with them. That's me."

These eighty men provided confirmation of my findings and gave me the confidence to continue exploring the broader implications these responses might have.

WHERE DID I FIND FOUR THOUSAND MEN?

People often ask how I found four thousand men. What parts of the country did they come from? What positions did they hold? In which companies? What ages?

When I decided to expand my study, the 4,126 men were selected from an available pool of more than ten thousand executives. Because I have worked all over the country, the survey sample is diverse and representative of all geographical areas. I have trained executives and managers from supervisory to senior management positions. Many of the men were recruited from my training workshops.

The majority came from Fortune 500 companies, while a small group of entrepreneurs, professionals, and technical people are represented in the sample. The breakdown is as follows: 1,349 senior-level executives, 1,893 middle managers, 784 professionals (lawyers, accountants, and doctors), 63 technical managers, and 37 entrepreneurs. Their ages ranged from twenty-seven to seventy-eight.

More than two-and-a-half years into this project and approximately two thousand interviews later, I hit a snag. Even though the interviews allowed me to delve into people's underlying thoughts and feelings, I needed a deeper understanding of the many factors affecting their reactions and decisions, an understanding that develops only over time.

To solve this problem, I asked fifty-six clients if they wanted a year's free counseling. In exchange for their time, I would explore in depth the problems and conflicts they faced in their professional and private lives. Forty-three accepted. All forty-three work (or worked) in Fortune 500 companies or are leaders in their fields: I interviewed fifteen corporate presidents or senior executives, fifteen middle managers, nine professionals, and four entrepreneurs. Their ages range from thirty-one to seventy-five. Eight are single, twenty-one are married, eleven are divorced, and three have remarried.

WHY WOMEN ARE NOT INCLUDED

To my women friends' displeasure, I did not include women in this study although many are coping with similar issues and problems in their lives. I decided the only women included in this study would be the men's wives, lovers, and women colleagues.

But even if I were to begin the study today, I would probably not include women. Although many similarities seem to have evolved recently, I believe there are some significant differences between the sexes: their rearing, their attitudes, and their methods of approaching life.

Therefore, rightly or wrongly, I did not want to turn this project into another comparison between the sexes. I felt it would dilute the importance of what these men had to say.

SEXUAL PREFERENCE

I debated long and hard about whether or not to include any cases about gay men. On one hand, gay men are often portrayed negatively. My experience with the successful men who also *happen* to be gay and are included in this study was extremely positive. Gay men not only have to sell their soul the same way straight men do to make it in the corporate world, but the price they pay to suppress their sexuality is an omnipresent factor in any decision socially or professionally. I wanted my reader to have an inside view of a gay businessman, learning that when it comes to business, power, work, and identity issues, the similarities vastly outweigh any differences that might exist. And the source of those differences has nothing to do with sexual orientation.

On the other hand, I didn't want to tell a story noting that a particular man was "gay" and have my reader (if he were straight) consider for a moment that the situation and feelings might not apply to him. Singling out gay men, by denoting their sexual preference, in my mind, would be a great disservice to all my readers. I don't say, "Justin Whitmore, a straight man in his early forties . . ." So I constantly asked myself, Why should I say, "Chris Kennedy, a gay man in his early forties . . ."

So I decided not to highlight whether a man is straight or not. Often it can be deduced when I mention a wife exists. However, there are many men who still live in the closet. For the public— their neighbors, business associates, clients, and family—they masquerade as "straight" men, keeping their "other" life separate and hidden.

I'm sorry that we still live in a world where most people find it difficult to accept people who are different from them; whether it be in philosophy, politics, sexuality, race, or religion. Bringing up this straight-or-gay issue only reminds me of the times men told me how they discriminated against other men if they didn't belong to the "right" country club, if they didn't go to the "right" school, if they didn't think along the same political lines. I hope this book begins to bridge the gap between all men, helping them understand and accept one another, no matter how they choose to live their lives. Above all, I hope the commonality of values, such as integrity and caring for others, will be the overriding force that brings men together.

HOW THE INTERVIEWS WERE CONDUCTED

Whenever I tell people how many men I interviewed, they are amazed. But breaking down the numbers shows the task was not overwhelming. If I had worked a forty-hour week, conducting one-hour interviews with 4,126 men, it would have taken me 103.15 weeks, or a bit less than two years. However, over the actual period of almost six years, the numbers are less daunting: I interviewed 723 men per year.

Every man answered questions covering organizational culture, individual achievement, managing others, and personal feelings about job responsibilities and relationships.

Here's a sampling of the questions:

1. Do you ever feel your company expects you to put your ethics or values on the line? If so, how?

2. Do you think your company cares about its people?

3. Have you made sacrifices to achieve success? Would you make them again?

4. How do you handle conflicts?

5. Do you ever fantasize about leaving your job and doing something else? If so, what?

6. Have you ever asked your subordinates how they feel about your management style?

7. How much value do you place on personal growth?

8. Why did you get married? Have you ever had an affair? If so, how many? What tempted you to do so?

9. How do you feel about women in the workplace?

10. How do you react when you find yourself in a competitive situation with a woman? Would you be happier if women would stop competing for the same jobs?

With the group of forty-three men, our arrangement was a little different. We had an agreement to talk once a month. If something prevented us from meeting in person, we would talk for an hour on the telephone. We made a commitment to each other that nothing would take priority over our agreement. Often traveling on business we would meet at an airline club. Or, having offices on both coasts, I would arrive at my West Coast office at 5:30 A.M. so I could speak with men who lived on the East Coast or in the Midwest.

While the four thousand men provided general answers to the questions, the forty-three men offered a unique and important aspect to the study. During the two years I followed their lives, many of the men were my clients. For the in-depth interviews, I used no standard questionnaire. Since I was the in-house consultant to the companies they worked for, I knew the players discussed and the situations that caused their frustrations. I could appreciate the conflicts and understand their leadership needs or personal problems. Given I was frequently trusted with the confidential details of the business problems they worked on, we could work out solutions and see them implemented. Together we could evaluate their success or failure.

For example, an accounting manager who felt rejected by his wife found that it seriously impaired his leadership abilities at work. With a staff of twenty-three women and seven men, he avoided asserting himself because he feared the women would reject him as his wife had. We worked on ways to deal with the problem at home while also figuring out why he brought it into the office.

I have been asked countless times: How did you get men to open up and talk? I must say that this was rarely a problem. Contrary to popular opinion, men are not insensitive, emotionless creatures. They are caring human beings who are in the midst of questioning who they are and what they want out of life. I found these men longed for someone they could talk to, someone who would *not* tell them what to do but who could understand them and listen to their feelings and thoughts. They longed to explore their problems, to find their own answers. When I asked questions, the men did not perceive it as prying. Instead they sensed that I genuinely cared.

More important, I was learning from these men. They were offering something to me, and I made sure they understood I appreciated their honesty and trust.

THE DATA

I must confess I was behind the times in documenting this information. Only in the past year did I use a computer. Before that

I used the tried-and-true method of card cataloguing learned in grade school. Every bit of information was transferred to three-by-five cards. By the time this process was completed, I had organized the material into 207 major issues and 680 subcategories.

Then I developed a notebook that was used as a cross-reference for the index cards. In this notebook, you could look up any major issue and find the list of subcategories underneath. For instance, if you looked up *competition*, you would find subheadings of: defined, related to productivity, verbal styles of, power and competition, corrupt styles, reasons for, not only in sports, avoidance of, and so forth.

As for the "forty-three," their lives were "reduced" to a summary index card. This card highlighted their major conflicts, outlined what they struggled with, listed their wives, children, lovers and co-workers. Each subject had a backup file that included transcripts, detailed notes, and correspondence.

WHAT TRUTHS DID THE STUDY YIELD?

Whether you are a man or a woman, the courage displayed by the men in this book will draw you into their hearts and minds. When these men take off their masks, revealing their self-doubts and fears, they bring us intimately into their lives.

I saw marriages that might have ended in divorce turn into mutually satisfying, fulfilling relationships. I saw men leave the "ideal" job to live out their lifelong dreams. I saw men bounce back from being wounded by women and learn how to *survive* rather than simply *cope* with their grief. I saw men stop believing that women are always better at feeling than are men. I saw men learn how to master their emotions. I saw men move up the success ladder because they learned to manage people in a way that brings out others' talents.

And so *Quiet Desperation* looks at how men are questioning their roles, wanting to establish an identity separate from work. It looks at how men are disillusioned by the fruits of their success, for it has often resulted in emptiness and confusion. They never thought success would bring unhappiness. Although these initial feelings took them by surprise, many are doing something to change how they feel, which means they are changing their lives.

In short, these men have not run from their conflicts but have courageously faced the emotional pain one must go through to find an inner sense of peace and confidence, and they are redefining what it means to be a man in today's world.

Throughout *Quiet Desperation*, men speak out about the most pressing issues in their lives: those dealing with conflicts of identity, power and relationships.

These men offer ways for other men to find their own truth.

Some people will see themselves in the men portrayed. By seeing, feeling, and being part of someone else's discovery process, we are given a safe haven in which to explore our own feelings. In other chapters people might not relate to the situation described. This provides a different learning opportunity; offering us the chance to question what we feel, what we would do, and in what values we believe. In the end, we have lived through the conflicts and struggles, so we know the triumphs are well deserved.

Quiet Desperation, thus, is a book about men who have the courage to face the problems life presents to one and all. It is a book about men who were not going to be the men sitting at their own retirement dinner, inwardly wondering what it all added up to, why they sacrificed what they did or how they let a relationship with their children slip through their fingers. As they saw career women wanting to have it all, they, too, wanted *their* version of it all. They were never going to say to themselves that it wasn't really worth it.

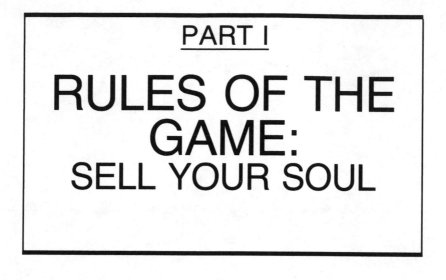

PART I

RULES OF THE GAME:
SELL YOUR SOUL

CHAPTER 1

IS MY LIFE A LIE?

This book is called *Quiet Desperation*, because most of the men I interviewed have been making changes quietly and often in isolation. Few have opened up to their wives or talked to one another about intimate feelings. Instead they have handled their inner turmoil in the proper male fashion, stoically and silently. So they have suffered inside.

And the source of that suffering comes from the fact that men are cut off from who they are. They have been taught to deny their inner world, to avoid their feelings, to live according to prescribed ways of being.

An unspoken rule has guided their actions with one another: "I will never challenge you to be honest with yourself, which ensures that you will never challenge me." They have helped one another perpetuate the game of self-denial and dishonesty.

However, in the process of the interviews I conducted, I continually found men who were challenging the myths that had been previously embraced without question. These men no longer wanted to lie to themselves. Much of my motivation to conduct this study and subsequently write this book came from the desire to describe how these men were dispelling the myths that had guided their actions and feelings for years and were carving out new and better ways to live.

Before I go on to describe for you how they destroyed the myths that caused their suffering, let's look at the definition of "myth" and examine some of the myths that guided these men and possibly are guiding your life.

According to the *American Heritage Dictionary*, 1980:

MYTH:—A notion based more on tradition or convenience than on fact; a received idea.

For instance: Do you believe that men are natural-born leaders? Do you think romance is the stuff that makes a good marriage? Do you think men who show emotions are weak and out of control?

THE MYTHS—IN GENERAL

- *Men are natural-born leaders*—Very few.
- *Successful men have better lives than their less successful counterparts*—Not necessarily.
- *Men at the top are lonely*—Not all.
- *Successful men base their decisions solely on rational factors*—Not many.
- *Men who repress their feelings are stronger than those who respond emotionally*—Not so.
- *Men don't need feedback or approval*—Many do.
- *Men are not dependent on women*—Many are.
- *Affairs will break up a marriage*—Very few.
- *Romantic love makes a good marriage*—Sometimes.

In the rest of this chapter, I describe these myths and challenge them with the findings that resulted from this study. In the chapters that follow, examples of how men have dealt with the issues they are questioning are described in detail.

THE MYTHS AND THE STATISTICS

MYTH: MEN ARE NATURAL-BORN LEADERS

We have been told, "Men are natural-born leaders." But of the men I spoke with, 53 percent admitted to having difficulty telling people what to do. And 71 percent think leaders are made, not born.

I asked senior and middle managers, "How do you communicate your expectations to others?" Of the senior-level executives, 68 percent simply expected people to obey their directives. Only 3 percent were uncomfortable telling people what to do and 29 percent felt they could improve in this area. On the other hand, 55 percent of the middle managers expected people to do as they were told; while at the same time, they found this style ineffective. Of the rest, 21 percent were uncomfortable being the "boss" and 24 percent knew they needed to improve in this area.

Put another way, executives and managers are comfortable hiding behind their title or status to get something done. They expect people will listen to them because of their position, but many men I trained and interviewed questioned whether someone would honor their request if they were stripped of title. These answers are not surprising because we have lived in an era where obeying authority was one of the key ingredients to climbing to the top of the pyramid. However, there is a generation of workers who no longer subscribe to blind obedience. Instead they prefer to challenge, question, and control their own work.

In recent years many top executives have become aware of the fact that expecting people to merely follow their orders hurts morale. In turn, they are making the effort to delegate more decision-making authority. This is not an easy task, for who truly wants to give up control when they have had it for so long? Bob Crandall, the chairman of American Airlines, is an excellent example. Brilliant, quick-minded, and strong, Bob ran American Airlines with tight policies and procedures. Before deregulation the airline industry was routine, predictable, and bureaucratic. Managers' jobs were based on making sure everyone adhered to the policies and procedures established. But in the age of deregulation, when the airline industry is constantly changing, Bob Crandall recognized the need to "push the decision making down to the people who are dealing with the customers." Much of his energy is dedicated to making sure this happens. As a result, his efforts have been most successful in restoring enthusiasm and commitment among American Airlines employees.

MYTH: SUCCESSFUL MEN ARE HAPPY

Daniel Yankelovich, in his book *New Rules*, states:

By the late seventies, my firm's studies showed more than seven out of ten Americans (72 percent) spending a great deal of time thinking about themselves and their inner lives—this in a nation once notorious for its impatience with inwardness. The rage for self-fulfillment, our surveys indicated, had now spread to virtually the entire U.S. population.[1]

When I asked, "Do you feel your life has meaning and direction?" or, "Have you made personal sacrifices to achieve your success? Would you make them again?" initially the answers were not what I had expected.

Only 9 percent of the entrepreneurs have any regrets. Sixteen percent would like more personal time, but three out of four claim they wake up every morning wanting to live life to its fullest and not regretting any of the sacrifices or choices along the way. Few are workaholics and many spend weekends involved in family activities. On the other hand, I discovered of the senior-level executives (1,349 men out of 4,126 interviewed), 68 percent are happy in their professional lives, but feel their family life suffers as a result. Of this group, nearly half admitted they regretted spending so many hours at the job and if they were to do it over, they would spend more time with their wife and children from the onset. Many brushed aside my questions with varying rationalizations, such as: You can't look back, You only have one chance to live life, or, I did what I had to do.

One CEO told me, "The perks are great. I bring my wife along on all my business trips. But she might as well stay home since I never have any time to see her. After forty-five years of marriage I hardly know her. My secretary and I know each other better and we aren't even intimate. And sometimes the headaches of this job are not worth it. I know when I retire my phone will stop ringing because no one will need anything from me then. I have nightmares about that day coming. But as long as I come to work every day, I'm a happy man."

Fifty-eight percent in the middle-management and professional ranks feel they wasted years striving for and achieving their goals, only to find their life empty and meaningless. Where their fathers went to work to earn a living, the generation of middle managers today expect much of their fulfillment to come from their job. Senior-

level executives are only beginning to realize that the work environment has to be a place that offers challenge, involvement, responsibility, and commitment for today's employees.

Jim Gabbert, who owned a broadcasting empire, radio and TV
stations up and down the West Coast and in Hawaii, told me, "I
went through a midlife crisis. I woke up one morning and asked
myself if it was worth it. I wanted to learn how to fly. I wanted to
travel. I wanted some time with the people in my life who mattered.
I had amassed an empire. I knew if I continued I would make
millions, but it wasn't worth it to me anymore." When I asked Jim
if he would do things differently next time, he responded, "That's
difficult to answer. I only know how to live my life based on the
experience I've gained. I don't know any other way. So, the answer
would be, I'd do it the same."

Jim has taken a young man under his wing, teaching him the
ins and outs of the broadcasting business. This young man, Mark,
is in Jim's words, "a workaholic." "I keep telling him to slow
down. He doesn't have to put so much time into his work to do a
good job. You can work less and still accomplish the same amount
without making so many sacrifices. He won't listen to me."

I admire Jim for not looking back and saying "if only . . ."
but instead being able to realize that he wasn't living his life as
satisfyingly as he could. Rather than put himself down, he has
channeled his knowledge into restructuring his life and becoming a
role model for up-and-coming young stars in broadcasting.

MYTH: MEN AT THE TOP ARE LONELY

I think there is some truth to this myth. But I have found the
men who are lonely bring it on themselves.

The division president for a major bank told me, "I don't trust
anyone who works for me. There is no one for me to talk to, to
confide in. And don't even suggest I try to find someone to talk
with. How can you solicit opinions from people you don't respect?"
Then he added, as an afterthought, "I don't need anyone to talk
to." I left his office three hours later, after hardly saying a word
but learning his entire life story.

At one point, I had had the opportunity to ask him if he had
hired or inherited his team. When he told me he had hand-picked
them personally without anyone's help, I no longer felt any sym-

pathy. It was obvious he had created the problem by picking people who were weaker than himself. In the course of my interviews, I discovered the loneliest of men were those who feared being up-staged by others, who had the need to be the best but didn't want any competitors; so they would pick weak people.

On the other hand, the president of a leading computer man-ufacturer told me, "People stopped calling me when I became pres-ident because they thought I was so busy, they should leave me alone. I made sure to correct that misconception fast. I need people to bounce my ideas off of and I like being challenged."

In this particular case it is difficult to accurately state any statistical findings because the answers were often circuitous or evasive; therefore, the understanding was left to interpretation. Ad-mitting to loneliness is difficult and embarrassing for many people because it is associated with not being loved or wanted.

MYTH: DECISIVE MEN BASE THEIR DECISIONS ON RATIONAL FACTORS

Not many do.

The core of this myth is that rational decisions are better than decisions made contrary to logic. Seventy-three of the senior-level executives disagree with this statement. These men confessed to being subjective rather than objective when making decisions. I say "confessed" because they acted as if doing so was a sin, rather than a natural act.

Unless other men admitted to trusting their gut reaction or depending on their intuition, nearly 81 percent of the men confessed that they wouldn't let others know that they based their decisions on factors contrary to logic.

In business, stories go way back about the use of intuition. Andrew Carnegie carried a deck of cards and played solitaire to calm his mind before making a decision. And when Conrad Hilton was bidding for the Stevens Hotel in Chicago, a number popped into his head. He used the number and purchased the world's largest hotel with a bid that won by just two hundred dollars.[2]

In recent years, though, the men I have interviewed between the ages of twenty-five and thirty-five readily admit they trust their feelings. I will often hear them use the expression, "If I listen to what my gut has to say, I would . . ." As so many of the men I interviewed discovered, their intuition is a gift that needs to be cultivated; it is a mental process outside of reason. It doesn't contradict logic, it simply rearranges it.

Although we might not see the majority of middle and senior executives confessing that they depend on their intuition, over time this ability will gain more credibility.

MYTH: MEN WHO SHOW THEIR FEELINGS ARE WEAK

Of the men I interviewed, those who are the happiest in work and at home, who are emotionally secure, who deal with the problems life manages to hand out, are men who depend on their feelings as guides.

Men who are comfortable with their feelings and in turn, with themselves, generally value self-development. I often asked them, "How much value do you place on personal growth?" Their answers would tell me whether they had any understanding of their feelings and motivations. Those who answered affirmatively frequently would elaborate about an exciting insight they had about themselves or someone else and how that helped them approach their work or their relationships in a better way.

Interestingly, of those over forty-five, only 6 percent place a high value on personal growth. Nearly 71 percent don't really care to spend any time being introspective and 23 percent think it merits some attention. And over fifty-five years old the numbers are even smaller.

Conversely, men between the ages of twenty-seven and forty-five place a high value on personal growth, 62 percent to be exact. And 34 percent think it needs some attention. Only 4 percent felt personal growth was a waste of time.

The other area that was of interest to me had to do with intimacy. I asked, "How often do you let people close to you know how much they mean to you?"

One man said to me, "You sound like my wife. She tells me I never tell her how much I love her. I told her, 'I told you back in sixty-six when I asked you to marry me.' But that doesn't make her happy." He wasn't teasing. Fortunately, not all men are that out of touch with their feelings. For the most part, I discovered that men are yearning to express themselves emotionally. The only problem is that they don't know how. But they aren't letting that stop them. They are learning how to understand the logic of feelings, listening to their inner voice and letting it guide them to a greater understanding of themselves.

MYTH: MEN DON'T NEED FEEDBACK OR APPROVAL

Before I began this study, I would talk in my training workshops about the importance of feedback. My comments were always met with resistance. Men would tell me, "I just believe in the saying 'No news is good news,' and I pray."

Then one day I was out in the field with a district sales manager for Ralston Purina. I had been hired to coach and counsel the managers in the western region. At the end of the day we stopped for coffee to discuss his performance. I had gone over his good points and then suggested areas he could improve upon. His eyes lit up as he said, "For twelve years I have been in this job and someone only tells me once a year how I'm doing, unless I screw up, of course. I wish you'd teach my boss how to give us some feedback. Out here in the field alone all day long, we sure as hell need it."

Until that time, I thought men were tough and never needed to hear how they were doing. In my heart I knew differently, but no man had been honest enough with me to confirm my suspicions. This district sales manager gave me the courage to ask other men, "How important is feedback to you?" "Do you give others feedback?" And, "Do you sometimes wish you received more input or suggestions from your boss or the people you work with?"

It took a little probing to get to the heart of their answers. More than 60 percent of the middle managers admitted they wanted more interaction with their boss. As one man said to me, "Like, I wouldn't mind him occasionally mentioning how he thinks I'm doing." Four out of five senior executives replied, "You don't get this high needing to hear how others feel about your performance." Yet, if I pushed the issue, they might admit, "I get tired of being surrounded by yes-men. I wish they had a little courage to speak up." It was difficult to get a clear-cut answer, "Yes, it is very important to me." So in this area I had to use my psychological skills, more than at other times, to interpret the answers.

Although I only interviewed sixty-three technical managers, two out of three said they depend on feedback from their bosses and from their peers. "You can't create in isolation," said one technical manager. And those in the professional category also realized the importance of feedback.

In response to my question, "Do you give feedback?" I was shocked to discover five out of seven executives and managers prefer to lie to an employee about his or her poor performance, rather than to give constructive criticism. Moreover, I was surprised by the reasons. Some 18 percent were worried that their employees wouldn't like them if they were critical; 34 percent weren't sure how to give helpful feedback; 11 percent simply admitted they hoped the employee would improve over time; 8 percent were uncomfortable over the thought of potential conflict.

One executive told me he and his boss decided to give a three-thousand-dollar bonus to the worst salesman, hoping that would be his incentive to improve. They never told him that they were unhappy, or why; they thought he would get the hint. When I asked them if they realized they had reinforced his poor performance, it hadn't even crossed their minds.

Of the 29 percent who are honest with their employees, 68 percent hated being critical but felt it was their job, while 32 percent felt they were making a contribution to their subordinate's development. Looking at this last statistic another way, that's 9 percent of the men interviewed who view feedback as a positive aspect of their management responsibilities.

MYTH: MEN ARE NOT DEPENDENT ON WOMEN

"He brought his wife along. He depends on her to be his emotional radar," said the president of a major bank about his boss.

When I asked men, "Do you feel emotionally dependent on anyone in your life?" 27 percent told me they don't count on anyone. But 41 percent claimed their wife was the only person they confided in. Of the remaining 32 percent, 17 percent avoided answering the question and 15 percent admitted their lover was their confidante over their wife.

I found this latter statistic rather intriguing, so I pursued it further. It seems some men feel they must wear a mask at home, hiding their vulnerabilities and emotional needs. Therefore they seek comfort outside in the arms of a woman who listens to their concerns or satisfies their emotional needs. But after they have unburdened themselves, they replace their mask of bravado and return to "acting" like they have always been in control.

When I asked, "Do you like being needed?" and, "How do you feel about people depending on you?" these questions, too, revealed a different source of a man's dependence. Three out of four men stated that they "need to be needed." Their dependency lies in the fact that without people needing them they question their purpose and meaning in life.

One man told me he had been unhappy for twenty of the twenty-one years he had been married. When I suggested he consider divorce, he replied, "I couldn't do that. I like the fact that she couldn't get along without me."

MYTH: AFFAIRS WILL BREAK UP A MARRIAGE

Would you have ever guessed two out of three men have had affairs? Only one-third would marry the same wife? And less than 3 percent have left their wife for their lover?

Men rarely leave their wives for their lovers. And frequently affairs help keep a marriage together and, in some instances, even help to strengthen a marriage.

An affair can ruin a marriage, however, if a partner flaunts it in front of the other. No matter what the intention is, emotional damage will occur. Trust will be destroyed.

Overall, the majority of men interviewed do not feel monogamy is a natural state. Approximately one-third of the men interviewed choose to be monogamous. The remainder have had between one and four affairs. Some men make extramarital sex a frequent activity.

Ned Cutter had been married for thirteen years when I first interviewed him. Eight years later, after twenty-one years of marriage, he was still actively pursuing women, while he maintained a steady relationship with a divorced woman in Washington, D.C., a city he frequently traveled to on business. "I've got to be frank with you, Jan," Ned began. "I love women and I am not satisfied with having just one woman. My wife never confronts me. I think she probably doesn't want to know the truth. And I'd never tell her because I care for her and don't want to hurt her. Women don't need sex as much as we men do, so we have to get it someplace. And I like diversity, something my lover provides. When I get a little bored, it's quickly conquered by meeting a new girl.''

In the end, because of the emotional dependency that exists, acknowledged or not, the men return to their wife. Sometimes they are stronger, more self-confident, more sexually proficient or less demanding—enabling them to find ways to make their marriage a fulfilling relationship.

MYTH: ROMANTIC LOVE MAKES A GOOD MARRIAGE

"Ever since romanticism replaced the arranged marriage, the assumption has been that people marry for love. This is largely a myth,'' wrote Gail Sheehy in her book, *Passages*.[3] Sheehy conducted 115 interviews, which is equivalent to only 3 percent of my sample. Despite this discrepancy in sample size, our conclusions are identical. I simply heard the same answers 4,011 more times than she did. And my 4,126 responses break down as follows: 10 percent married for love, while 47 percent married for practical reasons, 36 percent married out of insecurity, and 7 percent married for selfish reasons.

I must confess I am a romantic, sentimental sap. No way around it. And until I conducted this study I believed romantic love was what would make marriages work. In the course of conducting these interviews my illusions were shattered. I discovered that couples who married for practical reasons were as happy or happier than those who married for love. Loving someone doesn't always guarantee compatibility, good communication, and commitment—the three C's that make for a good marriage. Loving someone doesn't guarantee that you will like him or her and want to be best friends.

"We weren't in love with one another when we decided to get married. But we did enjoy each other. I don't know whose idea it was. We both seem to have thought of it simultaneously. The fact of the matter was, we shared common interests and thought it was time for us to marry. We hadn't been seeing anyone else, so we thought of reasons why we should break up. We couldn't come up with any. A week later we got married and here we are twenty-three and one-half years later. Not a bad track record,'' said Stan Rosenblum.

His wife, Elena, chimed in, "I thought of Stan as a friend. I always was a tomboy hanging around with him and his friends. I never cared much about having dates in high school or college. Stan was always there. We've known each other thirty-seven years. Sometimes I think that if we got married when we first started hanging around together, we'd be married thirty-one years. I have to tell you I couldn't have made a better choice for a lifelong companion if I had done like my daughters do by making out their lists. I got lucky."

Of those who married for love, 37 percent claimed to be disillusioned by their marriage. And 12 percent said they would marry for different reasons next time. Slightly more than half think they made the best choice of their life.

As Fred Schwarzmann and his wife, Ruth, said simultaneously, "We've been married for thirty-five years and have never been bored. But marriage is more than a fifty-fifty partnership. Each person has to give at least 75 percent, if not more. If you think you only have to give 50 percent, you usually give less."

For these couples, divorce was never an option to help them through rough times. Like Fred and Ruth, the happily married couples valued friendship and companionship, insisted upon open and honest communication at all times, and were committed to one another for life.

In the end, I came away from the interviews with those who were happily married believing good marriages could be had if a couple approached their relationship with open eyes, few expectations, and the desire to give far more than 50 percent.

MYTH OR REALITY?

The study is done. The statistics are in. And the comments are analyzed.

Men today are making changes in their lives, both personally and professionally. They are questioning their roles, reevaluating their career goals and dreams, altering their life-styles, and redefining their personal relationships.

Men, of all ages and professions, *are* in transition.

The reality is far more exciting and enlightening than any of the promises once held by the myths I've described. At this time, men are carving out new ways of working, managing, and living. In so doing, they are enriching their own lives as well as the lives of those with whom they live and work. Most important, they are enjoying life more.

CHAPTER 2

I DON'T WANT TO PLAY
THE GAME ANYMORE

For some women the rules of the game never worked. For other women, the rules stopped working long ago. Over the past ten years we have witnessed how the women's movement has helped women break out of their confining roles and create new opportunities and life-styles for themselves. It now appears that the impact of the women's movement has carried over to men. As if by an unexplainable force, men have stopped accepting the unquestioned expectations placed upon them.

It gives me great pleasure to see the changes men are making in their lives because I know it takes an enormous amount of emotional risks and courage to break out of the mold.

Jeff Flox is an example. He dropped out of the corporate world when his boss said, "What you have to realize is we are all whores. If you can accept that you will prostitute yourself to the right people and you will get somewhere. If you don't you are going to get fucked anyway and not get paid for it." Jeff chose to be true to his values and be guided by integrity. He now runs the art department for a world-renowned color lab.

Before I go on to introduce the other men in this book, men who are the inspiration for their peers today, let's look at how men have traditionally dealt with the dilemmas that seem to be an inherent part of playing the game.

For years men have been subjected to rules and regulations about how they are supposed to be and what they are to do to succeed. They had to suppress who they are and what they believed in, learning to second guess their bosses and tell people what they wanted to hear. They learned to agree, even when it meant defying their own principles and values. And some even lied or cheated to save their hide or that of their superiors.

To get ahead they abided by those rules, fulfilling their duties and obligations; making sacrifices in their own careers "for the sake of the company or for their employees." To succeed, or for some to survive, they had to deny their unhappiness, rationalizing it away by telling themselves they had fulfilled their obligations, they had done their duty by being a loyal soldier or good company man. They sacrificed their own values and ideals to climb the pyramid of success on someone else's coattails. In doing so, a big piece of their soul was extracted.

In making personal sacrifices they suddenly found themselves feeling empty, unfulfilled, and even depressed. These are men who previously believed they had to postpone their personal dreams until they retired, until the kids were finished with college, until they gained financial independence. They have gone through life playing the game of "either-or"; either their needs or mine, either what's good for them or what's good for me. The question they were always asking themselves was: Them or me?

Of course it is not spoken of in these terms. Instead one talks about it in terms of playing by the rules. Except for the men who are considered mavericks in their professions, it is common to hear men subscribe to canons such as, "That's the politics," "You can't fight the system," "You've got to go along with things," "Tell him what he wants to hear." But if we take the mask away, we find that conformity was the name of the game and the measure of success. The pressure to conform is often hidden under the guise of being a team player, being a loyal soldier.

David Riesman, in his book *The Lonely Crowd*, brought this problem to our attention back in the early 1950s. At that time he talked about the typical American character's desire to "fit in."

Arthur Miller aptly describes this same predicament in *Death of a Salesman*. Willy tries to cover up his competitiveness, like most men of two or three decades ago, by being "well-liked." When as an old man he is "cast into the ash can" by virtue of the changing policies of his company, Willie is totally bewildered and keeps repeating to himself, "But I was the best-liked." His confusion in the conflict of values—why does what he was taught not work?—mounts up until it culminates in his suicide. At the grave one son continues to insist, "He had a good dream, to come out number one." But the other son accurately sees the contradiction that such an upheaval of values leads to: "He never knew who he was."

And so I found men who after years of dedicated service, after building the company, after turning their firms into the best and most respected, wonder, "What's important to me?" "Where have the years gone and what do I have to show for them?" "Who am I, if I'm not my job?"

One sixty-one-year-old corporate vice president explained it this way: "I've been a slave all my life. Women think we are the privileged sex. But have they ever got it wrong! *We* are the slaves, sacrificing our needs for the company and for the family, working fifty, sixty, seventy hours a week. And is anyone grateful? No, they are not. I see no benefits for the time and sacrifices I've made. No one loves and appreciates me for the years I have slaved. They just expect more from me. I'm fed up. I think about how I'd like to walk away from it all and start over. But I don't because I can't live with feeling guilty. I could never cope with the guilt if I really did what I wanted."

Until this corporate V.P. helped me to understand this dilemma, I might have believed that men had lost awareness of themselves. They would rather die at their desk than free themselves from their compulsive patterns. As I continued to question this man's fear of doing what he wanted, he confessed, "I wouldn't know how to survive on my own. I just wish there was more time for me to do my own thing. No, what I really mean is that I wish there were time for me to find out what my own thing is and then to be able to do it without fear of guilt, loneliness, and loss of love."

Listening to him, I realized I was wrong about men. As a woman, I had been taught to be reflective. My sixty-one-year-old client taught me that many men have neither the opportunity nor the proper training to be introspective. He taught me the most important aspect of this dilemma: Men have not lost awareness of themselves. They were never given it in the first place. No one ever taught them how to find out what was important to them. They have not had the luxury to "find out what their own thing is." If these men are to rid themselves of their guilt, they must first be taught how to identify what they feel and to be aware of the thoughts that guide their behavior. You can't change what you don't know, so being able to recognize the problem is half the solution.

It was this initial honesty, the fact that these men shared a very private part of themselves with me, allowing me to feel with them what they were experiencing, that sent me on my own exploration. I was intrigued by both the subtle and dramatic changes that were occurring, and I was sympathetic to the emotional pain and confusion I sensed men were experiencing as a result. I was excited by the desire men demonstrated in wanting to give inner meaning and purpose to their lives.

However, at that time, the only context I could put it in was, "Is there a men's movement being born?" I remember asking a colleague if he had noticed this to be true with his male patients, particularly the business executives. He abruptly dismissed my notion. I am grateful that something inside me refused to let my colleague discourage my curiosity. Instead I decided to pay closer attention to what men were saying and feeling. I continued to ponder the same questions over and over: What is it that men are feeling but are not articulating? What conflicts are men feeling about their personal and professional lives? What is motivating men to alter their dreams and goals?

I was compelled to find the answers to these questions. For over ten years I listened as men spoke about their destroyed dreams, their hidden secrets; confiding in me the painstaking conflicts that plagued them by day and haunted them by night. The conflicts came about when men realized they no longer wished to be dutiful husbands, while others found themselves thinking that they didn't want to be loyal employees who had no control over their jobs. Others were hit by an unexpected traumatic event such as depression, divorce, dismissal, or death; feeling out of control, they struggled through the emotional pain, listening to their inner voice, sometimes for the first time in their lives.

The conflicting thoughts and emotions men shared with me made sense for the first time. I finally began to understand that there really was a quiet revolution of men breaking out of the straitjackets that had been harnessed on them years earlier. I understood how painful it was for men to decide that they didn't want to play the game anymore.

It was then that I saw men were silently suffering in the search for new meaning and purpose: a search for their own truth.

WHO AM I?

As the famous Chinese philosopher Lao-tzu said,

He who knows others is wise;
He who knows himself is enlightened.

—The Way of Lao-tzu

As the men I interviewed shared their private selves with me, I watched them struggle with their inability to interpret their experiences, to know what they were feeling, to face their inner reality.

Without insight into oneself, we walk through life with blindfolds on. But, when we are able to understand what we are experiencing, accepting rather than rejecting the pain, fear, or confusion, we find a way to be in control of our emotions and of ourselves.

Rollo May in his book *Man's Search for Himself* claims, "It may sound surprising when I say, on the basis of my own clinical practice as well as that of my psychological and psychiatric colleagues, 'that the chief problem of people in the middle decade of the twentieth century is emptiness.' By that I mean not only that many people do not know what they want; they often do not have any clear idea of what they feel."

I was pained by the feelings of emptiness, depression, or confusion I saw so many men trying to deny. They did not articulate these feelings; instead I had to dig deep, not taking all their comments at face value, looking for nonverbal clues, passing comments or apathetic descriptions that would help me understand how they really felt.

I am reminded of a poignant example, in which the president of a major bank was asked to resign. He asked me to meet him for cocktails to talk over what happened. While were were having a drink, he discussed how he didn't care that he had, ostensibly, just been fired. He then added, "I am the one who has made the bank so great." I asked him why he was biting the skin off his hand if he wasn't upset. Again, but in a hostile tone, he told me he didn't care what happened. The dichotomy between his inner feelings and his outward behavior was unapparent to him.

Or in another instance, John Bertrand, a mild-mannered, intellectual data-processing manager, informed me, "I put feelings and philosophy in the same category—esoteric principles that can't be figured out. I don't bother to figure out what I'm feeling anymore. You've got to be practical. It takes too much time and it's not worth the energy investment."

I probably could have accepted John's argument had there not been both physical evidence and verbal clues that this man was struggling to keep himself "emotionally together." Physically, he was extremely overweight despite the fact he rode a bicycle to work everyday, which was approximately sixty miles round trip. Verbally, he had said some things that led me to believe all was not well at home. And, although it was hearsay, people at his office told me his wife had a violent temper and he didn't know how to deal with her.

"I sometimes feel like I can't stop eating. I'm never satisfied these days," he mentioned laughingly. I took his comment more seriously and suggested he take notice if certain situations triggered his desire to eat; writing down how he felt after he ate but still felt unsatisfied. The first month he kept promising to do as I suggested, even though I never asked or reminded him. But during the second month he kept a food journal. To his surprise he discovered that his insatiable feelings arose when he was angry with people but didn't tell them. John was "stuffing" down his anger with food.

Sometimes we have patterns in our life that on the surface make perfect, logical sense, but underneath have a deeper significance. Greg Evans got to the office to begin his twelve-hour day at seven-thirty every morning. But before going to work it was important for him to get in his five-mile run. Since it took at least forty-five minutes to get to work, Greg had to arise no later than five-thirty. He often didn't return home before 7 P.M. This made for a long day.

One day we had a discussion about how much sleep one needs. I remarked that if I get more than six hours I feel fatigued. Greg was shocked. "I need at least ten," he told me.

It was my turn to be shocked. "What time do you go to sleep?" I inquired.

"No later than eight P.M.," he replied. "We don't have a set dinnertime, with three teenagers coming and going, so it's not that I have to get home in time for dinner. I have a light snack and hit the sack."

Something didn't feel right about Greg's explanation. I was alerted both to the amount of sleep he required and the unsolicited explanation about the family's lack of a formal dinner hour.

In time Greg confided, "I've noticed I get depressed Friday afternoons and it doesn't lift until late Sunday." A silence fell upon the room that seemed to last forever. For some reason, I was afraid to speak, thinking if I did Greg might withdraw. He finally spoke, "My wife doesn't seem to want anything to do with me . . . in bed that is."

His comment opened the door for me to ask, "Your employees adore you and your running makes you feel good. Is there a possibility you use your running and work to avoid the pain of rejection?"

"I never thought of it that way, but now that you ask, it does make some sense," Greg responded.

One can use many different activities to avoid personal problems, and Greg happened to have picked two healthy diversions. But not all men make such emotionally healthy choices. I have consulted in companies where the pressure becomes unbearable, but no one will admit the stress is getting to him. "Bite the bullet," the men say to themselves or one another.

However, one can't run from his feelings forever. Dr. Nicholas Cummings, the past president of the American Psychological Association, and internationally respected psychologist, explains it this way: "Ignorance is bliss. But any intelligent person eventually realizes that he can't go on fooling himself or attempting to fool others. No one can run from the reality of the mind completely. So his ability to deny his feelings and actions ceases as he is haunted by the truth. Some people describe it as being in 'living hell.' They make a decision that they don't want to suffer anymore. And to end the suffering means they have to learn how to understand their feelings and motivations."

The most important finding my study yielded was:

The men who were introspective, who valued their logic and intuition, were happier and more self-confident than their less introspective counterparts and better able to deal with the stresses of life. However, those who appeared outwardly successful, but ignored their inner life, were often confused, empty, or discontented, which resulted in their feeling overwhelmed or depressed and caused them to run from their problems.

Since conducting this study, I have witnessed the suffering men endure because they are denying their feelings. I have seen them live lonely, isolated lives because they shut people out, refusing to become emotionally involved, protecting themselves from being hurt. To the contrary, I have also watched men put an end to their quiet desperation by learning how to understand their feelings, finding a core of security.

RESOLVING QUIET DESPERATION

The late Carl Rogers, my most valued mentor, taught me how to trust and believe that individuals can find their own solutions. Thus, as I shied away from taking the role of expert, I have attempted to let the men speak in this book. At times I have described my work with a particular client and explained why I suggested certain approaches. Other times I have described what men feel and how they think, in the hope that you, by relating and identifying with these men's despair and triumphs, will find solutions appropriate for yourself.

Thus the emphasis of this book is on having the men share their feelings and insights with you, for that is the best way to learn and the safest way to decide when, what, and how you want to change.

You will meet a new breed of men, whom I call "responsibility rejectors." These are men who might initiate a divorce and courageously face the scorn and rejection from peers, family, and friends. Or they might reject the "acceptable ways" to achieve success and live out their real career dream. With fortitude and determination they endure their pain, learning more about themselves and becoming examples for men who are following in their footsteps.

Concerned about being a whole person rather than a partial man, many are striving to create a well-balanced life. Those who felt their own father's absence while growing up don't want to be absentee fathers; those who knew their fathers had extramarital affairs are marrying later in life, when they feel they can be monogamous. At work, they don't feel a need to hide their nurturing side; they care about the growth and development of their employees despite whether anyone regards them as weak. These men know that emotional courage and intuition are signs of strength.

In the chapters that follow you will meet these men: Men who explain why they need people to need them, and as a result fear their wife's independence or an employee taking the initiative without consulting them. Men who have dealt with the obligations imposed upon them and found ways to alleviate the guilt when choosing their responsibilities. Men who have abandoned the prescribed dream and created their own. And men who have entered the corporate world on their terms, rather than the corporation's.

They are men like Mark Sullivan, who, as a successful real-estate and financial adviser, gave up half his fortune because he cherished his freedom and happiness more than his material wealth and successful appearances. He discusses his feelings about his daughter's temporary rejection of him, his wife's threats to commit suicide, and his guilt about changing from a full-time provider to a part-time father: "I felt guilty for five years after we got divorced. I got on with my life, but she continued to mope around. My son blamed me for his mother's unhappiness. I almost went back with her when she attempted suicide, but someone told me that was her way of manipulating me. I don't know why it took all that time for me to come to my senses, but this friend was right. She had me under her thumb all those years, playing with my emotional heart strings. I finally said, 'No more.' "

They are men like Greg Morris, a successful sales director who always wanted to run his own ma-and-pa grocery store in the mountains and become the artist he always dreamed of being. This man, who had worn pin-striped suits and closely cropped hair, sent me an article from his town paper that described how he tossed away the successful corporate life for the back roads of Oregon. I stared at the picture of this man, a man I had worked with for five years, and didn't recognize him with his long hair and beard. When I went to visit him, Greg said, "I was so fucking dependent on the company that I didn't know I could ever take care of myself. If this business fails or burns down, I could go down the street and start again. I've got courage; the courage the company took away from me by demanding loyalty and teamwork.''

They are men like John Lazar, who dreamed of being an entrepreneur, took the risk, and learned that it wasn't for him. He had worked at Xerox for thirteen years and found it to be stifling and bureaucratic. Not knowing that any other corporate culture existed—particularly the type of environment he longed to work in—John thought his only way to freedom was to be his own boss. So John left Xerox and started his own real-estate investment firm. It seemed like a logical step, for he and a friend had been investing in the California real-estate market for years, making a fortune. But often timing plays a key role in one's success. A few months after John opened two offices, one in the San Francisco Bay area and one in Sacramento, interest rates skyrocketed and the real-estate market took a dive.

John assessed his position and decided to close up shop, cutting his losses before they got out of hand. He liked working for a big company, but only if that company gave him the freedom and authority to make his own decisions. In looking to reenter the corporate world, he decided to work for Clorox Corporation. Over the years we have spoken about how different his experiences at Xerox and Clorox have been. At his present company he is given the freedom to make decisions. He feels like his own boss.

John reflected, ''You don't have to get out of the corporate world if you want to find yourself or have the freedom to be yourself. You have to find the right company whose executives encourage their managers to take risks, who give them the control over their own little piece of the big corporate pie. As I look at my friends who are still stuck in the companies that control and stifle them, I think back to the days that I didn't believe another type of corporate culture existed. I find myself trying to talk them into leaving, trying to convince them that there really are better places to have both security and freedom. One doesn't have to be sacrificed for the other.''

At times I have felt men are quite oppressive of anyone, male or female, who has a position subordinate to themselves. I have sensed their oppressive behavior results from their own feelings of being oppressed. As more men reject this pressure, courageously questioning their lives, they threaten some of their peers. Many of my women colleagues and friends have not been privy to seeing how men oppress one another, how they often expect their peers to live according to the prescribed set of rules and join them in their own misery.

As more men find ways to unharness themselves from the confining roles they took on without question, and as more men accept the differences between themselves, their need to oppress others is diminishing. And as I encounter these men who are living a fulfilled, contented, and exciting life, I see how they encourage their peers to do so.

They are men like John Rollwagen, chairman of Cray Research, who went to good schools, MIT and Harvard, whose I.Q. was better than most, whose family lived in the better part of town. John was raised with the "right ingredients" and had acquired the formula for success. And outwardly he was successful. But at about thirty he suffered a period of self-doubt. A few years later he began to recognize that his marriage was falling apart. This perfect life wasn't turning out so perfect: "I went through some real personal conflicts. I was out of touch, plotting my sense of life. If you look at my life curve, it starting heading down around thirty and it lasted for almost ten years. By 1975 I was way below the base line of zero. My self-esteem was in question. I remember feeling scared and insecure. In 1980 I left home."

Fast forward. John is one of the happiest, most contented men I interviewed and one of the easiest CEOs to approach. Atypical of most CEOs, he is unaffected by his position and its perks. He is not impressed with himself. I think that comes from going through a humbling period where you are born with the silver spoon, only to find it silver plated. John told me, "Instead of applying the formula I was taught, I began to realize the answers came from inside, not from outside. I'm different and I like it, but it took some painful soul-searching to get here."

They are men like Trevor Harding, whose need to be perfect almost cost him his career. He drove employees mad, to the point that many refused to work for him. He drove his wife into the arms of another man for support and love. And he nearly drove himself crazy until he accepted how his need to be perfect was his need for approval from his father; approval he desperately needed but never received.

When Trevor realized he had internalized his father's critical voice, making it his own, he began to psychologically free himself from this self-imposed torture.

The changes men are making are changes that offer freedom to all who come in contact with them at home and at work. They offer the women at work and home support rather than discouragement to explore their dreams and achieve their goals. The desire for power over others as a measure of success and means to control their world is being replaced by a new definition and value: the desire for power over oneself.

Today many men of all ages are choosing what they *want* to feel responsible about and *who* they want to be responsible for. They are no longer accepting the rules and obligations unquestioningly. These men want a balanced life; they are working hard to be emotionally honest with themselves and they are trying out new life-styles and careers in search of the ones that are the right fit. Most of all, they have stopped accepting the myth that men who show their feelings are weak. They have learned that understanding your feelings is the way you understand yourself and others.

In one of the workshops I conducted with Dr. Rogers, he said to a participant who had expressed great fear about opening up his soul to the group of 125 people, "You will probably offer comfort to others, for the most personal is often the most general."

I hope you find this to be true for you.

PART II

THOU SHALT NOT FEEL:
COMMITTING EMOTIONAL SUICIDE

CHAPTER 3

SOMETHING HAS TO BE LOGICAL TO BE RIGHT

Sports and other physical activities have often been the only acceptable avenues for men to emotionally express themselves. In all other situations men are to keep their cool, hold their cards close to their chest, and bite the bullet. It is okay for a man to pat another man's butt on the football field; but any sign of physical contact off the field and he runs the risk of being called a homosexual. It is okay for a man to pound his fist on the table in a fit of rage, but it wasn't okay for Edmund Muskie to lose his cool. It cost him the presidential bid.

I am reminded of the time I conducted a workshop comprised of executives from power and gas companies in the Southeast. While explaining the importance of trusting your gut reaction in dealing with people, one man asked, "How do I know that it's a gut reaction I'm having and not indigestion?" Many of the men in the room howled. They loved to hear one of their peers put down this woman, who was advocating a "female" quality as an important one for executives. But that night, as we congregated for dinner, one of the men went up to the microphone in the grand ballroom and announced, "Jack Dunham, there is an urgent message for you from your internist. He says that what you're feeling is not indigestion, but merely a gut reaction." Again many of the men roared with laughter.

41

This example only serves to illustrate how ambivalent many men are about when to trust their feelings; when to be logical, and what value to place on feelings. Their ambivalence surfaces because they are raised to believe that if one is rational, then he, of course, is objective. And if he is objective, then he, of course, is always right. As a result, men become emotionally incompetent, denying their feelings and essentially shutting down a key part of their being.

THE IMPORTANCE OF BEING RATIONAL

My salvation, in many circumstances throughout my life, has been trusting my intuition. Therefore I couldn't comprehend the importance men placed on being rational and objective to the extreme of denying their intuition. So I set out to understand this "natural" way of being, for men that is, and this "phenomenon" to me.

I made the mistake of trying to find some deep, complex meaning behind this behavior. There wasn't one. As Pavlov conditioned his dog to salivate upon hearing a bell, men are conditioned to deny, discount, or disregard their feelings.

When little boys reach school age, or for some before, they must begin acting like a man. And they are doing nothing more than acting. Their intellectual process is allowed to develop over many years. They are allowed to explore various viewpoints and encouraged to be analytical. Mistakes and failures are not accepted. They are taught to value the rational over the subjective.

At the other extreme, their emotional learning process is stifled and a social role adopted before they have a chance to evolve into emotionally mature human beings. They are rarely given the opportunity to discover how they feel about a given situation; instead they are told how they are supposed to feel, or in most cases, how they are not to feel.

Real men never succumb to spontaneous emotional responses. They rarely give in to their intuition or gut reaction; for doing so would be equal to admitting they are weak, unstable, and feminine; logically speaking, that is. Instead they are told, "Men think and women feel." So anytime they express their feelings, they are likely to hear, "Stop acting like a sissy." Or, "Act like a man." Others are raised to be silent and stoic: never discuss your problems, don't count on anyone else, avoid showing any emotion. Consequently they shut themselves off from these survival signals; instead they learn to obey the commandment restricted for men only: THOU SHALT NOT FEEL.

This importance of being rational can be traced back to 1620 when Francis Bacon argued that a true model of the world should be based upon fact, not upon how a man's own reason would have it be. Bacon encouraged people to look for the "objective knowledge." Following Bacon, René Descartes believed that the key to understanding the world, to deciphering its hidden secrets, to controlling it for human purposes was to be found in one word: mathematics. Mathematics would offer us a precise method of determining life's factors, ending any confusion.

When we hear executives say, "Just give me the facts," or, "All I want is the bottom line," we can attribute this to Bacon and Descartes and others in this mold. Our worlds of business, medicine, and education all attempt to establish themselves on the basis of *facts*. If something is an art, we attempt to turn it into a science.

As Desmond O'Reilly, the vice president for data processing at one of Silicon Valley's top firms, explained it to me, "Being objective is being factual. If you are factual then you are right. But to be subjective is an expression, perhaps of mere reflections, personal feelings, and perspectives. And that is wrong."

I knew after enough interviews that it would be difficult to challenge this widely held premise, but I couldn't resist questioning Desmond. "It is wrong to be a human being? It is wrong to feel nervous, miserable, sad, glorious, enthusiastic, spellbound, relieved, thankful, optimistic?" I asked.

"No, perhaps it is not wrong. But it is better not to succumb to the emotions. One shouldn't let his emotions get control over his life. He should try to be rational, logical, and objective at all times," he replied.

Our society tries to make everything objective and quantifiable. As a result, men act as if the subjective—one's preferences, desires, values, and beliefs—plays no part in the decisions they make or the way they behave. However, what they state and how they actually behave are contradictory.

THE IMPORTANCE OF FEELINGS

Michael Maccoby, in his book *The Leader*, states that the leader of the future must learn how to be sensitive to other human beings: "If we are going to decrease, for I do not believe we can truly eliminate the problems in our society, men must learn to develop an attitude of caring and realness. Façades must be discarded, feelings must blend with thinking."[1]

Dr. Willard Gaylin, in his book *Feelings*, offers this viewpoint:

> "Feelings, particularly the complex and subtle range of feelings in human beings, are testament to our capacity for choice and learning. Feelings are the instruments of rationality, not—as some would have it—alternatives to it. Because we are intelligent creatures—meaning that we are freed from instinctive and patterned behavior to a degree unparalleled in the animal kingdom—we are capable of, and depend on using rational choice to decide our future. Feelings become guides to that choice. Feelings are fine tunings directing the ways in which we will meet and manipulate our environment."[2]

But men aren't taught to view feelings as instruments of rationality. And so they spend their life running from their inner world.

Their avoidance of feelings can lead to a rash of injuries or physical ailments, for it is more acceptable to complain of a backache or a hangover than to express frustration, helplessness, or insecurity. Their body often takes the brunt of their emotional denial manifested in physical symptoms: heart attacks, lower back pain, high blood pressure, stomach problems, or hives. Or they engage in self-destructive activities: overeating, alcohol, substance abuse. By running from their feelings, men are committing emotional suicide, joining the ranks of the walking dead.

I often suggest to men that they look at the importance of identifying their feelings as signals for survival: "Feelings are the clues that tell you if your rational, logical, and objective decision is 'right' for you. They tell you that, although someone's words sound okay, something else is going on and you should be cautious. They tell you when you are bored, angry, guilty, tired, upset, envious, used, proud, touched, moved, exhilarated, fulfilled, contented, surprised, or thankful; to name a few. Feelings tell you about yourself.''

Feelings don't have to be our enemy; they can be our ally. A colleague of mine told me about one of his patients who had been struggling to make peace with the feeling part of himself. This patient had a dream in which he was locked up in jail and couldn't get out. The only thing was that he was a woman in his dream. They spent some time discussing the dream, especially trying to interpret why he saw himself as a woman. After great deliberation, the patient concluded, "If I don't come to peace with the feeling side of me, and let it out, I'm going to feel locked up forever."

The men who have unlocked their feelings, who have taken the time to understand how they feel rather than judge their feelings as stupid, irrational, or overemotional, have become more accepting and happier with themselves. In turn, they have stopped being judgmental with others, at home and at work. On a personal level, they have attained more self-knowledge, more self-confidence, and more self-worth. On a social level, equality is slowly being achieved. A mutual understanding between the sexes is developing. These men have realized there is much to gain by understanding and experiencing their feelings.

In this book, however, you will meet men who have learned how to trust their feelings.

They are men like Thomm McHenry, who was depressed for almost two years before realizing he had started believing his own press and lost touch with himself. Born with solid self-esteem, he began doubting himself. This wasn't good for the president of one of Boston's Route 128 computer firms. But as the spokesman for this highly successful company, Thomm began to think he was the company. When betrayed by his own chief operating officer, he took stock of himself and what had gone wrong and he returned to the values and feelings that had originally gotten him to the top of the pyramid.

They are men like Larry Murphy, who was seduced by the perks of his position and the power it wielded. He was the youngest, the best, and the brightest. So, why did he wake up each morning feeling empty and lethargic? Larry came to realize that he defined himself by the titles and toys he collected. As he began to place greater value on his inner life, his happiness returned. He began answering to his own needs and criteria for success rather than forcing himself to meet society's standards.

They are men like Josh Roberts, who became a millionaire before he was twenty-eight. Josh had no time to worry about how he felt. Besides, engineers logically evaluated things. But Josh, in running from himself, felt the need to control others. And his employees resented this. They told him so. Josh had never been confronted before—who would have thought to speak up to the boy wonder? And Josh went into a tailspin. He had to come to grips with his insecurities, breaking down the walls he had built to shield himself from the anticipated pain. Through great struggle Josh learned to give credence to his feelings.

IT DOESN'T HAVE TO SOUND LOGICAL

There I was in my jeans and oversized shirt, no makeup and my hair a mess. I had been writing twelve to fourteen hours a day to get the book done and not much else was on my mind. I was standing in line to get my visa for France, when I struck up a conversation with two men in business attire. I mentioned to them I was writing a book. After explaining the subject matter I asked them what they thought about the myth, "Something has to be logical to be right."

I struck a chord with one of the men, Mark Baldwin, a scientist for Chevron, who offered some insight as to how scientists approach their work: "In science you know you've got to trust your gut feeling if you're going to be good. The scientists who think they need to gather more and more data before they can make a decision rarely get ahead."

Tom Nakagawa, an architect, added, "For something to be right it doesn't have to sound logical. I frequently go with my gut instinct. There are people who don't trust their own judgments, so they have to massage a problem over and over before they'll feel comfortable enough to act. They gather reams of information to support their point, hoping they will convince others how right they are. It gripes me how often that ploy works. People get intimidated so easily when someone raises a point they hadn't considered."

Mark continued, "But you don't tell anyone you came to your conclusion based on a hunch. If you do they'll try to dispute it logically. The game is easy enough to figure out. You've got to be able to back up your gut feel with the logic that got you there. Besides, all intuition is, is logic scrambled up. After you reach your conclusions you search for the logical points so you can defend your position.''

I responded, "I couldn't agree with you more. I think our society values logic to the extreme.''

Mark nodded in agreement and offered this thought: "Science is an art. Technology is the science. Technology is developed based on already established scientific facts. But as a scientist, you are searching for the answer. More often than not you take the Edisonian approach. It's also the shotgun approach. When Edison created the light bulb, he wasn't sure of the right or logical way. So he generated this idea and saw it through. When it didn't work, he generated another idea. He didn't have a hypothesis. He was looking for an answer and he didn't even know the right questions to ask. Researchers or scientists who have a hypothesis can always find a way to support it with logic. But true discovery is done when you trust your gut feel and explore different avenues before stumbling upon the 'right, logical' answer.''

Mark elaborated, "We men play one-upsmanship with logic. You can find a logical point in everything if you want to. So we try to trip one another up by trying to find the logical point that the other guy didn't consider. But just because something is logical doesn't mean it's right.''

Tom turned to Mark and said, "Boy, is that ever true. Some guys at my office get into these contests about who can come up with the most logical reason we should go ahead with a project. But most of the time we base our decisions on some subjective reasoning. It's not that logic doesn't have its place. It does.''

Our hour and a half together was coming to an end as we were making it to the head of the line for our visas. As I later reflected on our conversation I was struck by the comments these men made to me. They both were in fields of precision: architecture and science. But their fields also required they be creative. For Tom to be successful he couldn't draw a building someone else had already designed. And for Mark to be successful he had to find the solutions to Chevron's scientific problems that no one before could solve.

Creativity is a big buzz word in business these days. I think creativity is absent from many companies because they depend too much on the logical approach, on structure, and on policies and procedures. But men who are willing to take intellectual and emotional risks to look at problems from angles no one before thought to consider are the men who will lead us through the next decade and beyond. These are the men who are unwilling to reinvent the wheel or give the boss the answer he wants to hear. These are men who want to discover the undiscovered. And they are able to do it because they know one of their "hunches" will pay off big.

HOW DO I BEGIN?

I had just finished a speech on goal setting. As I was packing up my papers, a tall, Nordic-looking man approached me. His voice faltered as he asked, "How do I begin to answer the questions you asked of us? I never thought about what I wanted or how I felt. I don't have any idea what is important to me."

I asked, "Do you have time for a cup of coffee?" Then I added, "I think it's better if we talk away from the crowd."

While walking to the coffee shop I saw the tears well up in his eyes. "My wife complains that I'm angry and mean to her and the kids. I don't know where the thought came from, but right in the middle of your speech I saw myself screaming at her, 'Can't you see I'm afraid. I don't know what I want from my family, from you, or from myself, for that matter.' " He continued, "And then I saw myself break down and cry."

Over the next hour we spoke about his life, his father and mother, and his own family. As our conversation was concluding, he said, "I don't mean to diminish the importance of everything you said, but the most important thing I learned from talking with you is I need to stop worrying about finding the right answers and learn to ask myself the right questions."

"I would only modify that by suggesting you eliminate the concept of right and wrong questions and answers," I responded. "We live in a society that forces perfection upon us," I continued. "But mastery only comes through practice. How can you discover the answer to something if you don't ask the question? And when you are asking yourself the questions, only you know which one is right for you. You have to try out different questions. You have to explore. When the question 'fits,' only you will know—and then the answer will come.

"Sometimes the right answer is, 'I don't know the answer to that question.' And then the fun begins as you begin discovering the truths within yourself."

QUESTIONING THE ETERNAL TRUTHS

There are many intellectual and emotional barriers that must be broken through, reevaluated, and discarded before you can become comfortable "in your own skin." I suggest you begin to question the messages and premises you have been raised with that prevent you from knowing your private self. By challenging these "eternal" truths, many have come to reject the notion that men don't feel. Moreover, doing so has helped them to alleviate the haunting emptiness and confusion that plagued their moments of solitude.

Here are some questions to help you along:

1. Were you told it was a sign of weakness to discuss your problems with anyone else?

2. What messages were you given about feelings?

3. Do you remember any particular situations where someone told you you were inadequate for feeling as you did?

4. How did your parents respond to your feelings of, for example: joy, excitement, animation, adventurousness, curiosity?

5. How did they respond to your feelings of: sadness, confusion, helplessness, fear, anger?

6. Do you remember if there were acceptable and unacceptable feelings for you to have?

7. Do you feel emotionally dependent on anyone in your life? If so, whom? How? In what ways is this expressed?

8. How do you respond to your children when they express emotion?

9. How important is it for you to understand your inner world?

10. What value do you place on feelings as a result of reading this chapter?

CHAPTER 4

IT'S NOT GOOD TO LET ANYONE GET TOO CLOSE

Trust is the most important aspect of any meaningful relationship. More specifically, it is a mutual condition that must exist between a manager and his subordinates, a husband and wife, and between friends.

A husband who doesn't trust his wife to listen and be supportive will not disclose his personal thoughts and feelings. If he doesn't trust her judgment, he will not confide in her. As a result, they will grow apart. A manager who doesn't trust his subordinates will not delegate responsibility or authority. Instead he will resort to controlling them. When employees don't feel trusted they are likely to become territorial, derisive, and antagonistically competitive.

Rollo May, in his book *Man's Search for Himself*, discusses the destructive aspects of this attitude:

> —this type of individual competitiveness—in which for you to fail in a deal is as good as for me to succeed, since it pushes me ahead in the scramble up the ladder—raises many psychological problems. It makes every man the potential enemy of his neighbor, it generates much interpersonal hostility and resentment, and increases greatly our anxiety and isolation from each other.[1]

Raised with a competitive spirit, where winning is more important than caring, competition more important than friendship, men search for their opponents' vulnerable points to be used as ammunition in the future. As Anthony Rich, an investment banker, told me, "I store confidences away to be used at a later date, especially if it's to my advantage. Any bit of knowledge is fair game to be used against your perceived enemy in order to declare a victory." Although this man did not admit it, the implication was there: "It's okay to betray someone you treat as a friend if it means winning or losing." Consequently, this intense competitiveness and desire to win breed fear and distrust between men.

The president of a major airline called to talk with me about something troubling him. As he began to confide in me, he said, "My senior vice president of marketing calls this 'opening up your kimono.'"

In general, men are discouraged from "opening their kimono" with one another. They are told to never count on anyone but themselves. But I found that when I encouraged men to talk with one another about their haunting conflicts and issues, that which was troubling them suddenly seemed less important or disappeared. They unburdened themselves of feeling vulnerable by exposing their private side and finding someone who understood them. Most often the men I interviewed were shocked at how a simple step could alleviate their loneliness and pain and provide clarity and insight.

THEY'LL ONLY HURT YOU IF YOU OPEN UP

Although there is some truth to the assertion that men distrust others because they themselves can't be trusted, another important factor comes into play. Men don't believe they are in control of their feelings, that they choose to feel as they do. Instead they think feelings are something that come over them, that they are made to feel as they do by a mysterious external force. They attribute the power and ability to others, believing someone else made them feel fear, hurt, happiness, or anger.

As Eleanor Roosevelt said, "No one can make you feel inferior without your consent." The same holds true for every other emotion. Unfortunately people often project their feelings, values, or attitudes onto someone or something else. By not "owning" their feelings, but by externalizing them, blaming outside forces, they reinforce their belief that they are out of control. The only way to feel in control of your reactions is to "take responsibility" for creating your own feelings. Please pardon this bit of jargon I am using from the human-potential movement, but I find these words do convey the concept that helps change people's view from feeling threatened to being in control of themselves.

It is the difference between seeing things from a child's viewpoint or from an adult's. A child is at the mercy of another person. Children are not taught to distinguish and reject someone's opinions. Instead they are conditioned to be dependent on their teachers, parents, and friends. Self-reliance is rarely encouraged and hardly ever taught. So we have to learn this in adulthood. Once we do, we begin to see that we are emotionally independent from another's opinions and actions; which means we are in control of both our thoughts and our feelings.

Men fear getting close to anyone, women or men, because it's another way they might put themselves on the line, becoming vulnerable. Countless men told me they longed to be close to others, but if it meant feeling out of control, they didn't want anything to do with intimacy.

As Tom Strecker, an executive at Ralston Purina, summed it up, "If I don't know what I'm feeling, I lose my sense of security. When I know what I'm feeling, I feel in control. Because I know I am the one who controls my feelings, I am unafraid of people, of what they say or how they act toward me. That doesn't mean I don't feel rejected or disappointed. That doesn't mean I don't feel apprehensive or intimidated. It does, however, mean that I delve a little deeper to understand what I'm thinking that causes me to feel as I do. And when I do, I'm in control again."

I DON'T NEED TO TALK TO ANYONE

"You should be able to work things out for yourself no matter what they are," my friend Don told me adamantly.

I happen to disagree with him. I think we do need to talk to other people. And I don't believe this because I am a psychologist. I feel this way because after talking with over four thousand men I learned how much men hold inside, how much needs to be expressed, how much they really do want to confide in someone they trust.

Frequently when Don and I would get together he would stage these protestations. And frankly I was bothered that he was always reminding me he didn't believe people should discuss their feelings with one another. Granted, I am very aware of both my thoughts and my feelings and I don't hold back expressing myself. I often wondered if my comfort with discussing how I felt caused discomfort in Don. So when he protested, I would listen and accept his feelings at face value. But one night after listening to him go on forever, I thought to myself, The gentleman doth protest too much.

As usual the next time Don and I met for dinner he balked about people who need to discuss their feelings. This time I timidly challenged him (since I didn't want to scare him off), "Don, do you think I don't care to listen to what you have to say?"

He replied with great force in his voice, "I think if you have a problem you should know how to work it out yourself. And if you can't get it worked out you should go see a counselor. But you should never burden your friends."

"So you do think I don't care to hear what's troubling you?" I responded.

"It's not that. When I was a kid, my father made it very clear that one never put their problems on anyone else's shoulder," he began to explain. "Whenever something was wrong, he sent us to our room and told us to figure it out ourselves. He only wanted to hear our solutions."

"Is that why your eyes glaze over whenever I express feelings that might be considered negative?" I inquired.

"It's not worth thinking about the negative. You can't do anything about it. Besides, you can always find the positive in a situation," Don answered.

I had no intention of letting him operate from this premise without challenging him head on. "Don, maybe I don't think being angry or sad, frustrated or overwhelmed are negative feelings. Fact is, I don't judge my feelings. They are what they are. If I'm overwhelmed, I might learn that I've taken too much on. If I'm disappointed it might mean I've realized how much someone or something means to me. I can't help wondering, since you're judging other people's feelings, are you afraid people will judge you if you open up?"

Don's black eyes darted out at me and then he quickly looked away. He turned back to me and said, "You're right. I'm afraid someone is going to tell me to go to my room and resolve those feelings; and once they are resolved, then I can tell them about my solution."

"So you do feel I might think you're a burden if you open up to me?" I asked again.

Don looked away again and then changed the subject. I asked my question again. "I guess I do," he admitted.

"Hear me loud and clear. You are not a burden. I want to know you better. And to do that I need to understand you. I want to be there for you, not to give you advice, but to be your sounding board, to help you discover how you feel. And I am not interested in passing judgment on your feelings, just in learning more about you."

Over the years I have had to work very hard to develop trust between Don and myself. I have had to prove I will be there for him when he needs me. He trusts me to understand him. Don never needed me to give him advice. He needed me to help him uncover what he wanted to do, what he thought was the right solution for the problem he wrestled with at the time. In time Don has learned that he really did need someone to talk with, someone who would listen to him.

I think many people are reluctant to reveal their inner thoughts because most people don't know how to listen. Instead they make the mistake of trying to be helpful by giving advice. I know that unless I specifically ask someone for advice, I prefer that he or she help me understand the conflict, problem, need, or whatever I am wrestling with inside, to play back to me what I'm saying, to help me see the contradictions I might be thinking or to face the feelings I am running from.

Many men would ask me how I understood what they were saying when they couldn't articulate it. Dr. Carl Rogers refers to the skill as reflective listening, whereby the speaker does not identify what he is feeling, but the listener attempts to "name" it for him.

Here are some wonderfully touching and revealing quotes: "I think of myself as a package that no one would want to open" (Feeling unlovable). "I imagine myself walking off" (Wanting to run away). "I feel like I just had an arm amputated" (Feeling rejected). "You never listen to anyone" (Wanting attention).

In due time Don changed his protest from "I don't need to talk to anyone," to "I need to trust the person to listen and understand me." And I think that is something we all want from others if we are going to "open our kimono" for them to see us emotionally exposed.

MEN WHO ARE FRIENDS

A friend of mine, Serge Fraser, came to San Francisco to conduct some focus groups. Serge is an advertising account executive for a big Chicago agency, as well as the boyfriend of my childhood friend Sara. Over the course of dinner we were catching up on one another's lives during the two years that had passed since our last visit.

As I was telling him about the book, I commented on the difficulties men were having in learning to trust each other. Serge nodded in agreement as I spoke. "I don't know if my story will help you at all, but I've recently become aware of what an ass I am. Sara has helped me to understand myself a little better. And she's always so supportive and understanding," he began.

Frankly, I was a bit taken aback by his self-condemning comment, but I reserved comment and asked him to continue.

"But it was a friend of mine at work who was instrumental in getting me to see how cut off I was from my feelings. Phil and I were working together day and night for over a year. He's the creative director at the agency. Well, being together that much we struck up a friendship. With Phil, you've got to care. He's a demanding friend. He gives a lot but expects a hell of a lot in return," Serge started to explain.

"One day Phil got after me about my apathetic, cocky, aloof attitude. I used to be passionless," Serge admitted to me matter-of-factly. "But Phil wouldn't let me get away with it. He became the catalyst and instigator, preventing me from shutting myself off from life. He told me I had to learn to care or I was going to waste my life away. He kept after me time and again, forcing me to uncover what I was feeling. Phil continually accused me of being arrogant and unresponsive. And I was. I acted aloof to cover up my insecurities. But underneath that arrogant face was a guy shaking in his boots."

Serge began fiddling with his paper clip. "I guess I learned to be insensitive from my father. I hated him. I still have a lot of anger waiting to explode at him. About three years ago, when I was twenty-nine, my father went into this Betty Ford–type clinic. All my life he had a drinking problem, and when my mother threatened to leave he decided to do something about it. The entire family got involved. My two sisters and I took time off from our jobs and came home for the summer because he needed the family's support. We were all in therapy three times a week. To support his effort, we had to give up drinking as well. This went on for three months. We all made a hell of a sacrifice.

"That bastard got out of the hospital and stayed dry for three weeks. Then he got drunk one night and it was all over. Not once did he ever make a sacrifice for us. Emotionally, I mean. And we put ourselves on the line for him. We gave up our lives for him, something he never did for us. Was I ever disappointed. And now he apologizes. I don't want to start caring again. I don't ever want to get hurt again."

Continuing, he said, "A few years ago when my parents got divorced my mother accused him of being a lousy father. You know what he answered—'I was a good father. I put a roof over their heads and I gave them an education.' But he was never there for us. I still don't communicate with my father. He was here this past weekend visiting my aunt, who's in a nursing home. He stayed with my cousins—that's how close we are. One night, while he was in town, we had dinner and he apologized for not being there for us. It's about time he said he was sorry. I let him have it.

"Oh, I'm sort of getting off the point," Serge said apologetically.

"No need to apologize with me. I know that these digressions relate to how Phil helped you get in touch with your feelings. The story about your father explains to me how and why you shut yourself off from caring about others. You trusted, you cared, and, in your mind, the disappointment led to hurt. Please go on," I responded.

Serge continued, "That's it. I was disappointed. I had a lot of hope that once my father dried out, we'd have a relationship. I thought life was like the Nelson family or 'Father Knows Best.' I thought I was the only one with a lousy family. I came to find out that most families are not like the Nelsons. When I was growing up, there was this family down the street. Their house was a mess.

Their dad was a blue-collar worker. They didn't have the luxuries we had. But those kids had love. That's something we didn't get.''

Suddenly Serge stopped talking. Finally he looked up and asked, ''Why did it take me so long to realize those kids had it better than I did?''

I answered, ''Don't get down on yourself. It didn't take you 'so long' to realize it. There were other things you needed to understand before you could realize nice houses and white-collar jobs don't automatically create loving families.''

Serge nodded in agreement, but as his head hung low I could see he was still hurting. I encouraged him to continue.

''I don't let anyone get close to me because I don't know how to get close to them. I never ask personal questions,'' he explained as he folded his arms in front of himself on the table. Almost as an afterthought, Serge added, ''Two years ago I would have never been able to comfortably discuss these things with you.''

I smiled and then asked, ''Besides having your father as a role model, teaching you how to act cold and aloof, why do you think you felt uneasy about expressing your feelings?''

''I didn't want to feel rejected or to fail, so I erected this wall. I was afraid I wouldn't 'do it' right,'' he confided.

I responded, ''So many people are afraid that their feelings are not 'right.' But in the world of feelings there is no right and wrong. There is no I.Q. rating to them. When people judge our feelings, they do so to try to make us wrong, to make us feel stupid or to say we are irrational. People make judgments because it's a way of distancing themselves from their own feelings. For example, if someone divulges a confidence of yours in front of others and you get angry, you have every right to be angry. But they might not like being confronted with their own mistake. Instead they project their feelings of being wrong onto you.''

''My old man did that the entire time we were growing up. It wasn't until the family went through that therapy while he was drying out that we all learned his drinking wasn't our responsibility or fault,'' Serge remarked.

''Then, when I met Phil, I realized he cared about me. I could trust him. I even went out of my way to be thoughtful, despite how afraid I was I'd get kicked in the face for doing so—and it paid off. I don't stay so closed.

''I make an effort to get to know people. I realized you can't ask the questions unless you know what to ask. I have to admit it took a lot of hammering at me, but now that Phil's got me going, I am fascinated by this whole process of trying to be more sensitive. And now that I know a little more about myself, I'm asking those questions that I thought were too personal because I know how good it feels to have someone interested.''

A while later a friend of mine showed me some of her poetry. One poem in particular touched me because it reminded me of Serge. I sent it off to him. And I have included it here for you.

To learn to escape insecurities
the tedium and tyrannies
To draw upon myself
when loneliness abounds

To recognize my potential
and make it
Work for me
And those I love

To make wasted minutes
productive hours
To be positive
with consciousness of growth

I want to feel me living.[2]

I'VE FINALLY LEARNED TO LET MY FEELINGS SHOW

Justin Winchester, a New England WASP of the first order, told me, ''In my family, one never expressed any emotion. Stoicism was the key word. Mother was cold and aloof. My three brothers and I would call her Stonewoman. Everything was very formal in our house. Even the servants addressed us boys as Master Justin, Master Jonathan, and Master Charles. Father would have our nanny bring us down to the library before dinner for a few moments of conversation. He'd ask about our day and tell us about his. Then he'd do the same with my sisters. We children would eat separately from our parents.''

He continued, ''When our dog was killed by a car, all three

of us broke down and cried. Father and Mother scolded us for behaving so shamefully. From that point forth my brothers and I made a pact to never show any emotion again. That was all well and good, but as adults, we don't even know how to show positive feelings. My kids think I don't know how to care about anything. But they're wrong. It's in here, but it doesn't know how to get out.''

I must confess that I, like many women during the seventies, viewed men as cold, insensitive, callous people—and I became frustrated because I couldn't connect with them on any level. They wouldn't let me see who they were and how they felt. There was nothing real to respond to. Had I not conducted this study, I might have been insensitive to Justin's dilemma.

In particular, one of the men in my study, Gary Moore, made a very important distinction for me that profoundly affected my view of how men deal with their emotions. Gary was one of the forty-three men whose life I followed for two years. I loved going to visit him because everyone who worked with him was so happy. His entire staff adored him and he adored them. None of them took their work too seriously, yet at the same time his division was number one in the country.

During the first year I spent with Gary, we practiced ways he could counsel one of his employees who had been alienating his co-workers. On a more personal level, we discussed how he might go about living out his dream to be the artist he always dreamed of being. Over the recent months I had been working with him, prodding him to be more caring and compassionate, both with his employees and family members. Finally it happened.

Gary recounted a conversation with his daughter that was particularly moving. She was really crushed over being rejected by her first boyfriend. ''I took her in my arms and told her to cry, that it would make her feel better. And I rocked her until she fell asleep. When she woke up, still in my arms, we talked about how much it hurts when someone you like doesn't like you.''

I responded by saying, ''Well, you have finally learned to be sensitive.''

Gary corrected me, ''I have always been sensitive. It has been through your help that I have learned to let my sensitivities show.''

What was seemingly a semantic difference was instead a very important distinction that changed my view of how men relate to others and how I could better counsel the men I worked with. I came to view men as people who didn't know how to trust their feelings, rather than as people who shut themselves off from feeling.

Seven years have gone by since Gary first educated me and subsequently changed my view of how men deal with their emotions.

Throughout the rest of this book men intimately reveal to us the struggles they experience and how they overcome them. You will meet a sample of the growing number of men who don't subscribe to the myths about feelings, who can comfortably discuss their emotions, and who have the desire to be a whole person rather than a partial man. As men are discovering themselves, they are becoming exciting people to know.

And now let's move on to the specific issues, one by one.

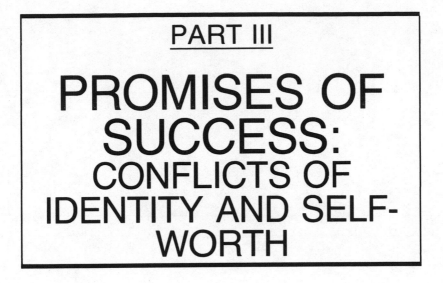

PART III

PROMISES OF SUCCESS:
CONFLICTS OF IDENTITY AND SELF-WORTH

CHAPTER 5

WITHOUT MY JOB, I'M NOBODY

Bill Russell, during his career with the Boston Celtics, would be stopped by fans on the street. "Aren't you Bill Russell, the basketball player?" they would ask him.

"No," he would answer, "I'm not a basketball player, I am a man who plays basketball." A deceptively simple statement, it reflects an attitude not commonly shared by men today. For men to separate themselves from what they do is not as easy for most men as it was for Russell.

The reason for this is simple. In our society, a man is normally defined by what he does.

For instance, the president of a major computer company feared being ousted by his board of directors. He invited me to his office to discuss how he might handle his problem. Upon sitting down in the sunken living room, which was an extension to his penthouse office on the top of one of Los Angeles' skyscrapers, he said to me, "I *am* the company. My dismissal is equivalent to the loss of face. I can't bear the humiliation. Who will I be in this community? If my employees don't need me, what am I worth?"

Unfortunately this president was ousted by his board of directors. He suffered a serious depression, withdrawing from life and at times feeling suicidal. But his feelings are no different from those of his peers who jumped from their office windows when the stock market crashed in 1929.

All too often, men confuse their roles with who they are. They take on titles such as hero, provider, breadwinner, lover, husband, father, warrior, empire-builder, mover-and-shaker. In the course of "becoming a man" they learn to define themselves in relation to the degree that someone or something else needs them: family, company, employees. Should they have to relinquish a role or two, a temporary identity crisis can occur. Worse yet, when men think about who they would be without their roles the unsettling answer is often, "I'd be nothing."

The promises of success—identity and self-worth—are the supposed benefits for fulfilling their roles. However, in the course of my interviews, men discussed with me how the male responsibilities and roles assumed by obligation or social conditioning are far from fulfilling. Instead, they have become the source of a gnawing, unrelenting sense of discontentment.

Guy Stewart, forty-six years old, successful investment banker, woke up in the middle of the night in a cold sweat. Startled by a dream in which he was in jail and the only way he could get out was to be able to tell the guards what he wanted from life, he saw himself crying for he was unable to do so. They stood waiting for an answer he could not give, an answer that would be his ticket to freedom. Guy recounted the dream to me, "Ever since grade school I've felt like I was in jail. Everyone has decided how I will be successful, but no one asked me what I thought. I married the best catch." Then he paused, clearly disgusted with himself, and continued, "I don't need to list all my credentials to tell you how great my life is. The truth of the matter is, it isn't. I've lived my life for everyone else: my company, my family, my kids. I haven't lived it for me. The toughest part of facing that truth is: I don't know how to begin."

My intent in this chapter is to show you how men are unharnessing themselves from the provider-achiever manifesto and creating a life that is more fulfilling and meaningful. In the process they are learning how to determine what is important and to be less dependent on external forces to define who they are. Some are even rejecting the life sentences they were told they had to assume.

THE NEED TO BE NEEDED

Many men define their worthwhileness, their importance by the amount of control (being needed) they have over others. Control and dependence have been two qualities men consider necessary in defining their relationship with their family and their employees.

However, a man's need to be needed is being challenged. Women want to create an independent life for themselves. Employees want greater freedom to make decisions and initiate actions. For many men, the sudden realization that people, at work and at home, want more control over their own lives, and the realization that people need them less, threatens each and every man's identity.

As a result, men are forced to examine their need to be needed. They are reevaluating the sacrifices they have made. They are admitting that the provider-breadwinner role has given them meaning, purpose, and security. They have needed other people to be dependent on them. And they have used the dependence of others to provide themselves with feelings of importance and power.

One day at lunch, an IBM executive described his reaction to the burdens he has endured over the past twenty-seven years. His children had just completed their college education, and for the first time he and his wife were alone in the house. Before lunch arrived he drew a diagram on the table. He divided the placemat in two. On one side he listed the IMPORTANT reasons for being needed: to earn a living, to love his wife and kids, to care for them by providing the expected creature comforts, to protect them, to give meaning to his and their life, to share pleasures and sorrows. On the other side he listed the BURDENSOME duties: making all the decisions, worrying about money, telling the plumber what to do, mowing the lawn, fulfilling all social obligations, disciplining the kids, all of this after spending the day fighting the battles at the office.

Looking at the diagram, he admitted, ''I like being responsible for the things on the important side of the list. And really, some days I don't even mind the burdensome duties. But I sometimes think one of these days I am going to break because I feel responsible for everything and everyone. If only moments of relief would come my way, but they don't. With the kids grown and my wife starting to work, I'm having to cope with no one needing me like they used to. Maybe I was more comfortable complaining about these burdens.

I need to be needed. When I'm not, I feel people have stopped valuing me and my existence no longer matters.''

Again and again I heard men tell me they felt that to do what they wanted would make them unlovable, that taking care of others is what makes them worthwhile. A thirty-five-year-old real-estate tycoon was frighteningly honest with me. He had retired a year before to explore who he was without obligations to his business partners, family, and friends. He summed it up this way, ''Need me when I need you to validate me, when I am feeling down about myself, when I need to be reminded that I am important, competent, and able. But leave me alone when I don't want to be burdened with your needs. I only want to consider your needs when they are compatible with mine. And don't forget, it is true that we men are dependent on women for our worth and purpose. We are only supposed to pretend that we are not. If only dependency could be a two-way street, I think we'd all feel a lot better.''

A thirty-two-year-old hotel executive described his ambivalence this way, ''I wanted my wife to be dependent on me. When she needed me I knew that I mattered. I liked doing things for her, especially when she couldn't do it herself.''

As our conversation continued, he revealed that he and his wife had divorced. ''After a while her dependence got to be too much for me. I wanted her to be able to do something for herself instead of always needing me. But I had set it up that she had to ask my permission to spend money, to go out with her friends, to do whatever it was she wanted. Soon she was doing more and more things without asking me or without my help, and I began resenting it. She got angry because she didn't know whether she should let me know when she needed me or not. According to her, I acted resentful when she depended on me.''

The same attitude affected his management abilities. He continued, ''The people who work for me tell me I confuse them all the time. Sometimes I delegate too much; sometimes I don't delegate enough. I know I feel better when my people come running to me with their questions. Then other times I wish they would leave me alone.''

This man is not alone in his ambivalence. Like most men, he grew up being told that his worth came from the roles he played and the purpose he served in others' lives. I refer to this dilemma as "The Male Credo," which is the belief that it is a man's obligation to be responsible to and for others' needs above and before his own.

Most men I interviewed previously believed they had to postpone their personal dreams until they retired, until the kids were finished with college, until they gained financial independence. As they unquestioningly accepted the responsibilities and obligations imposed on them, sacrificing their own needs, these men have never learned to determine what they feel, what is right for them.

One man explained it this way, "Even when my father was alive, I felt responsible for the family. When he died, I felt that it was all on my shoulders. I had to keep the family together, making sure everyone's needs were taken care of and ensuring their happiness. My mother raised me to put others' needs before my own. So whenever I do for myself or think of my own needs, I get this sensation. It doesn't always come right away. But it's this foreboding sense that the ax will fall because I have done something wrong."

"What types of situations trigger these feelings?" I asked.

"Oh, when my wife wanted to move to the suburbs and I wanted to stay in the city. In my mind I felt I was being selfish if I fought for what I wanted. If I get what I want, sometimes I realize, again after the fact, that I get self-destructive. Sort of a self-imposed punishment. Oh, I might drive recklessly, drink beyond my limit, pick a fight with my wife. Other times I give in. It's easier and less painful that way. Besides, that way I don't have to feel guilty."

Many men I spoke with intentionally ignore their own needs in order to avoid the anticipated guilt. They tend to put a negative value judgment on their needs, feeling they are betraying the male credo: putting others' needs above and before their own, if they make a decision to put their own career before the company's goals, or consider their own advancement before an employee's. Whenever they consider what is best for themselves, they feel guilty.

This guilt comes from feeling they have done something wrong. We are all raised with values that shape our behavior. When we deviate from those values, our internalized parent surfaces to remind us that we are betraying the imposed definition of what it means to be a good person. To conceal their guilt for wanting to be taken care of, men become demanding and self-centered.

THE SELFISH FACTOR

To my women friends' dismay I often defend men when they are accused of acting selfishly. I do so because I understand how difficult it can be for men to express their needs. Men often act selfishly and self-centeredly because they feel no one will anticipate their needs. Freud referred to this as a "reaction formation": taking on the opposite behavior of how one really feels.

A successful venture capitalist and president of his city's symphony summed it up for me: "We are selfish and self-centered because we feel we don't have a right to our own needs. If I give up the demanding little boy in me, then who will take care of my needs? Who is going to put what I want ahead of what they want? I don't know how to ask. You go through life knowing everyone is counting on you and you can't let them down because doing so would make you a failure. I can't bear feeling guilty when I decide to put my wants ahead of my employees' or partners'. It's easier to act like a spoiled brat. People will let you get away with that."

Men may use self-centered behavior to hide their resentment about constantly taking care of others. In the past they would deny their own needs and resentfully give in to their company's or family's wishes instead of complaining about these burdens or saying what they need (an "unmanly" thing to do). But by not explaining themselves, men have succumbed to an emotional straitjacket.

Increasingly, men are realizing how self-destructive this behavior has been and they are beginning to learn how to emotionally fend for themselves, how to consider others' needs and still voice their own. They are finding ways to satisfy both parties.

I was hired by a national real-estate company to help the chairman determine whether he should fire his president. As I delved into the problem, I discovered the president was a diplomatic, accommodating man who was apprehensive about voicing his disagreement with the chairman. The chairman, who was fifty-eight, thought he had an incompetent sixty-one-year-old president who never did his job. Instead, he had a president who did not have the courage to assert his beliefs because he thought his role was to support the goals of this brilliant chairman. This might seem like a simple example. However, it affected everyone who had to work with these men (ten office managers, two secretaries).

To correct this situation I established ground rules for these two men to use to communicate with each another. According to the rules, the president had to say what he thought about each directive from the chairman. In turn, the chairman had to encourage and inquire about the president's views. In short, he had to stop expecting the president to "buy off" on every idea. Instead, the president was to select the top three out of ten ideas to work on and explain the reasons for his choices.

I knew my plan was successful when the chairman told me the president had finally stopped acting as if only his ideas were the ones that mattered. And when the president told me how much better he felt in voicing his ideas and his disagreements with the chairman. It was extremely rewarding to see the myth of "I am too old to change" proved wrong again. These men wanted to find a way to improve their nineteen-year business association and were willing to change their behavior to do so.

The problems faced by these two men are not unique. When I began conducting Assertiveness Training Seminars for managers, I was surprised by the number of men who were uncomfortable being assertive. (Assertiveness is defined as being able to consider both the other person's needs and your own.) Instead these men were either extremely compliant (busy taking care of anyone else's needs and ignoring their own), or very aggressive (ignoring everyone else's needs and pushing their needs on others).

Over the past ten years I have watched men search for both professional and personal autonomy. For some men this means leaving the corporate world to take career and financial risks that require support and sacrifice from the family. Others take emotional risks that include divorcing their spouse or finding new ways to make their marriage work. And, some men are learning how to communicate about what they are feeling. They are rejecting silent, stoic self-sufficiency. They are asking for support, understanding, and compromises. They are saying, "It's my turn." They are looking for ways to unharness themselves from the role of provider-achiever, the roles that have defined them, the roles they took on without question. Now they ask for what they need and find people only too willing to give it to them. Now they find that they are able to give and care with sincerity and desire rather than out of obligation.

REJECTING LIFE SENTENCES

Dennis Derringer, a successful thirty-year-old entrepreneur, told me, "When I was twenty-six, I gave up a job as a prominent stockbroker, making two hundred fifty thousand dollars a year, driving an eighty-thousand-dollar car. I went to Harvard B school. After a year of working on my M.B.A., I looked around at these privileged kids. I was one of them. We acted the same, talked the same, dressed the same. If this was what my future would bring, I had to get out now. None of my friends understood. They took my decision personally. When my parents found out I quit business school, they weren't exactly pleased. And then when I told them I was going off to find myself, that was the end. They didn't speak to me for over two years. It hurt, but I knew this would pass. If I had stayed at Harvard, I'd be hurting for the rest of my life."

Dennis spent four years changing his life. At thirty, he runs his own business and loves getting up in the morning because he is going to have fun with all the people he works with. He dresses in baggy pants and oversized shirts. He talks to me about the time he takes to talk with his people if something is bothering them; he believes it helps them work better. Dennis's business provides him with an income that meets his needs.

It wouldn't matter if Dennis made a million dollars a year or just enough money to get by as long as he was doing what he wanted. Too often people evaluate the external trappings without understanding the internal workings motivating the person. Dennis took risks most people did not approve of and he became a stronger, happier person because of his courage to deal with the rejection received.

I wish I could give people some easy answers about how Dennis dealt with the rejection and loneliness but, as he and I discussed, change is a painful process that takes a long time to work through. Change requires emotional courage. But the pain experienced in change helps create a stronger, more mature person. It is difficult to erase years of conditioning in one sentence.

Dennis was willing to openly discuss with me how he weathered the rejection from his parents and peers. As a college student of the seventies, part of the "me decade," Dennis participated in the human potential movement and took drugs, an activity that was part of the culture. "I am so glad I took drugs because it opened my mind to ways of looking at life that I could never imagine. Strangely though, I would not recommend that someone take drugs to find themselves. I used them as a crutch for a year or two to help me 'expand my mind' and to numb the fear that looking into my feelings was betraying what it meant to be a man. The drugs helped me to see I wasn't happy. Money and cars don't mean much when you have this sense of dissatisfaction constantly lingering. There were times I wanted to jump out of my skin.''

I was curious about whether the drugs had provided the turning point for him. So I asked Dennis, "Was there a particular moment you decided to reject doing what was expected of you?"

"No, not exactly," he began. "When you are in B school, you are expected to have plans. I was reviewing my past year at Harvard and realized I hated my life. It was this increasing sense of discomfort that finally caught up with me. I was more successful at twenty-six than my father was at a similar point in his life. I was supposed to be happy. I had 'made it' in all the ways you are supposed to. But I couldn't stand looking around at these clones of myself, all spouting the same ideas. Suddenly, my eyes opened up to the fact that we were all living a charade. Like hell if I was going to continue this game."

Dennis's values had changed. They were different from those of his peers or of men ten to twenty years his senior. While others embraced the value "Sacrifice your needs; postpone your enjoyments," Dennis was embracing the value "Be true to thyself."

Values are a powerful force in any of our actions. They influence our motivations. At the same time another powerful force, the need for approval (i.e., love), influences our behavior. Dennis wrestled with watching his father and his B school friends emotionlessly carry out their roles at the same time he doubted his feelings and criticized himself for quitting Harvard.

"How did you cope with this guilt and rejection?" I inquired.

Dennis leaned back in his chair and pensively responded to my question. "I coped with my fear by calling myself an 'emotional risk-taker.' I needed a positive image of myself plowing through this internal debris. Since I couldn't yet break away from the roles expected of me, I created one that mixed my old world with the world I wanted to be in.

"I've always been somewhat of a rebel. I like being different. My arrogance helped. Of course, since then I have learned that arrogance is a cover for insecurity. So what? It helped me then and I grew from it. We men are good at shutting ourselves off from what we feel. And I don't know what it is in me that won't let me escape from reality for very long. But, I did ignore my fear of being alone once my parents stopped speaking to me. I pretended I didn't care. I'd have these dreams where I'd see my father lecturing me for being different. He'd tell me I wasn't any son of his because I wasn't being a man facing my responsibilities and preparing for my duties in life. I'd wake up in a cold sweat.

"There was someone who helped me sort this through, an older woman friend, Louise. She told me that according to dream theory, all the people in my dreams were me. How could I be my dad? I wondered. Yet this helped clarify something for me. I had been trying to live out my father's life and I was now struggling to find out how *I* wanted to live my life. So my father in the dream was me lecturing and crucifying myself. I set out to make peace with that part of me. That wasn't as easy as I thought, because I felt like I was this bad boy, betraying a man who provided me with comforts and a good education. He spent his life preparing me, grooming me to be better than him. And I was rejecting what he gave me."

Dennis told me that this realization prompted him to call his father. His father was cold and aloof, but Dennis did not retreat. His father finally agreed to meet with him.

I wanted a blow-by-blow description of the meeting and Dennis complied. "The conversation went something like this," he began. "I sat down with him and felt like I had a speech prepared. I had rehearsed it in my head so many times. As I was shaking and felt my shirt getting wet, this little voice inside me said, 'Come from your heart.' So I said to him, 'Father, I know how difficult it must be for you to see me reject everything you have prepared me for and given me. I am not rejecting you and I am not ungrateful. Please understand, I need to find the way to live my life, doing it my way. Not yours or anyone else's. I feel insecure trying to be like everyone else. It's not working for me. Give me time. I wake up in cold sweats feeling like I am betraying you. And in some ways I am, if betrayal means being different from you. Let me be me. I keep thinking I need your blessing, but maybe you'll never give it to me. I don't feel like what I am doing is completely right, but I do know the other way is wrong. Be patient, and you'll see. I'll find a way to integrate what you've given me, in time.' "

Dennis paused. As I watched, his eyes filled with tears. "His response blew me away. He told me he didn't want to see me because I was doing what he always wanted to do but couldn't. That was really a blow. It sure set me back. Here I had opened my heart, made myself vulnerable to the most important person in my life and boom, I was smacked in the face. That's when I really felt rejected. Even though we are on speaking terms, I don't think I ever recovered."

One might wonder why this was so shattering to Dennis. No matter how old we are our parents' approval remains a powerful force in our lives. Dennis had hoped he and his father would be closer as a result of this experience. Some people, even our own parents, are unable to be happy for us when they see we have done what they are afraid to do.

When this happens we have two choices: We can continue to seek their approval or we can grow (up) from the pain and learn to depend on ourselves. There is nothing that psychologically frees a person from being dependent on others and from projecting his needs onto others better than learning to separate from his parents. It is one of the most vital processes we can go through.

Because Dennis had already done much of his psychological homework when this final blow came, it only temporarily shattered him. He recovered relatively quickly. In fact, within a few days he regarded it as a test to see if he could take risks in the face of rejection and survive.

CONDITIONAL LOVE CAUSES BACKLASHES

As I explained to Dennis, many of us are raised with conditional love. Conditional love means being loved according to others' standards, not for who we are. When we don't live up to others' standards, they find ways to invalidate or reject us, as in the case of Dennis and his father. After all, Dennis was not rejecting his father, only his father's ideas. However, his father was unable to separate his ideas from himself, and so interpreted Dennis's lifestyle as a personal rejection. At the same time, his father was unable to admit this to himself. Instead, he had to find fault with Dennis.

Parents often use conditional love as a manipulative tool to get us to behave. As children, we are dependent on our parents for our feelings of self-worth but as adults, we only need answer to ourselves. Part of growing up is letting go of our need for our parents' approval and becoming our own parent.

I suggested to Dennis, ''Talk to the child in you. Let the adult in you be your guiding force. Think about the messages your father gave you about what was important. Challenge them. You can change your thinking, and, when you do, your perspective, feelings, and behavior will follow. Growing up means eliminating what doesn't work for you. Your father feels betrayed, but that doesn't mean you have betrayed him. You have rejected the premise that you must take on the prescribed roles and sacrifice your needs for others.

''Let's not ignore the fact that your peers rejected you as well. You had to seek out people who were going through the same transition. If one group of friends rejects you and another supports you, who is right and who is wrong? Neither. But if you feel a haunting sense of wrongness, then you are more likely to give credence to the disapproving group. And although you join with those who feel as you do, you are likely to project your own self-doubt onto them: 'Even though these people agree with me, maybe we all are wrong.' Oversimplified, you are making your peers extensions of your disapproving father.''

I was curious to see if Dennis had weathered the transition. Thus my final question to him was: Have you found a way to integrate your past needs with your present ones and are you happy with that balance?

He looked up to the ceiling and around the room before he smiled and answered, ''Yes, I work on it every day. I have a lot of fun and I care about people. When I talk with my dad, I tell him how the business is going. I've learned that he won't ever understand what I'm feeling and that if I try to tell him, I'm threatening him. Since I don't feel like I need to be punished anymore, which I guess means I don't feel guilty for betraying the old man, I share with him the part he can relate to.

''At work, I'm surrounded by many people who share my values and ways, so I've stopped feeling alone and afraid.''

Men like Dennis are choosing what they want to feel responsible about and who they want to be responsible for. Often responsibility and choice have been perceived as mutually exclusive elements. More and more men are redefining their responsibilities to suit their own needs while considering the welfare of others. They are coping with the turmoil that such a transition brings. Men have felt for years that they have a right to take time off under certain conditions—after long stretches of productive work, or if they feel they have earned it. To let the lawn go unmowed because watching the football game with the boys would be more fun, to sleep late on a weekend morning, to postpone some paperwork until tomorrow, to take a morning or even a day off from work without feeling guilty, these have become battles worth fighting. These men are still searching for the freedom to answer to themselves, the freedom to do what they want without guilt.

DREAMS BECOME REALITY

On a grander scale some men are making major changes in their life-style and career. One of my clients, a former litigator for one of the most prestigious law firms in New York City, always wanted to run a neighborhood bar. When he told me his dream, I had to contain my surprise. Thomas Kimball was a Boston Brahmin. His great-grandfather, his grandfather, and his father had all preceded him at Harvard Law School. He sat on every important board and gave to all the right charities. He married Muffy Houghton, whose family had been in the social register longer than the Kimballs. And now, it seemed, he wanted to run a tavern.

Could this possibly be a fantasy about what life might be like had he been born ''normal'' like the rest of us? I challenged him, discouraged him, and tested him until I was convinced this was what Thomas really wanted to do. Then I helped him deal with the conflicts that haunted him: ''What will my family say?'' ''How will the kids react?'' ''How will my colleagues respond?'' ''Will we be eliminated from the social register?'' ''Will I be asked to resign from my board duties?''

Thomas discussed his dream first with his wife. After she recovered from the initial shock and worry about what people would think, Muffy treated Thomas's dream as I did initially, with disbelief and as a flight of fancy. Thomas asked me to speak with her. I suggested she spend a romantic evening with Thomas listening to how unhappy he had been all those years following in his forefathers' footsteps.

Until Thomas finally discussed his dreams with Muffy, she

had never questioned the life she had with him. They had taken on their upper-class roles without question. Listening to Thomas's unhappiness jolted her perfect world. But Thomas had anticipated this. He told Muffy that he would support all of her charity efforts, attend benefits with her, take from the family trust an agreed-upon sum for her to disperse as she chose in order to maintain the life-style to which she was accustomed. He made it clear that all he needed from her was support and understanding. She didn't have to change at all. She simply needed to accept that she would no longer have a prestigious litigator for a husband. This was a minimal risk situation for her. She had already achieved her own standing in the social community, and even if they divorced she would not have lost it. However, Muffy was caught up in appearances, and her insensitivity almost cost her her marriage.

I knew enough about their marriage that I counseled Thomas to accept that he might have to make a choice: the bar or his marriage. Unfortunately it almost reached that point. After numerous discussions, Thomas told his wife that he was prepared to leave her. This was the first time his wife had not gotten her way in their eighteen-year marriage. I encouraged him to ignore her manipulations; eventually she would learn that Thomas had his needs to consider as well.

Many times he felt like giving up, but a new surge of anger rose, an anger that represented Thomas's internal change: "I'm finally considering my needs and I see that you are not." Finally Muffy accepted the terms he had presented in the beginning. Six months later Kimball's opened.

The first year was rough. Although his wife had gone along with Thomas's wishes, she did not really accept the changes and she made life difficult. Thomas was ready to ask for a divorce. I didn't approve of how Muffy was treating him but I also knew that she loved him dearly and he loved her. She was reacting like many men do during the first year or two when their wives begin working. Adjusting to change that you do not initiate takes time. As most of the people in Thomas's life accepted his new "profession," life got better at home. The kids had felt torn and didn't know whose side to take. But as everyone saw Thomas change from an aging forty-five-year-old into a youthful man who looked ten years younger, his friends and family joined in his pleasure. After a while, you would find Muffy bringing a friend to Kimball's after a charity meeting.

Men like Dennis and Thomas are not "responsibility rejectors"; instead, they are "responsibility choosers." They have redefined The Male Credo to mean a responsibility for oneself as well as for others. They are men who have stuck around to deal with the scorn and rejection from family and colleagues because they decided to make a change in their work or home life. They are also men who are envied when they have taken the risks that other men dream about. They don't define themselves by what they do or by who needs them. They are role models for men today.

CHAPTER 6

I GET DEPRESSED WHEN FRIDAY COMES AROUND: THE WORKAHOLIC

"Thank God, it's Monday," rejoices the workaholic.

Workaholics do not like being away from their work. At work, they are extremely happy and challenged. Away from it, they go through withdrawal, feeling empty and useless. For many who know a workaholic, it may be difficult to believe he has these negative feelings for often he is accomplished, dynamic, and charismatic.

A typical workaholic described for me the first fifteen minutes of his vacation in Maui. "I sat staring at the waves, feeling my entire body go into convulsions," he remembered. "I never ached like this before. Oh, I had been heartbroken once in my life, and I thought that hurt. No, nothing was as bad as this. I tried to think about something, anything but my work. But when I did, all I thought about was that I didn't have a single friend. No one invited me to do anything or go anywhere unless it was work-related. Worst of all, I shook in fear that if I really set about changing, I wouldn't know how or where to begin. I don't know how to make a friend or just 'hang out,' as my daughter says. I don't even know my wife of eighteen years."

More than any other type of man I interviewed, the workaholic needs his work to validate his existence. As one workaholic described it, "When I'm working, I feel alive. I have my days and

80

weeks organized. I know what I want to accomplish and set forth doing so with blinders on. Let anything get in my way and I'll railroad it. But when I stop working I feel lost, I don't know what to do with myself. I'm not one of these people who has hobbies or enjoys lounging around. I have to be productive. It's as if something is consuming me.''

Workaholics often tackle their work with gusto and passion. They have fifteen projects going on at one time, with a few more waiting on the sidelines. The workaholic doesn't know how to play, how to have fun, how to enjoy himself. He often uses work to hide from the loneliness he feels. The workaholic leaves no room for a well-rounded, balanced life.

One man told me, ''I always have the best intentions of going on vacation with my family, but as the time comes to leave, I start to worry. The first couple of times I'd take the family to the airport and send them off by themselves, promising to join them in a day or two. Once I didn't even go. I couldn't break away from what was happening at the office. In recent years I've gotten much smarter. I have our driver take them to the airport. That way I can avoid dealing with their disappointment that I'm not leaving with them.''

This man hasn't gotten smarter. He has succumbed to his cowardly way of dealing with people—avoiding confrontation, avoiding consideration, and avoiding compromise. Most workaholics are the same. Even while growing up, they were consumed by their work. As a result, their social skills are minimal. In fact, many aspects of their personal life and relationships suffer.

For instance, the workaholics I spoke with told me how they prefer work over sex. Roger Cashman, a young, attractive chief operating officer for a consumer-goods firm, recited the virtues for me. ''Results are the most important thing. You've got to get things done and done well. Don't let distractions get in your way. Once while I was making love with my girlfriend, the solution to a problem came to me. I stopped what I was doing to figure it out on the computer. I can lose my erection anytime if I think about work, but it never worries me. Pisses Sheila off a little—but then she gets over it. She knows how I am.''

Frequently the origin of workaholism is rooted in early childhood experience. No one is immune to the emotional problems that can come with growing up and coping with life's demands. Many workaholics were raised by parents who only praised them when they did something well. As a result, they have come to view their own worth in terms of what they do and how they do it.

One man told me that when he was ten years old, "my father was convinced I would be a failure and made no bones about telling me so. He was proud of my older brother. I was the ugly duckling while Tommy was the bigshot. Tommy died in a swimming accident, and it crushed my dad. When he'd get angry at me, he'd tell me, 'God should have taken you instead of Tommy.' I set out to prove him wrong. From that point forth I made sure I was the best at everything I did."

And this sort of problem continues into adulthood. There has been much talk about corporate cultures over the years. One type of "culture" that has not been identified is the corporate culture that extols the virtues of workaholism. Men in this culture brag about how many years they have gone without taking a vacation. They are intolerant of others who don't work as many hours as they do. In fact, they expect people to be as they are. There is no room for alternative work-styles.

However, I have yet to find a study that says workaholics get more done than those who work normal hours. I have found only one book that plays up the benefits of workaholism—and it was written by a workaholic. One might say it offers a subjective viewpoint on workaholism. I have, unfortunately, seen the repercussions others endure from working or living with a workaholic, and I challenge the acceptance of the virtues of workaholism.

WORKAHOLISM DEFINED

Workaholism is a chronic, pathological condition, caused by the habitual, excessive dedication to one's work at the expense of everything else. (Everything else can include physical and mental health, family, friends, and other activities.)

Workaholics are very similar to alcoholics. The only difference is the substance they abuse. One is regarded as "healthy and productive" by our society and one isn't. But any "substance" upon which one is overly dependent is, by definition, an unhealthy crutch.

Workaholics need to alter their work and life-style to prevent or eliminate problems it can cause. If you suspect that you are a workaholic, I suggest you undertake an in-depth exploration of your motives. I don't like seeing men have their spouses walk out on them because these men have ignored their own emotional needs and the needs of those they love. I don't like seeing a man suddenly realize how important a loved one is only to discover it is too late to repair the relationship. These situations can be prevented, if, and only if, the workaholic will take a little time to determine why he *needs* his work to validate himself, and make some changes in his values and priorities.

ARE YOU A WORKAHOLIC?

1. Do you work anytime, anywhere?

2. Would you work all the time if you didn't need to eat or sleep?

3. Do you wonder what to do with yourself when you are not working?

4. Do you look forward with pleasure and anticipation to the moments when you can work and not feel burdened by outside distractions?

5. Do you fantasize about work when you are on vacation, making love, or watching a movie?

6. Do you find it difficult to think about things other than work?

7. Do you resent the advice of others who tell you to slow down and not to work so hard?

8. Do you work to escape from worries or trouble?

9. Has your physician ever recommended that you work less?

10. Do you use stimulants or depressants?

11. Is the amount of time and energy you spend at work affecting your family life?

12. Do you feel dissatisfied with the work-style of those around you?

13. Are you frustrated by others' lack of passion about their work?

14. Do people you work with disappoint you?

15. Have people ever told you they feel they can't live up to your expectations of them?

Before I give you the scoring key to this test, I'd like you to know that it was adapted from the Alcoholics Anonymous test, which helps one determine if he is an alcoholic or not. According to their scoring key, if one answers yes to more than three questions, one is not considered a social drinker; he is either a borderline alcoholic or a confirmed one.

My scoring key is not that severe. When it comes to workaholics, I think degrees of workaholism exist.

If you answered yes to less than three questions, read the chapter with interest and for insight. But don't worry too much. If you answered yes to three or more, read through this chapter with a discriminating mind, challenging yourself along the way. After you have finished the chapter, reread the questions, being scrutinizingly honest with yourself. I suggest this because sometimes the primary symptom of the workaholic is "denial" of reality.

If you answered yes to 6–10 questions, workaholism has permeated your life, but I suspect you are also intensely involved in other activities with the same compulsiveness (perhaps disguised as passion?) that you put into your work. On the outside everything might seem okay. But is everything okay on the inside? Only you can answer that.

If you answered yes to 11–15 questions—I suggest you take this chapter to heart. Reread it a few times. Spend quite a bit of time evaluating your answers to each question. You might want to write a brief answer to each question, elaborating on your feelings and beliefs. Use it as a guide to understand yourself a little better.

BEING HONEST WITH YOURSELF

Denial is refusing to accept reality on two levels. The first level consists of your external reality, that which is actually happening before your eyes. The second level is your internal reality, that which you are feeling. The state of denial is in full force when you feel like your family is making demands on you to spend some time at home and you think you have been. The only problem is you bring work home every night and sequester yourself in the den.

"I can't help it" is the statement that catches any psychologist's ear, raising a little flag. Often the person is admitting that he is out of control. Paradoxically, however, he doesn't realize that is how he is feeling. And the workaholic tries so hard to have everything in control. Fact is, life isn't that way.

While denial ignores or blocks feelings and reality, dishonesty, lying to oneself and to others, fills the void. Being dishonest can mean telling everyone everything is great when you know it isn't. It can mean adopting the attitude, "If I don't think about it, maybe it will go away." When you lie to yourself this results in a third factor: self-destruction.

Rarely is the workaholic aware of these symptoms until it is too late. A friend of mine valued work above everything else in his life. His marriage was disintegrating before his eyes and everyone else's around him. Yet he refused to admit this. When his wife told him she was unhappy, he was devastated. It came as a complete surprise to him.

Of course, if I were he I wouldn't have liked the way I was told. They had put their house on the market. After they accepted the offer his wife told him, "I'm not moving with you. As soon as we close on the house, I'm moving into my own place. You might as well find a place big enough for you but with rooms for the kids to visit."

He had counted on her to be there always and forever. It never crossed his mind that his marriage might need maintenance. All relationships do. He had never been happier in his life, he told her with great bewilderment. She said, "Of course, you take and I give. I'd be happy in that kind of relationship too."

My friend was depressed for months. He threw himself into his work. When he wasn't working, he was getting stoned with some friends from work. It took almost a year for him to pull out of his depression. During that time he continued to delude himself and those around him. In fact, he carried on the charade at work for more than six months that he and his wife were still together.

He had to "hit bottom" before he picked himself up and looked at his life. Unfortunately it is often divorce or disappointing events that cause a workaholic to take notice of his life. Until then he is consumed by his work. Obsessed with his goals, he forgets that, as in the board game called Careers, you must collect "happiness hearts" in addition to fame and money for a balanced life.

No matter what you scored on the previous test, a little self-awareness can go a long way. Taking your emotional pulse on a regular basis, preferably daily, you can prevent minor instances from getting out of hand.

SOME LEARN THE HARD WAY

Christopher Hegarty, a noted speaker and former chairman of a major corporation, learned about his own workaholism the hard way. In fact, Chris refers to himself as a recovered workaholic.

When we spoke, he took me back in time to when he was still denying his workaholic tendencies. He told me about some situations that helped him see how he was destroying his life, himself, and subsequently his family. "I remember the time my wife asked me to spend more time at home. I became violently upset. I was working for her and the family and she didn't seem to realize that," Chris began. "I believed that. But I now know that I needed to work to do that for myself, to prove I was a success. I actually believed that. That's how I had myself fooled."

Chris is right. Many workaholics fool themselves by rationalizing, justifying the reasons they are working. What all the effort comes down to is: Work is used as the narcotic to run from low self-esteem. It is the temporary fix that makes the workaholic feel good.

He continued, "The next stage was becoming more understanding. If I wanted my family to have greater understanding of me, I had to have some understanding of them. On rare occasions I set aside small blocks of time to be with them. But even when I was with them I was not really there." Instead of developing more understanding for his family members' needs, Chris understood how he was present in body but not in mind. Like Chris, many workaholic fathers tell me about how they took their kids to the park; they read the Sunday paper while their children play. Or they go on vacation but spend the entire time on the telephone with clients and office members. Unlike Chris, they don't realize they are physically present and emotionally absent.

When Chris's attempt to be understanding and to set aside more time failed to work, he admitted to himself that he was, in fact, a workaholic. "I realized underneath everything I felt like a fraud. I was constantly trying to prove my worth by being a productive, achieving executive. Once I admitted this to myself, I became unwilling, for my own selfish reasons, to continue this game."

In Chris's case this realization came too late. His wife had grown to resent him so much that they divorced. And he told me how his oldest daughter, who at the time was four-and-a-half, helped him realize the damage he had caused to himself and his family. "One day we were driving on the freeway and my daughter was in the back seat. She came up from behind and put her arms around me, asking, 'Daddy, how come you don't want to live with me anymore?' I pulled over and cried while my daughter tried to comfort me."

After some time passed, Chris developed seven rules for himself. He has allowed me to list them here:

1. Continuously tell yourself the truth. Don't say the way things should be, but admit how they are.
2. Prioritize your life.
3. Enjoy the benefit of being disliked.
4. Separate yourself from your work.
5. Have the courage to admit you are wrong.
6. Strive to communicate.
7. Develop the capacity to laugh at yourself.

Chris has recovered. He works hard without using it as an escape. "I no longer look at work as a way to validate myself," he says. "I ruthlessly prioritize my life and I have learned to exquisitely enjoy my leisure. I no longer bring the office home."

DON'T WAIT UNTIL IT IS TOO LATE

The chairman of a major printing company went to see his son at graduate school to tell him that he thought it was time for them to have a relationship. For years he had paid no attention to his son. His work always came first. Now that he was retired he realized the years had gone by, his children had grown, and he didn't know anything about them. Although he didn't admit it, he was feeling lonely.

Often workaholics approach their personal relationships as they do their business plans. Simply because he decided it was "time" to have a relationship, he thought it would happen. Workaholics don't realize that closeness and understanding of one another come after years of work, openness, and trust. He was shocked when his son simply said, "I'm sorry, Dad, it's too late."

For some workaholics it's not too late.

Jim Garrick was raised in South Dakota. His parents impressed upon him how important it was to do something well, or not at all. Jim simply loves to work, and to work hard. As an only child, he learned to occupy himself with various activities and interests. To this day, he still needs many projects going on concurrently.

All Jim ever dreamed about was becoming a good small-town doctor. He never dreamed about or coveted success, and he still doesn't. He holds on to the fantasy of one day returning to a small town. Reality, however, is a little different. Jim is the director of the most prestigious sports medicine facility in the country and author of the best-selling book *Peak Condition*. He is a top international orthopedic surgeon (he operated on Joe Montana's knee) and he lives in the wealthy San Francisco suburb of Hillsborough.

Jim Garrick has a reputation for being brilliant, charismatic, and down to earth. Those who are jealous of him say he has an "ego," but Jim is one of the most modestly successful men I have ever met. He also has realistically dealt with being a workaholic, coming to grips with many of the issues other workaholics run from. And in the time I have known Jim, I am continually impressed with how he has learned to pay attention to his feelings—sometimes admitting to intentional avoidance and other times finding practical solutions for all involved.

I met Jim when he treated a hip-flexor injury I sustained while weight lifting. When I returned for a checkup, Dr. Garrick walked into the examining room, greeting me with his usual jovial smile.

"Aside from finding out about my hip flexor I have something to discuss," I began. "I'm writing a book." As it turned out, so was he. So we chatted about the publishing business and the writing process. Then I gave him a brief description of the study, concluding, "And I have pegged you as one of the few happy ones, so I was wondering if you'd like to let me follow you and your life for a while?"

He shook his head sadly. "You should have talked with me six months ago. I was a lot happier then. I'm not sure I'm right for your study."

I asked what had caused his recent unhappiness. "I've always loved working," he said. "Leisure time is for grasshoppers. Yet last weekend my son and I went to fishing camp. I've always been a workaholic, but now I'd rather be home with my son than here. I don't understand why it took this long for me to realize how important he is to me. He's supposed to go away to college year after next." The tears welled up as he continued, "I'm not going to let him go away to college without getting to know him better."

I was touched. I thought how typical it is for workaholics to feel momentarily desperate when overcome by their feelings. "Jim," I said, "you are fortunate to notice how you feel before your son goes away to school. Most men realize too late how important people are to them. By then they are depressed, lonely, and regretful. You won't be one of them."

I continued, "It's typical of men like you, who are extremely accomplished, successful, and respected, to be defined by what they do. Many of them believe that their personal worth accumulates with their successes. It is often not until such a man reaches his mid to late forties that he begins to feel secure within himself. By that time he has accomplished his goals and dealt with his disappointments.

"But as a workaholic, you proceed through life ignoring your emotional needs. As a result, these postponed feelings surface without warning and can't be ignored as they had been in the past. Relationships suddenly take on an importance that they didn't have before. I don't know you well enough to say what has caused you to feel this way at this time. But you're feeling overwhelmed because your feelings have caught you by surprise. The fact that you are mindful of your reaction is half the solution. We can get a handle on it and find ways to gain control of these feelings you have about your son, as well as other reactions that might be surfacing."

Jim seemed relieved by what I had said. "How fascinating," he responded. "I'm glad to know that I'm not in as bad shape as I thought. I'd be happy to be in your book."

Of all the workaholics whose lives I followed, few were as insightful or realistic as Jim. As I discovered during further discussions with him, he has been receptive to comments his wife had made over the years, respecting her advice and valuing the difference in their approach to situations. This has helped him weather situations that normally would be frustrating for a workaholic.

There is very little point to advising a workaholic to replace work with play. But I have found workaholics are much happier when they can integrate caring for people with the dogged determination and incessant activity that characterize their life.

Approaching mental health from a preventive standpoint can help avoid the devastation when certain feelings spring up by surprise. Don't wait for that moment when you suddenly realize how important certain people are to you. Don't wait until you only have two years to get to know your son and enjoy his company. Don't wait until your four-year-old puts her arms around you to comfort your sorrow. Don't wait for people to resent you because you ignored them.

ACCEPTING OTHERS AS THEY ARE

As I have already stated, a workaholic needs his work to validate himself. If we could put the workaholic in a room alone and prevent him from interacting with others, we could limit the damaging effects of the workaholic's attitude to himself alone. However, since this rarely is possible, we must address how his compulsive nature affects those who work with him.

Because he is insecure, the workaholic not only uses his accomplishments as validation, but he believes that there is only one way to accomplish a goal—his way. When I teach managers how to delegate work, I emphasize the importance of not worrying about how one accomplishes an objective, but only that the desired results are achieved. The workaholic always challenges me on this point.

He is intolerant of the differences in others because, although he is unlikely to attest to this, he measures differences in workstyles from a "right and wrong" perspective. In essence his intolerance is saying: "If you are like me then we are right. If you are not like me then one of us has to be wrong. Since I need to be perfect, I will make you the wrong one."

Juan Estevez had worked hard to become a manager in his company. Born in Mexico, his family immigrated to California when he was four years old. Raised in the barrio, Juan strived to excel and bring importance to his family name. In the course of his pursuit, he destroyed his marriage and was fired from his job. The feedback from those at home and at work was the same: You are so demanding and unaccepting of others.

I met Juan in one of my management training programs. Six months later he called, asking for my help. As we discussed his problems, Juan continually complained about how unhappy he was with the way others performed their work.

"Do you let them know specifically what you are dissatisfied with?" I inquired.

"Oh, I couldn't do that. Besides, I hint enough, so they should get the point," Juan responded.

Juan, and other workaholics, hint at their dissatisfactions because they are afraid of conflict, afraid of not being liked. At the same time, they are unaware of how demanding they are, because in their mind they see this as just expecting others to do the job as well as they, themselves, do it. In Juan's case, his desire to be a nice guy was in direct conflict with his expectation that people be like him. He expected others to be as curious and involved in their work as he was; but not everyone is motivated similarly.

Juan did not realize he created his own frustration. He wouldn't tell people what he expected because he didn't want to hurt their feelings, but at the same time, he wouldn't confront any problems head-on.

But two of his subordinates had convinced him that they should open the Midwest office service center. The company was small and Juan had opened the three other service centers himself. He had to relinquish some of the responsibility. He had to learn how to delegate.

I convinced him of the benefits of delegating by emphasizing that it would free him to explore some other business areas he thought had potential. And if he gave the other managers some responsibility and authority, Juan might also pique their curiosity to think about the business a little more. Working from behind the scenes, I had Juan call a staff meeting. He had been avoiding it because he didn't want to hear any complaints. At the staff meeting he assigned a project to each of his seven managers, asking them to look at various business aspects and make a presentation to their peers two weeks hence. And Juan had the managers evaluate the responsibilities of the division; then they divided them according to the strengths of each person. It took constant reminders to convince Juan to oversee the activities, not to do everything himself. "Give them some freedom to run with the ball," I counseled.

Most important, I had Juan open the staff meeting by voicing his expectations, reviewing what was going well, and describing his ideas for the future. Weeks before the meeting we reviewed what he wanted to accomplish and how he should set about doing so.

I saw Juan the morning after the first staff meeting. He was proud of how well he had handled things. As he recounted the meeting, I saw how well he had applied what we discussed. His employees were relieved to have Juan listen to their complaints and respond with some possible solutions.

As the months went on, Juan learned to "let go" of responsibilities and give them to others. Through working with Juan, I have developed some general guidelines for workaholics who are faced with management responsibilities that make them uneasy. Here's what you need to do:

1. *Stop expecting others to work your way.* There is not a study that exists supporting the belief that workaholics are more productive than those who work less hours. So, focus your concern on results, not process. Give people the freedom to get things done their own way. Don't bother yourself with how they do it.

2. *Discuss your expectations.* Don't expect people to read your mind or imitate you. Assume the leadership role you have earned. Let people know what you want; discuss your vision of how things should be. Ask others how they see themselves making a contribution.

3. *Delegate.* Now that you are going to discuss your expectations of others, you can follow up by giving them more responsibility. Unburden yourself. You don't have

to do everything. Remember, if you let people work their own way, then more people can help you meet your objectives.

4. *Take time for people*. Most workaholics don't take lunch breaks. So, have a working lunch. Invite people into your conference room for sandwiches. Talk about how things are going. Don't make the meeting specific and goal oriented. Allow for casual interaction. This is when you stop living in the ivory tower and learn what is really happening in the trenches.

5. *Learn to listen*. You don't have to solve every problem that comes your way. Sometimes all someone needs is an ear. Be there. Stop acting like everything you are doing is a matter of life or death. In the whole picture, how important is the little thing you are doing at this moment? It is often very important to the person you have given some time to. Listening means understanding what's important to another person. Let him or her know you understand.

BE OBJECTIVELY INTROSPECTIVE

Unless a workaholic is introspective and possesses objectivity about himself, he is likely to be caught by surprise when problems surface, leaving him overwhelmed and confused. Many of the problems he encounters could be avoided by developing self-awareness, altering his values, and bringing some balance between his work and home life.

If you suspect you are a workaholic, here are three ways to perform preventive maintenance in your personal life.

1. *Do an inventory*. Ask yourself: Am I uncomfortable in social situations? How much do I give to my marriage, kids, friends? How many close friends do I have? When was the last time I saw my friends? Do I put work before everything else?

2. *Prevent problems from starting*. Make time for lunch with business friends and talk about things other than work. Honor your commitments. Don't break your plans because "work is calling." Spend "quality" time if not "quantity" time with your kids. It is not how much time you give to someone else; it is what you give when you are with them. Let people know they matter. Give of yourself and you'll be surprised by the return on your investment.

3. *Set a weekly goal.* Address one aspect of your life at a time. For example, on week one, call two friends from college days. Week two, take your kids to a movie. Week three, spend an evening alone with your wife. Week four, honor all social commitments, refusing to cancel anything because of work.

If you feel that changing your behavior requires more intensive action, you might want to consider some of these approaches that have helped others:

1. *Go to therapy.* Whatever your hangups are about therapy, get over them right now. It is not a sign of weakness to seek help. It takes strength and courage to be honest with yourself. To reach out is always an act of strength. The most common reason for drowning is that people don't yell for help. If you are emotionally drowning don't wait until you hit rock bottom.

To find a therapist, ask a friend you know who is already in therapy. Call your internist. Don't answer ads in publications. You want someone qualified and experienced. Once you have gathered some names, interview a few of the psychologists first by phone and then in person. All too often I hear people complain after the first few visits that they don't really like their psychologist. In the beginning don't think something is the matter with you if you feel this way. Find someone you feel comfortable with. Look for chemistry between you and your therapist.

2. *Keep a journal.* Writing down what you are thinking and feeling helps you gain perspective on your problems. It is also a way to unburden your mind. If you write something down you don't have to commit it to memory. Don't ever feel you have to write in your journal every day. Write on an as-needed basis. You can write nasty letters to people. You can be conceited. You can explore your fantasies. You can create life as you would like to see it and compare it to how things are.

3. *Find a place for spirituality.* Alcoholics Anonymous is one of the most successful programs for dealing with addiction. Other programs such as Overeaters Anonymous, Cocaine-Users Anonymous, or Gamblers Anonymous all build their foundation around AA principles. They advocate spirituality—believing in a power greater than yourself. Read books that deal with this subject. Go to church, meditate. It doesn't matter how you pray or what you believe in. Find your way to believe.

4. *Set your priorities.* Reevaluate your needs. Take time for things in life other than work. Find out what's important to your family and friends. Make some short-term goals for yourself. Too many workaholics spend time looking into the future and letting today pass by. Don't be a person who looks back on his life and wonders what it was all about. Learn to enjoy some of the simple things and stop using work to prove that you are worthwhile. Above all, remember that work is only something you do, not who you are.

CHAPTER 7

PEOPLE TELL ME I'M TOO HARD ON MYSELF: THE PERFECTIONIST

- *"Do it right or don't do it at all."*
- *"After completing a project, I usually think of how I could have done it better."*
- *"When people compliment me, I think, But I have so much to improve on."*
- *"At times, I feel that I am not good enough, especially when I look at others' successes."*

Do any of these statements ring true for you?

If so, you might have a perfectionist streak. What does it mean to be a perfectionist? It means feeling that, no matter what you do, it is not good enough and that the only way you will become a great person is to do everything perfectly.

If you are a perfectionist, there may be a little voice inside your head that edits your comments, judges your actions, and tells you what you should be doing or saying. When someone compliments you, you may respond by pointing out your flaws. Or, you may set goals for yourself only to be upset because you don't accomplish everything in the established time. You refuse to acknowledge that Superman would be unable to tackle the feats you set for yourself.

Perfectionistic managers drive their people hard. As fathers they don't give their kids too many compliments because they want them to work toward something. "Criticism builds character," says the perfectionist. Or at least it does for him. In fact, if someone told a perfectionist to give up that critical voice in his head, he wouldn't, because it's what motivates him, what lets him know that he is doing the job well. It is the driving force behind his success.

If this is beginning to ring a bell, you are not alone. In fact, 52 percent of the men in my study indicated that they had perfectionistic traits. Major psychological studies show that 70 percent of all people have feelings similar to those cited above for at least a period in their life. One of the more recent studies on perfectionism showed that two out of every five successful people in all walks of life experience these feelings.

The positive side of the perfectionist complex is that those who have it often accomplish more than their peers. The negative side, however, is that over the course of the perfectionist's education and career he feels that, despite advanced degrees or honors, promotions and achievements, he still hasn't really made it yet.

Ask yourself these questions: Do you find yourself creating more challenges and goals for yourself? Have you ever felt like a fraud? Have you ever felt your success was a fluke? Have you ever felt your success happened because of luck and timing? Have you ever felt less qualified than your peers even though many people tell you how bright, talented, or effective you are?

If you identify with these characteristics, the case study in this chapter is designed to help you recognize how your need to be perfect affects those people you work and live with and how the critical voice prevents you from seeing how good you really are. The chapter also explains how to develop a more supportive, nurturing attitude toward yourself and others. It will help you understand the feelings and motivations that cause you to behave as you do and to determine when and where they began.

MEETING THE CANDIDATE

I was working with Leland Whitmore, the divisional vice president of a major financial institution, helping to restructure a sales force of five hundred people. Leland was a maverick in a staid, archaic organization. While his peers were the chairman's clones, wearing sexless, box-shaped Brooks Brothers suits, Leland paced the halls in his hand-tailored suits from Italy, with longish black hair hanging over his shirt collar and bright ties startling the eye.

Leland wanted to promote Trevor Harding, one of his finance managers, to the position of vice president of finance. However, despite Trevor's genius and technical expertise, his co-workers, upon hearing the rumor of this possible promotion, claimed they wouldn't work for Trevor. Many of them, it seemed, loathed dealing with Trevor because they found him too judgmental, unforgiving, and prone to issuing verbal assaults.

I am often brought in to work with these kinds of people. In such cases, two questions must always be asked. First: Does the "candidate" or the person requesting my services (often the boss) really need my help? Second: Does the "candidate" perceive that he has a problem?

I am adamant that the decision to work with me be the candidate's alone. It is irrelevant that the boss or I think help is needed if the candidate doesn't. Over the years, senior management has hoped that hiring me would instill fear in those employees they want to change. I generally recommend against this strategy because fear as a motivator has a short life. The changes it brings about are often temporary.

Besides, I prefer people who are open to criticism, using it as helpful information that brings about personal improvement. I prefer to work with people who want to change because they desire to be the best they can be. No matter how skilled I am, and regardless of my training, it is not only difficult to crack through someone's well-established shield, but it also can be detrimental. It must be done with concern and respect. Otherwise the person may retreat even further into his protective shell.

Leland and I had something else to contend with. I began this project in 1979. At that time it was a relatively new concept to provide managers with private coaching. That was a problem in itself. And compounding the problem was the fact that I was working with everyone in sales, not singling out any individual as better or worse than his peers. In this instance, Trevor was not in sales, and he was singled out. This concerned me greatly. I tried to do everything possible to ensure I would not be viewed as a threat.

The best I could do to normalize the situation was to allow

Trevor as much control as he wanted. After the introductions were made and Leland explained to Trevor the purpose of my services, I expressed my concerns and reservations. I concluded by telling Trevor that the choice to work with me was his alone.

I was surprised by Trevor's openness to Leland's suggestion. On the surface, he seemed comfortable with the idea of working with me, suggesting we have lunch at the Harvard Club at noon the next day.

BIRTH OF THE CRITICAL VOICE

During our lunch I learned that after graduating from Harvard, Trevor had gone on to Stanford for his M.B.A. He then joined the firm, proving to be a valuable asset to the mergers and acquisitions department. Trevor told me about his accomplishments, described his wonderful wife, Claire, and their perfect marriage, and expressed pride in himself on his steady rise through life, a life that he assured me was going very much as he had planned. That was, until Leland and I had sat down with him.

With this opening Trevor sent me a strong warning: Tread lightly because I guard my insecurities carefully. Heeding this warning, I decided to take a circuitous route to uncover the source of the problem by finding out about Trevor's upbringing.

He told me his father had been a successful, prominent Bostonian who raised his children under the Protestant work ethic. "Boy, do what you are told," his father had said. "Be responsible, never brag about your achievements, and you will be rewarded."

"I feared him until the day he died," Trevor said. "I can still hear him, half jokingly asking why I had brought a report card full of straight A's, when A+'s were the only thing suitable for a son of his. No matter how well any of us did, it was never good enough. I've got to be the best at anything I do. All my life people have told me I'm too hard on myself, yet I can't seem to stop it."

I now understood why the lunch began with an indirect warning. I empathized with Trevor, because although he had not verbalized how bad he felt receiving this input from Leland, I could safely assume that anyone raised by a father like his would be coming down pretty hard on himself as a result of Leland's suggestion.

Although Trevor went on to describe more about his upbringing, his feelings about his father, and the resulting inner turmoil, I already knew that the first thing we would have to contend with would be his critical voice. I felt it was important to explain to Trevor how his critical voice had developed. "Most perfectionists are run by a voice of this kind," I began. If the messages we received from our parents conveyed, "You are not good enough yet, but keep trying," we grow up continually striving for their approval. As a result, we grow up with a self-disparaging voice, the voice of the critical parent that gradually becomes our own.

I explained to Trevor that since he rarely received positive input as a child, he incorporated his parents' way as his own. As an adult he ignored, suppressed, and even ran from feeling good about himself. We all develop strategies or psychological defenses to reduce emotional pain caused by disapproval, rejection, or criticisms we may have experienced while growing up. As we probe deeper, we see the self-critic has put all his trust and belief in his parents' opinions, so as he moves into adulthood he feels it would be an act of betrayal to contradict his parents' thoughts and opinions. In Trevor's case betraying his parents would eliminate his chances of receiving the approval he so deeply covets. So he continues through life, unable to trust any positive feelings or thoughts he has about himself or about how others feel about him.

I suspect Trevor's father believed, as many parents did and still do believe, that criticism would motivate his child to achieve more, to be better. However, most parents do not realize they are not only teaching their child to treat himself like they treat him, but they foster his unsatisfied need for approval and affection. On the outside the child appears to be undamaged, continually striving to do his best. But on the inside he constantly fights this verbal whip and his feelings of inadequacy. The continual criticism creates a sense of inferiority coupled with the hope of one day receiving the coveted parental recognition.

Let me explain this another way. First and foremost, how you treat or talk about others is often a reflection of how you feel about yourself. Psychologists call this "projection." Projection is the process of attributing your own feelings, behavior, or attitudes to another person. A simple way of illustrating this is: People often use "you" language when they are in fact making a statement abut how they think or feel, which should actually be signified by "I" language. "You" statements are judgmental or critical in nature, often causing people to feel angry or defensive. Conversely, "I" statements tell someone what you want, expect, need, or desire without putting that person down or causing guilt. "I" statements do not put a burden on the other person.

For example: "You have disappointed me" can be expressed in a positive way, as, "I feel disappointed." "You aren't considerate enough to my position," could instead be, "I would like you to consider my position." "You really messed up this assignment," would be better expressed as, "I wanted this done differently, and I am unhappy with the results."

After explaining this to Trevor, I decided to use an example that would hit close to home with him. "Trevor, let's attempt to analyze what your father meant when he would tell you that you were never good enough. It began, I suspect, with your father's belief that being hard on himself had paid off. Therefore, what he thought was good for him should be good for his son. He was projecting his attitude onto you. Since he was critical of you, you can bet he was just as critical of himself. He drove himself equally as hard. What you are doing is acting like your father, and that's what we want to change."

Trevor leaned back and laughed. "This sure has been more enlightening than I ever anticipated. I only hope I can do something with what you've told me."

"Well, if that means I'm hired, then cut out the b.s. What do you mean, 'you only hope you'll do something with the knowledge'? I refuse to let you waste it or to get away with putting yourself down from this point forth."

"I want to ask you something, and I want an honest answer," Trevor demanded. "Why won't you come out and tell me I've been a jerk, that I've done it all wrong?"

"I don't think you are a jerk," I answered. "You are the critic, not I."

UNDOING THE DAMAGE

At our first official meeting, Trevor demanded that since we had uncovered why he was so tough on himself, he wanted to know how he was going to remedy the situation.

"Sure, Trevor," I responded, "your father does damage for twenty-five years, you pick up where he left off, and I am supposed to wave a magic wand and change the tide. A miracle worker I am not." Still I understood what Trevor wanted: relief from a way of life that had caused him emotional discomfort and turmoil.

The first hurdle always to be overcome with driven men is to convince them that getting rid of their critical voice is the right thing to do. They rarely believe me in the beginning, because they are convinced that this verbal whip is their primary motivator. When I point out that their motivation really comes from their desire for approval and recognition and that the critical voice is simply a tool, it becomes easier to "sell" them on the idea of trying out a new "motivational tool." I assure them that one can operate without the critical voice and still be ambitious and successful. The energy that previously was channeled into the critical voice can be directed into performance. The new tools are self-appreciation and recognizing and building on the positives.

"Trevor," I began, "we need to look at what you do and find ways to change your behavior. I suggest we start with doing some psychological research. You have all the information we need in your head. I will jostle your memory with a few questions. We can't change any behavior, or the feelings that bring on the actions, unless we know what thoughts cause your behavior."

I then asked him a series of pointed questions. Did your father expect blind obedience? Was your father competitive with you? Did he compare you to other children or to your siblings? What made you value your father's judgment above your own? Did your father discourage you from being independent in your thoughts and actions? Did he encourage you to be just like him? Are there things you want to do but don't because you fear that you might not be good enough at them?

As Trevor reflected on these questions, I could see that it was like a light bulb turned on inside of his head. He threw himself back in his chair and exclaimed, "That's why I gave up sailing. During the summers, we would have boat races up at the Cape. Father was always the captain, and my brothers and I obediently followed his orders. During the season's last race, we were neck-and-neck with another boat. The championship was on the line. Instead of looking to Father, I took it upon myself to pull in the jib enough to give us the cutting edge. We won the race and the championship. I was elated and turned to Father, expecting him to say something like, "Good going, son." It didn't happen. Instead he glowered at me disapprovingly. Later, he accused me of trying to steal the thunder from my brothers. I was crushed. I never wanted to sail after that, and in fact, I haven't. That was more than eighteen years ago. I never realized until this moment why it is that for half my life I've been avoiding something I once loved."

He went on, "The fact of the matter is that I don't do anything anymore unless I know I will do it exceptionally well. I am easily frustrated. If something appears difficult, I move on to something I know I will succeed in."

He stopped talking for quite some time, then began again. "This makes me wonder if my discomfort with people watching me work has anything to do with my father's disapproving stares. Do people grow up with memories like mine imprinted in their mind causing them to wonder if others might react to them similarly?"

"Yes, people carry those childhood scars into adulthood," I responded. "Until we resolve our psychological ghosts, we often do two things. First, we pick people like our mother or father with whom to reenact our unresolved situations. Sometimes this is conscious, other times not. For example, is there someone currently in your life who reminds you of your father? Do you do things that you hope will please him or her? Because your father was critical it is the criticalness that you respond to in someone, whether it be a man or a woman.

"Second, we misinterpret people's reactions because the emotional wounds remain unhealed. For instance, have you ever felt after explaining your work to Leland that you perceived him as disapproving only to discover he was confused? It's important to be aware of how we expect people to react to us.

"This isn't always easy, but I have a few suggestions to help you. The goal of this exercise is to challenge the ghosts lurking in your mind that you haven't been able to identify." I suggested that Trevor try the following:

- *Make a list of the people you care about.* Below each person's name, write down why he or she is important to you. Ask yourself if that person reminds you of someone else in your life. Ask yourself how you want him or her to feel about you. Spend some time reflecting on this.

- *Make a list entitled "What I Want to Be Admired For."* This list will help you discover what you consider important. Then challenge each item by asking, "Who did I learn this from?" "Do I really want to keep this on the list?" "What is not on the list that I want to add?"
- *Make a list entitled "What I Like About Myself."* This is often the most difficult to do because people so readily come up with what they *don't* like about themselves.

IMPACT ON OTHERS

Trevor responded well to the exercises and suggestions I gave him. We spent nearly two months making him aware of whom he looked to for approval, what he did to get approval, how he verbally beat himself up and what situations triggered this reaction.

My strategy was simple. Until he became aware of what he did to himself, I would not be able to encourage him to acknowledge what he did to others.

I met with Trevor a few weeks later. He burst into the office looking more relaxed than ever. I was thankful that the timing seemed good. After a short chat, we got down to business. "The time has come for us to get a little information from the people you live with and work with," I said. "I think you have a good perspective of yourself. Over the past two months, we have found ways to incorporate a more positive self-image into your thinking. You are ready to compare your own opinions with the feedback you get from others. You can't change your behavior or personal feelings until you know how you are perceived.

"I would like you to talk with your people and then I would like to do it as well," I continued. "We have to gather information before I can suggest new ways for you to manage them. You have to become more aware of your feelings and see how you act. My talking to them will help us discover if there are problems you are not being told about."

"I can't do that," Trevor protested, "because they tell me I never listen to them. My wife tells me this all the time. So I know my people probably won't even talk to me." When Trevor noticed this excuse did not make me waver from my position he asked, "What should I do differently?"

"Trevor, the inability to listen comes from feeling defensive. Describe for me how you react when people try to express their feelings to you."

"I'm not exactly sure. Some people have said I always act as if I know better than they do or I interrupt them to debate the point that they are making. Sometimes I look away when they are talking or get exasperated, impatient with what they say. Is that what you mean?"

"Exactly," I said. "I have some ideas about how you might approach the meeting with your people and help establish rapport with them."

- *Set the tone*. Explain that you know you need to work on your management style and that you need their input.
- *Show empathy*. Tell each person that it is equally as frightening for you to hear what they have to say as you know it is for them to tell you the truth.
- *Ask questions*. Listen to the answers; probe deeper for more explicit examples, if needed. Thank people for their input. Let them know you understand what they say.
- *Avoid negating, explaining, or defending*. No matter what past actions they talk about, you don't have to respond other than by listening. If you do anything else, it will circumvent your goals. Do not expect this to be easy. It won't be. Many managers don't have the courage to do this.

Trevor was apprehensive but willing. He briefed his staff that we would be meeting with them individually over the next two weeks. I wanted Trevor to hear their concerns and not be put off by any emotional charges, so I met with them first. I prefer to be a buffer or even a recipient of the frustration or anger they feel.

Upon concluding the discussions with his staff, Trevor and I met to exchange notes. I was excited that they had been equally open with Trevor and me, indicating that Trevor had not intimidated them and had not been defensive. It was not easy for Trevor to hear one person tell him, "I abhor the idea of being put down by someone so insecure who constantly needs to prove himself at my expense." Another person summed up the feelings we both heard throughout the interviews: "I feel like I have to walk on eggshells. For what

I can learn from him I wouldn't want to work for anyone else. For how he treats me, I'd take anyone else to be my boss.''

Trevor and I discussed the responses and what he learned from this exercise. Above all he was truly surprised that he had acted so similarly to his father. "Listening to them made me question whether they were speaking for me or about me. I really don't want to be so tough on them.''

As we worked together over the next six months, Trevor slowly learned to trust my judgment. When I complimented him or brought to his attention how he had changed, he no longer countered with a self-deprecating comment. When I revised his goals or suggested he reconsider his expectations, he adjusted them realistically, normally without a fight or an accusation that I was being too lenient. A few times he even agreed with me. This was progress, and I was glad to see it; but the path to success is not always straight, and many things can happen before the job is complete.

IMPACT ON THE HOME FRONT

As we entered the home stretch, a setback took place. The holidays were over, and we welcomed in the New Year with great anticipation. The first month was almost behind us when Trevor confessed to me that his wife had left him two days after Christmas. He had been living with this for almost a month but had told no one.

A month after Trevor and I had started working together, Claire confessed to him that she had been having an affair with the carpenter. This took me by surprise because Trevor had always spoken of his wife, the former Claire Woodruff, with admiration and affection. I was not surprised to learn, however, that Claire was a Radcliffe girl he had known most of his life. Her family was pure Boston Brahmin. Claire was exactly the kind of woman whom Trevor always hoped to marry. For him she was the perfect wife and, when the time came, she would be the perfect mother. Her mother had entertained presidents, ambassadors, and members of high society. Claire had been trained to follow in her footsteps. According to Trevor, she even outdid her mother. (I gingerly prodded Trevor to talk. He couldn't look at me. I felt awful because I could see he felt humiliated.)

It seemed that this was not Claire's first affair. Trevor couldn't bear letting anyone (even himself) know that his perfect marriage wasn't so perfect. So he hung in there, waiting for Claire to decide what she was going to do, tolerating her successive extramarital involvements. From what he described, he had more than "hung in like a trouper." He couldn't yet see that Claire was at fault here, too. He was still locked into the mind-set of blaming himself.

I asked Trevor what reasons she had given for leaving. He said she felt that she could be herself with the carpenter with no qualifications, no justifications, no judgments. She felt Trevor was always judging her, making her afraid to say or do anything.

Trevor and I talked for nearly three hours before he confessed, "I can't believe that what I was doing to my staff, I also did at home. The day after she left, I called my mother. Do you believe it, a man my age calling dear ol' mom for support? I wanted to know if she had ever felt that way about Father. I seemed to be doing everything else like him, so why not this? As she described how my father had treated her, I wanted to fall through the earth and disappear. It had been dismal for her. My mother never let on that she was unhappy. She said she'd always wanted to leave but decided to stay with Father for our sake. I thought I was going crazy. I wasn't sure if I was listening to Claire or my mother. They both were saying the same things."

This story left me devastated. I could only imagine what Trevor had been living with. His defenses would soon run out, for he had lived with this charade of perfection for too long. I feared Trevor would withdraw, pick on people, put himself down, or alienate the people he had worked so hard to get along with.

TESTING THE POSITIVE FEELINGS

Trevor was deeply depressed for more than two months. His staff found him intolerable as he took his anger out on them. I attempted to convince Leland and the others (including myself) to be as objective as possible. To help us be objective, I even explained that Trevor was using us to live out his self-fulfilling prophecy of "I'm really no good," that he was trying to prove us wrong for believing in him and for being supportive.

Leland was growing apathetic. I knew he felt hurt and disappointed. I tried to reassure him. The staff was balking. Finally, I dug in my heels and insisted, "People have never supported and cared about Trevor when he was obstinate. He's always proved himself right by alienating others. We can't let him win. Supporting him—proving him wrong—would be the greatest contribution we could make to his life. Trevor thinks reality is what exists in his head. He is having a hard time because life is not proceeding according to his internal script."

Trevor's internal script read like an unfavorable critic's review. His belief system was jolted by the mere fact that his boss, staff, and I continued to care and encourage him to weather his emotional storm. Trevor had to confront himself. He had to challenge the premises by which he operated.

BREAKING THE CYCLE

Trevor needed to examine his self-imposed negative feelings and question their validity. "Isn't it about time to bury the negative perception of yourself?" I asked. "Why are you refusing to see how positively people feel about you? What are the benefits of pretending that others feel negatively about you when they don't?"

His answer caught me by surprise. "I'm beyond hope. I thought everything was going as planned, but my life has fallen apart, and it's all my fault."

That was the beginning of the most negative diatribe Trevor had yet made about himself. In order to break the cycle, I used a technique that had previously been successful. I suggested he continue telling me everything that was bad about himself. When he finished, I recited it all back to him.

"Trevor, what would you think of a man who would say these things about himself?: 'I don't know why people bother with me. You and Leland are fools to stick by me. Claire was right, I should have listened to her. I can't seem to get anything right.' "

"I'd feel sorry for the poor guy. It would be a pity that people cared about him and he was unable to accept it, let alone appreciate them."

Feedback can be one of the most powerful tools a manager, wife, husband, lover, or consultant can use. It can provide the objectivity one needs. Listening to his own comments was the best medicine for Trevor.

"I should stop being so insensitive," Trevor said. "Life hasn't been very easy lately since Claire left me. I've been afraid to believe that anyone else would find me worthwhile. I can get some things right."

When we are not in the habit of doing something, as in Trevor's case, it helps to write down the new thought process so we can see it. I suggested that Trevor do another exercise to reinforce his positive frame of mind. Here's what the exercise consisted of:

- *Make a Daily "To-Do" List.* At the end of the week review your goals. Look at the ways you subconsciously set unrealistic goals. Do you berate yourself when you don't accomplish them? Reevaluate what you did get done and consider all the unexpected demands.
- *Make a "Done" List.* At the end of every day write down what you did accomplish. You can put anything you want on the list. Both trivial and important things belong there.

Do both of these exercises for two weeks. By comparing the "done" list with the "to-do" list, you will begin to understand why some things get accomplished and others don't.

Trevor and I met a month later. As I walked into his office, even before I had a chance to be seated, Trevor began updating me. He admitted that if he had not been doing these exercises, he might have overlooked how well he and his staff had handled another major acquisition.

He went on, "The fact of the matter is that I feel quite differently now. I have heard you tell me numerous times that Claire was not without responsibility for our failed marriage, but I couldn't believe it. I can see now that she ran to other men, opting to avoid expressing her discontentment with the situation rather than finding a way to make our marriage better."

He continued with mock anger, "Why didn't you tell me that finding the good in what I do and what others do produces these strange sensations called pride and exhilaration? For the first time in ages, I really want to get up in the morning. I like coming to work. I've genuinely enjoyed watching my people blossom. I have been going over one person's career goals and a few others have come to me with their problems. I think I've returned to the old me.''

"Oh, so the old you is this positive, supportive manager that we see now?" I inquired sarcastically.

"You'd better believe it, and he's going to stay around if I have anything to say about it." Trevor and I were laughing again. I had missed that part of our working relationship and was glad that his internal pressure had subsided.

It was a little more than a year since we had started working together. Trevor asked if I'd meet with his staff once more. He decided the discussion should focus on what he still needed to improve on, adding laughingly, "I'm feeling lonely without my critical ways, putting myself down, never feeling good enough. It's dangerous for me to feel too content with myself. Of all people, you should know that I have difficulty letting myself believe any progress has been made. I'm surprised at you. Had you forgotten that completely, in the face of all this improvement? Did you become stupid in the past year while working with me?''

Two weeks later the entire staff met on neutral ground. On the thirty-second floor of New York's Plaza Hotel, with a beautiful view of Central Park competing for our attention, I started the meeting by asking each person to tell me (and Trevor) one way Trevor had changed that made him easier to work with and for. The consensus was that Trevor had become a supportive manager who offered valuable criticism while still letting you know what your good points were. He was much easier to work with and no longer compared people to one another. He had always taught them a lot, but over the past six months the fearful learning environment had become one of mutual support.

A few months later Trevor Harding was finally promoted.

Trevor and I decided to have a summary meeting before we said our good-byes. At that meeting, Trevor realized that he had never known anyone who could be consistently supportive of his efforts, no matter what he did. We both agreed that I had served many useful roles over the past sixteen months, but most important, he began to integrate my supportive, encouraging voice into his own. I urged him to make friends with other people who were as supportive as I had been, because I didn't want his life to be devoid of the encouragement and recognition he needed and deserved.

Trevor's time and thought no longer went into counteracting the self-abuse he used to heap on himself so often. He had developed an appreciation of himself and a belief that he did not need to tear himself apart in order to gain motivation. He realized that the time wasted beating himself up and licking his wounds was now channeled into performing.

Now he had time to dream about his goals and build upon his newly acquired pride. Since he no longer knocked himself down, he didn't have to squander energy to build himself up again. He now appreciated and enjoyed himself with fewer down days and a greater enthusiasm for life.

IF YOU RELATE TO TREVOR

The critical voice is not something to be ignored. And it is often difficult to combat it alone. However, not every company will hire a consultant to work with their managers; so it might help if you find someone else who suffers from a critical voice and help one another to change. Or you might decide to seek counseling. Most important, if you relate to Trevor, here are some things you can do to help yourself change:

1. List all of the qualities you want to be admired for.
2. Think about the people in your life whose opinions matter.
3. Focus on your positive qualities.
4. Find a role model to learn new behaviors from.
5. Challenge the expectations you have of yourself.
6. Make a list of self-criticisms, and counter them with your positive qualities.
7. Ask people for feedback and simply listen.
8. Compare your "to-do" list with your "done" list.
9. Admit to yourself, and at least one other person, when things are not so great.
10. Take risks and make mistakes.

CHAPTER 8

IN PURSUING SUCCESS, I LOST MY SELF-ESTEEM

In some ways, the men I interviewed profoundly affected my views. In particular they dispelled the myth that success automatically brings self-esteem and confidence.

During the course of the interviews I would wonder: Why can a person be outwardly successful, yet insecure? Why do some people appear satisfied with their accomplishments, while others are never contented? A few men helped me answer these questions. These are men who learned to stop looking at and depending on external yardsticks to measure their self-worth. These are men who realized their lives were driven by misguided values, which only perpetuated their feelings of emptiness and insecurity. Through dogged introspection and honesty, they learned to believe in themselves and see themselves as separate from their accomplishments.

But some men never learn to believe in themselves, no matter what they accomplish. They see themselves as they want to be, rather than as they are. They spend their lives developing the best sales presentation, buying the best ski equipment, playing the hardest, conquering the most women; yet they never feel like they've "made it."

"You're only as good as your *next* accomplishment when you depend on anything outside yourself to measure your self-worth and identity," I would attempt to impress upon them.

I spoke with an accountant, who had recently started his own firm. As in all start-up operations, the path was arduous and slow. When I asked him what he hoped to gain from his commitment and hard work, he told me, "I'd like financial security and my self-esteem."

"Your self-esteem will only come once you build your practice and gain a reputation for yourself?" I responded half inquisitively and half rhetorically.

I felt sorry for this man. By the time I met him, I had interviewed so many men and heard this same comment so many times, I couldn't help saying, with a tone of frustration and concern, "You men have the order all wrong. Your self-esteem does not come from what you do, it comes from who you are. So what if you never become Arthur Anderson or Touche Ross, building a top accounting firm as they did. If you believe in yourself, it doesn't matter what people think of you. It's the values that guide your life. It's the way you feel about yourself that gives you any self-esteem."

"I know you're right. That is, in my head I know it. But I don't feel that way. And that's not how I see other men acting. I wish I knew how to jump off this treadmill, but I can't get my legs to stop running," he responded.

He was so right.

This needless suffering and emptiness is caused by misguided values men embrace as the gospel, values that place more importance on fame, wealth, and status than on honesty, integrity, self-development, and caring. By sacrificing their values for status, placing more importance on appearances than happiness, and spending time in empty or false relationships rather than with people they love, these men find themselves feeling empty and fraudulent.

Many peers and colleagues hold Mark Adams, an executive vice president in the entertainment business, in awe, for he exemplifies the ultimate in success: becoming one of the youngest (twenty-eight) EVP's in "the business," having an eye for creative works that bring large profits, owning a home in the Hollywood Hills and a Mercedes 380SL. Those he comes in contact with love and respect him.

There's not a place he goes where people don't know him by name and wait on him with special care. One day he took me to lunch at a well-known Beverly Hills restaurant. After we were seated, Mark said to me, "I know what to say in order to impress people. I know what body language to use so people will think I'm confident.'' Mark then demonstrates for me a relaxed, stretched-out position, before continuing, ''I know when to be witty and charming, when to nod or smile. I criticize myself; I compare myself to others: some younger than I have surpassed my accomplishments, some men have better taste than I, some others in the business get more done in a day or week. Yet, none of them would believe that I feel this way. I spend my life fooling people.''

Just like Mark, many men find themselves wondering, ''Without my tux and toys, who am I?''

Whenever men tell me they are questioning the time and effort they are putting into their careers, I suggest that they look at the values that might be causing that unfulfilled feeling. The 23 percent who claimed to be happy with themselves both inwardly and outwardly had one main characteristic in common: their self-confidence was a result of experiencing a period of self-doubt, a period of questioning their beliefs, values, and objectives. The satisfaction with their lives resulted after a long search for inner meaning and by overcoming their dependence on external yardsticks for success.

These ''satisfied and happy'' men listed their priorities, which included: having fun at work, valuing personal growth, cherishing family and friends. You don't find status, fame, or money on the list of motivators. And it is not that they don't want any of those external indicators. If one happens to come their way that's okay. But these men are not pursuing outward measures of success. They simply don't need crutches of confidence to define themselves.

But they know self-worth and confidence cannot be taken for granted. Contrary to the braggarts who put on their secure façade every morning and who will never admit to anything going wrong in their lives, these men have learned to be honest with themselves; an honesty that comes only from the pain of personal growth. It is acquired through hard work; by learning how to be introspective, how to understand your feelings, how to create your own rules rather than subscribe to formulas.

A PERIOD OF SELF-DOUBT

John Rollwagen was not one of the forty-three men whose lives I followed, nor was he one of the original four thousand. I met John in January 1987 after he participated in a panel discussion about CEOs, leadership, and the future.

When John said to the group, ''To admit problems exist means you have to be as comfortable with the good feelings as you are with the 'bad' ones. I believe in trauma. Sure, some pain is involved and that means you have to counsel people a little bit. But in the end it's worth it because you generally have created something great,'' I knew he had to be profiled in my book.

Upon conclusion of the panel discussion, I waited to talk with him. Since I have interviewed many corporate heads, I am aware of the demands people place on them, always asking for something: their time, their advice, their assistance. I never wanted to be perceived as a "taker," so in the interviews I always made sure to give back as much as they gave. But at request time, there was no way to convey this, and when I was about to ask John if I could interview him, butterflies swarmed in my stomach. But within seconds he put me at ease.

So often when men get to the top of the pyramid they become unapproachable. Protected by secretaries, subordinates, and sycophants, one has to permeate layers of shields before reaching the "ruler." Some of the men asked me to write letters to various members of the chain of command before they would give their approval for an interview. Others wanted to see how many hoops I was willing to jump through to get to them. Some secretaries had to be begged and bribed. To the contrary, John is one of the most approachable CEOs I have met.

I gave him a brief description of the book and asked if he would be willing to talk with me. "Sure," he said, "except I figured out that I'm home about ninety days out of the year. So if you could send me something to read first, I'd be happy to call you." True to his word, John called me shortly after he received the material. And over the next few weeks I spent some time getting to know him.

RAISED WITH THE FORMULA FOR SUCCESS

In John's words, "I've had it better than average. I went to good schools [MIT and Harvard]. I came from a good family, lived in the better part of town. I'm bright. I was brought up with a lot of the formula, the ingredients to be successful.''

At thirty-seven, John became the president of Cray Research. At forty he took over as the CEO, then a year later assumed the responsibilities of board chairman. Despite his privileged upbringing, the climb to the top did not happen as smoothly as one might expect.

"Over a ten-year period beginning in 1970 my life took a downturn," John started to explain. "Looking at my life curve there are three distinct periods. Growing up, life was great. I was always satisfied with every opportunity, every experience. I've had my quota of goodness that comes along in life. I'm a lucky person who has been given his fair share.

"By 1975, my self-esteem was way below zero. I remember feeling scared and unsure. I had taken a cut in pay. I was plotting my sense of life, applying the ingredients; but it wasn't working. I was in a job where my boss's management style and mine didn't mix. He had me kicking ass for him, and I'm not built for that."

It seemed that John was faced with dilemmas in his personal life as well. His marriage wasn't working. He knew he wanted out but was saddled with guilt.

"I went through all this responsibility and guilt. I thought we had made it this far, there had to be something we could put back together. But there wasn't. The first few years we were apart, we still did things together as a family. I thought that would lessen the pain on the kids and on my ex-wife. It only made it harder. Looking back, I handled it that way so as to make it easier on myself," he explained.

John is an electrical engineer by training. I had expected him to deal with things logically, rather than so emotionally. By that I mean, I was surprised by how adept he was in dealing with his feelings and with his self-understanding. So I asked, "Who taught you to trust your feelings?"

"I learned from my daddy that feelings were okay. But I use my logic as well. Let me give you an example. When I would get scared, my daddy would tell me it was okay. Then he'd tell me to stop for a moment and think about what the worst case would be. And he'd remind me there was nothing I couldn't deal with."

"So you use your logic to calm yourself down, but not to put yourself down," I surmised.

"That's right," John responded.

In 1980, John finally left home. It took him five years from the time he knew he wanted out of his marriage until the time he left. "It wasn't ever a question of do I or don't I [leave]. It was a question of 'How do I do this?' I don't like to hurt people."

And about the time John left was when his self-esteem started to come back. I remember asking what he thought was the turning point that directed him upward. "I think it happened when I realized that the way I was going to stop feeling afraid and unsure was to give myself a little time. The answers I needed would come, if I didn't force them.

"About that time I got together with Beverly [his second wife]. She helped me through this depressed period. She got me through this period of self-doubt by giving me permission to lighten up. She helped me laugh or she'd hold me when I was scared, tired, or upset.

"She was so different from my first wife. In my previous marriage it was more of a combat style. Mary would subtly judge me, usually quite negatively. My former wife was controlling and competitive. I spent my time steering her away from directly trying to compete with me. She'd say things to me, such as, 'Don't think you'll ever be head of a company.' And I'd get into the competitive trap thinking about how I was going to prove her wrong."

Continuing, John described Beverly, "She's herself. Beverly has her own career. She's an accomplished artist and writer. I met her when she was flying for Northwest, finishing her college degree, and putting the pieces back in her life since she had recently been separated.

"If I hadn't found Beverly to give me permission to be me, I wouldn't be able to give others permission to be themselves."

It caught my attention that John used the word "permission" to describe how Beverly helped him through his doubting time. I asked him to elaborate.

"She gave me permission to not take life so seriously. It was Beverly loving me and teaching me trust that instilled in me the values of helping people grow to be who they are," John replied.

And then John added, "Cray wouldn't be what it is today if I had stayed with Mary. Nor would it be [as great] if I hadn't found Beverly. I know the feeling around Cray reflects how I feel. If I'm depressed, the whole place is depressed."

Few corporate heads are aware that they set the tone for the entire corporation. Their values and attitudes permeate the philosophy, the policies, and the morale. Rollwagen knows this well.

Cray is a company where many people want to work. Last year Cray received thirty thousand applications for the eight hundred positions available. To quote from *Cray Style,* a written testament to their corporate philosophy, "Cray people trust each other to do their jobs well and with the highest ethical standards. We take each other very seriously. At Cray Research, we take what we do very seriously, but we don't take ourselves too seriously."

"My philosophy is simple and straightforward," John began to explain. "One, we give people the opportunity to tackle major challenges. The objectives are tough. And we make the work groups small. Two, we provide limited (but adequate) resources. And three, we offer no backup plan. Nothing is set up to hedge our bet. And nobody else is trying to do that project, so people are competitive and driven to be successful."

Elaborating on this, he said, "You have to trust people rather than supervise them. The way I communicate my philosophy to people is by telling them, 'It's your decision.' And blame is not the issue. Something gets screwed up, you don't ask, 'Who did it?' Instead ask yourself, 'What can we do now?' "

I asked, "What would you tell someone who asked you, 'What should I do to be successful like you?' "

John answered, "You have to find your own way instead of following a formula or just applying the ingredients. You have to find the right opportunities to use your talents, knowing you have the skills to find your own solutions."

"How can you tolerate being with other CEOs then?" I caught myself asking.

"I don't know if I know any," John answered. "I don't hang around with many. I think they shake their heads, looking at me quizzically, and write me off. I suspect some feel threatened. So many don't know how to be happy. I think they're jealous knowing I'm having such a good time."

"I bet they are," I said.

Then John added, "I like being different."

And John was different from many of the CEOs I interviewed. Where the others would talk the "new language of management," reciting passages from the latest pop management books, John was living it.

Although John was born with all the "right" ingredients, he had to learn on his own to place a high value on personal growth. Introspection means you have to work through emotional pain. It means you have to go through a trial-and-error period, with no guidelines or rules. In the end you discover the individual components that make up your emotional backbone.

A TEMPORARY CHANGE OF VALUES

"I was raised in a working-class neighborhood of Pittsburgh, where my father was a coal miner. Everyone loved Edward St. John. They called him 'good neighbor Ed.' He instilled in me values that had little to do with materialism and more to do with caring about others."

Success had come to Paul St. John at an early age. When he was twenty-eight, he became a manager at the investment banking firm where he worked. He made more money the year he was thirty-two than his father had made in ten years' time.

"Because we didn't have a lot of money when I was growing up, I was under the impression that money bought happiness. In trying to achieve that goal I discovered I lost my confidence, my self-esteem. Then I opened my eyes to what I had done, only to find out that I had stopped liking myself," confided Paul. "I used to be so concerned about status symbols. I would wear designer suits and make sure to take my jacket off and fold it so the label showed. Instead of offering someone a ride, I'd say, 'I can drop you off, my driver's outside.' In looking back I ask myself, Why did I need four suede jackets? I was happy with the house we were living in, so why did I buy a new one four times more expensive just to impress people?"

"Why do you think so many men fall into that trap?" I asked Paul.

"I can only answer that from the perspective of the world in which I spent most of my working years," he started to explain. "In the investment banking world, the money you make is the measurement of how good you are. And everyone knows how much money you make. They want to know you want more than you already have or you will lose your credibility. I've never taken my mask off in front of others, for they'd kill me. So by training, I was never satisfied. I constantly had to make more money. If I didn't make more money, I'd think I wasn't doing as well as my peers.

"I tried to hide how much I cared about people. As an investment banker you learn never to say what you feel. To care about people you were always thought of as 'weak' or as a 'wimpo.' Very few men in this business have intimate friends. We set ourselves up to be insular, overprotective, phonies with nearly impenetrable veneers, so our friends don't ever see our weaknesses.

"On the other hand, most of my peers and supervisors were inconsiderate, awful, or ignored their management responsibilities. I decided I would be different. Investment banking required that I be a 'barracuda' with regard to my work, but I had no intention of extending that aggressiveness to my management style. I was going to show people respect. If they had a problem, I wanted them to feel they could talk to me. I looked at them as individuals with different concerns and needs," he started to explain.

When I met Paul he had left his investment banking firm to become the president of a successful software company whose fame derived from its brilliant but reclusive owner. By virtue of who he worked for and the company he represented, Paul was asked to give speeches in the community and around the country. People always wanted to meet him, know him, and be seen with him.

However, it wasn't easy working for a creative genius, especially when your management philosophy differed from his. Frederick Castle, the company founder, had a great desire to control the entire organization, although he didn't want to be actively involved in any of the activities. Frederick gave lip service to caring about people and being progressive in his management style. He claimed to care about employees, but Paul frequently had to remind him to thank someone for his contribution or not castigate him in front of others.

Contrary to Paul's management style of delegating authority, Frederick would constantly usurp Paul's power. In truth, he was a martyr and a dictator. "He only wanted people to agree with him," Paul reminisced. "Frederick wouldn't give me much power to do the things I believed the company needed. My way of counter-manding Frederick's power plays was to work on people liking me. They were loyal to me and supported my ideas. Frederick didn't know how to unite a team. That was my role.''

As Frederick continuously treated Paul like the company's fig-urehead, Paul assumed that role. In looking back, Paul reflected, ''I was the company. If I lost my job, I [thought I] would lose face. So I was willing to do anything to hold on to it. And that meant not being willing to see that the person I bestowed the most trust in was stabbing me in my gut, right before my eyes.''

That realization did not come to Paul without much pain. I was a consultant to Paul until he fired me for telling him the truth —that he was being betrayed by his most trusted employee—a truth he didn't want to hear.

A few years later Paul called to tell me what happened. We agreed to have lunch; to discuss what had transpired and what he had learned. I was so moved by his story that I asked Paul if he would spend some time recounting what had happened so I could write about it. And Paul has been gracious enough to let me tell his story; a story of triumph over betrayal and of the pain of losing yourself in your job, all in the pursuit of success.

RAPED BY REALITY

Paul's management team was made up of the best and brightest young talent. What they lacked in years of experience, they made up for in enthusiasm and brain power. Paul enjoyed developing people and he delegated power and authority willingly.

Paul developed a strong relationship with Bill Crawford. Tall, handsome, and brilliant, Bill endeared himself to everyone, espe-cially Paul. I often referred to Bill as Paul's alter ego. As Bill became a trusted ally, Paul gave him more responsibility. Everyone in the company, except for Paul, recognized Bill's quest for power, at any cost and at the expense of anyone. Before two years passed Paul promoted Bill to COO.

Before his promotion, Bill had tried to hide his drive for power. With his new title, he relinquished all restraint and aggressively began his attempts to usurp the reins from Paul. But he simultaneously continued his charade with Paul. In Paul's presence he would act like the loyal puppy dog. And if threatened he would resort to drama.

A few people tried to warn Paul that Bill was sabotaging his efforts to run the company. At first Paul was going to sit back, holding on to his trump card, playing it at the right moment. He had placed a lot of faith and trust in Bill, and he was crushed by the prospect of being betrayed. Paul could not sit still, knowing Bill was undermining his leadership. When Paul confronted Bill, Bill, teary-eyed, adamantly denied the accusations.

Paul's father had raised him to trust people.

"I always trusted people," he continued. "I had never been betrayed or deceived. When I finally accepted that Bill was out for my job, I lost all confidence in myself. I couldn't believe that I could be so wrong at judging someone. I felt raped by reality."

Being betrayed shook Paul more than anything in his life, he claimed. It brought about a loss of faith in people.

IGNORING THE TELLTALE SIGNS

I asked Paul, "What caused you to ignore the warnings that everyone gave you about Bill?"

"I was angry at my wife, at anyone who tried to tell me the truth about Bill," Paul started in. "In retrospect I rationalized away the warnings by telling myself, 'Other people seem to have a personality conflict with Bill.' In truth, I thought if I listened to what they were telling me, I would have to admit I was wrong. And I didn't want to believe that Bill had misinterpreted all my good intentions.

"And I didn't want to talk about it with anyone. I was embarrassed. I saw this as my own failure and I was afraid people would laugh at me," Paul confided.

"Was there a turning point at which you finally accepted Bill's deceitfulness and did something about it?" I inquired.

"There was," Paul answered. "We were sitting in our hot tub during a snowstorm one evening and Roberta [his wife] and I started talking. She told me, 'I loved you all those years because you never cared about impressing people. You believed in yourself.'

"It was then that I realized I had had a temporary change of values. Roberta let me see myself, hear what I was thinking. She stopped being put off by my anger and drew out my concerns. She never challenged or criticized me but reinforced how important a person I was to her and that my job had nothing to do with it. I was caught in my own image, believing my own press, fearing that people would laugh. I didn't want to talk to her because I was embarrassed at feeling like a failure.

"When I realized my job had become more important than my self-esteem, I knew I had to do something. The first thing I did was fire Bill."

"How was that the solution?" I asked, half challengingly and half inquisitively.

"It wasn't the solution. It was the first step in admitting I had been wrong. Frederick had already begun to lose faith in my management abilities because he, like everyone else, saw through Bill. I had to be prepared to lose my job. But losing my job, for the first time, didn't mean losing my identity."

Paul eventually left this software company, but not before he regained his confidence by doing what he feared most: admitting he had made a mistake. It is common when going through such a situation to believe you are the only one who has ever committed such a gross mistake. To his surprise, people let Paul know how much they admired his courage in dealing with the situation.

"In the time I've had to reflect on what happened, I realized I needed to separate myself from what I do. I've taken some time off to think about what I want to do. At first it was difficult dealing with the guilt of not being productive. But then I started telling myself that I was being productive in a different way. I have the time to do things I have always enjoyed doing," Paul confessed.

"In my next venture, the status things won't be important. Enjoyment of the job is more important than money. And 'commonality of spirit' with the people I work with is high on the priority list. I don't want to feel like a stranger in a strange land. It's important for me to think along the same planes with the people I do business with. I want something that is more than just a job. Work needs to be fun. And it has to be a business that I believe in.

"I made both the software company and the investment firm more important than everything else in my life. I even listened to someone at work more than when my kid had a problem. I'm at a point where relationships are more important to me. I like spending

time with my sons. I took my family for granted. But not anymore,''
Paul explained.

"I don't know if it's because of age or what, but I've noticed,
as men move into their late forties, it becomes more important to
have male friends with depth and understanding. A writer friend of
mine and I were just talking about this. If he rang my bell at four
A.M. to tell me he needed me, I'd be there for him. We've been
friends for ten years and only now are we able to say, 'I love you.
I'd like to be your friend.'

"This was the most painful time of my life. And I don't know
if I'm saying that I don't need status or money because we are
financially comfortable at this point. I can't honestly say. But I do
know I don't have to prove anything to anyone anymore. I've proved
it to myself.''

A PERMANENT CHANGE OF VALUES

Feeling secure is an intangible quality that produces many
tangible results. The signs are easily recognizable. But getting there
is not simple. As we can see from the cases just told, much emotional
pain and self-understanding is required.

I believe a renaissance of values is taking place. But I question
how conscious and active it is. Of the men in my study, only 6
percent of those over 45 place a high value on personal growth.
And 71 percent don't care to invest the time in being introspective.
I can understand their response. Introspection means you have to
work through a great deal of emotional pain before reaching a point
of confidence and emotional security.

My hope lies in the fact that 62 percent of the men between
the ages of 27 and 45 place a high value on personal growth. As
John Rollwagen admitted, "Cray reflects how I feel." But unless
more men who are running our corporations and who are the role
models for the up-and-coming take some time to reevaluate their
values, things aren't going to get any better for the employees and
it won't be any easier for the good managers to do their jobs.

I know Gary Trudeau made fun of California Assemblyman
John Vasconcellas's task force on self-esteem. But if people didn't
have self-esteem problems, Daniel Yankelovich would not be reporting that 72 percent of the population is searching for self-ful-

fillment. The human potential movement and all the crazy groups, mostly from my home state, have given a bad impression of what self-understanding is all about. It is an important aspect of ensuring we live life with peace of mind.

It is impossible for me or for these men to provide neat little guidelines for you. So many of the "new-agers" think this *is* possible, but it is not. Growth involves a willingness to take chances, experience pain, admit failures, and move on.

In conclusion, if an individual looks to outside sources for his self-worth, he will never find self-esteem. If he can look inward and live his life guided by values of self-understanding, caring about others, honesty and integrity, he will have no need to prove himself to others or need others' approval. He will be guided by his own voice.

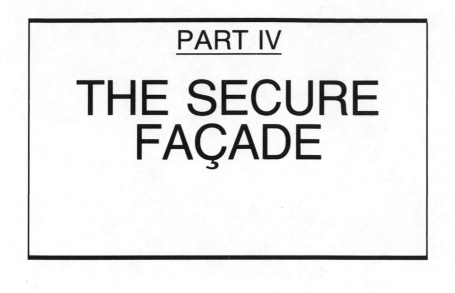

PART IV

THE SECURE FAÇADE

CHAPTER 9

IT'S IMPORTANT TO BE A NICE GUY

"What is your oxymoron?" I asked a group of fifteen managers.

Admittedly, it's not a question you're asked every day. An oxymoron, I explained, is defined as two incongruent qualities existing simultaneously. I had decided to form an exercise around the concept for this particular group of managers because, when I had met them individually, they all seemed concerned with the same issue regarding their management style: being liked rather than being respected.

I had been hired by a small film company to train their managers and conduct a team-building workshop. We sequestered ourselves in the presidential suite of the Sheraton Hotel. Stating oxymorons was the first exercise they would participate in over the next three days. I thought it was an important opening exercise because it would help them see that they all operated from a similar position: always playing the nice guy.

As we went around the room, people recited their oxymoron: amiable taskmaster; considerate driver; likable confronter; compulsively easygoing; kindly tough; sternly considerate; helpful disciplinarian; obliging controller. The conflicts therein were obvious to one and all.

I had been brought in to teach this group management skills, ways to communicate openly and honestly. They were a group of young specialists who wanted to create an idyllic, caring, supportive work environment. (Remember this is a film company, and their daily work is being the support staff to the people who create fantasies.) According to the company president, they had failed to assume levels of authority with one another or with their staffs. As a result, they acted behind one another's backs. This was too small an organization to let office politics stand in the way of getting things done. Besides, it didn't support their 1980s corporate culture ideals.

By the end of the exercise, the chief financial officer, who was rarely considered perceptive, exclaimed, "We all seemed to be concerned about being tough and nice at the same time." His comment opened the door for an explanation of the conflict they were experiencing and its resulting problems. I began by describing the origins of such problems. "Often our values attract us to others," I began. "From my interviews with each of you, I find that you share common values: caring about what others think of you, avoiding conflicts, being Mr. Nice Guy. Each of you, in one form or another, said you felt conflict between assuming your roles as division heads and wanting to be one of the group. Which should you be? Boss or buddy?"

The idea struck home. "I don't like hearing what you say," the president of the company interjected, "but I know it's true about me. At my former position they called me the Iceman because I was so ruthless. I seemed to have overcompensated for that by being the nice guy here and setting the tone for the rest of you." Motioning to his executives, he concluded, "I don't want you all to come out of this workshop acting like s.o.b.'s, but we can't go on as we have been. We need to find a balance."

I was grateful for his comment and continued with my explanation, "When you are stuck in this conflict, its impact on your management style is nonproductive. More often than not, you will opt to play things safe. We all know that when people do this, one of the games that results is 'Cover Your Ass.' And, when people play C.Y.A., they avoid saying what they think, which means they have to lie. They avoid becoming leaders. Further, they become poor delegators because they are afraid to tell people what they want from them. Doing so could cause conflicts or disagreement from below, and we all know that nice managers should never have problems with the people who work with them.''

The group laughed nervously, so I knew I had hit the right nerve.

''The rest of what I am going to say you might not like hearing either. But it's important that we know the pros and cons about being the nice guy. Nice guys spend more of their waking hours concerned about getting approval rather than getting the job done the right way. They will do anything to avoid making a mistake, which means you can't count on them to take risks. Risks mean potential failure and failure means making people unhappy. Because they are concerned about being liked, they can be manipulated with great ease. And because they are so 'agreeable,' when something is important to them, they counter their fear of being swayed with stubbornness.''

The moral of the story became the slogan for the workshop. The head of special effects volunteered his artistic skills, making a sign that hung for all to see over the next three days. The sign read: IT IS IMPORTANT TO BE RESPECTED.

THE NEED FOR APPROVAL

In my workshops I've found it helps if people know that I empathize with them. So I never hesitate to express my identification with a problem, whenever it's relevant. With these film company executives, I was pointing out a chink in their armor. I had to let them know that I, too, had once had that chink, but that I had overcome it.

''I believe that worrying about people liking you is wasted energy,'' I began. ''As for me, I wasn't raised in a home where everyone had to 'make nice.' I learned that it was healthy to disagree, and that conflicts can be resolved by finding points of compromise. There were times when my father yelled at me, 'You never seem to care what people think.' He was right. After all, he had spent years teaching me to believe in my own opinion.

''Despite being raised this way, I am not impervious to someone's opinion of me. I went through a couple of years during my late twenties constantly worrying about doing the right thing and needing people to think well of my actions. It began when I admired a former boss. Fact is, I thought he walked on water. I cared so much about what he thought of me and worried so much about getting his approval that when he gave it, I never even noticed. I stopped thinking for myself. I began to value his opinion above my own. This obsession carried over into all aspects of my life. I constantly worried if I was doing or saying the right thing. I worried how everyone felt about me, even people I didn't particularly care for.''

Several people in the room laughed. It was the kind of laugh that comes when someone identifies with what you've said. The chief financial officer interrupted, ''You sound like you're describing me some of the time.'' A few others nodded in agreement.

Acting on that cue, I distributed a handout that is designed to help people identify their own need for approval. The timing seemed right to use it as a discussion tool. The sheet was entitled ''Am I an Approval Seeker?''

It read like this:

DO YOU IDENTIFY WITH ANY OF THESE STATEMENTS?:
1. At least one of my parents withheld affection and I have grown up wondering why they didn't love me.
2. Because a parent never met my emotional needs I seek approval from other people who are emotionally unavailable to me.
3. Terrified of disapproval, which I tend to view as rejection, I do anything to keep peace.
4. I will go out of my way to be accommodating.
5. Deep down inside I feel no one loves me.
6. I avoid unpleasant situations or people I am unhappy with rather than risk hurting their feelings.
7. I like it when people need me, when I can be helpful.
8. I often find myself doing what others want me to do: ''I go along with the crowd.''
9. I blame myself when things go wrong rather than consider other possibilities.
10. I do things thinking about how others will react rather than for the pleasure I will derive from the activity or task.

Mike Webb, head of production, quickly took the floor. "My father was a mean s.o.b., and I decided early on that I wasn't going to grow up like him. He never cared about anyone but himself. Unlike him, my mother was loved by everyone. She seemed so much happier. I guess somewhere along the way I decided it would be better to be loved than to be mean and ruthless. But I never stopped hoping that my father would pay attention to me. He never did."

"This is the 'either/or' conflict we often face," I responded. "Our parents are normally our role models, the people whom we watch. From them, we learn how to behave. As adults, we either act as they did and/or pick people in our lives who treated us similarly to the way they treated us. If our parents didn't meet our emotional needs, we grow up feeling less than lovable. In adulthood, when people like us, we think something is wrong with them. We blame ourselves for reasons beyond our understanding. Then we hold on to this self-blame because it is fueled by the hope that we will figure out what we did wrong as a kid and correct it.

"Our parents also give us the values that guide our behavior while growing up. As adults, it is important to identify and challenge the inappropriate messages that are the motivations for how we respond. Imagine you are the company's corporate counsel. Your job requires that you deal with conflict continuously. However, as a child you were told you should always be agreeable. Conversely, you wouldn't be doing your job if you didn't find all the holes in someone's position. So, whenever your job requires you be the devil's advocate you feel as if you are betraying a long-held value. If you let us listen to your internal arguments we would hear an inner voice evaluating what you said or did according to your incorporated values. Sometimes personal values contradict work values, and that can be okay. Resolving this conflict happens when one begins to think in terms of 'appropriate' values or actions rather than in terms of right and wrong."

George Schwartz, the marketing man in the group, said, "I've got a good laugh for all of you. I've been sitting here listening to everyone, thinking I am my own person, only to realize that I'm a 'people-pleaser.' I worry all the time about making someone feel good, telling people what they want to hear. Need I go on? You all have this look on your face that I haven't said anything you didn't already know." As George laughed at himself, others joined him because they identified with what he said.

Then George asked, "Is it wrong to get meaning and purpose from trying to make people happy?"

"Not at all," I answered, "if, and only if, you don't give up your personal identity in the process. You have to ask yourself: 'Am I what I think others want me to be?' 'Do I consider others' needs, ideas, and desires at the expense of my own?' 'Am I constantly disappointed when people don't appreciate my efforts?' 'Do I disguise my competitiveness by attempting to be well liked?' 'Do I ever get frustrated or angry because people aren't as easygoing or as nice as I am?' If any of you answered yes to most of those questions, you can safely assume that, as George put it, you are a 'people-pleaser.'

"I'd like to describe for you how people-pleasers go through life. Simply put, they give their power away."

RELINQUISHING POWER

"What I mean by giving your power away is letting others' opinions alter your behavior, giving up control over yourself," I told the group. "The people-pleaser passes out scorecards to everyone but himself, then tallies up the opinions and guides his behavior accordingly. He forgets to ask himself what he thinks. In the purest sense, this is giving your power away," I explained.

"When we give our power away, we give others the power to judge us, to approve of us, to determine if we are in fact how we want to be. This is different from needing feedback, support, and encouragement. To accept others' compliments, criticisms, and helpful suggestions demands the ability to ask ourselves how their input compares with our own. But if we have never been taught to look to ourselves for the final score, we are without a point of comparison and without control over ourselves. Self-awareness is knowing what we believe to be true for and about ourselves. No one else lives with us twenty-four hours a day, every day of our lives. So why should anyone else's opinion carry more weight than our own?"

The room broke into applause. I had clearly struck on an important idea, so I suggested we use role-play situations to see and hear how people-pleasers behave. I needed a volunteer, and Simon Tyler, the chief financial officer, "offered himself up," as he put it.

When Simon and I had met one-to-one, he told me he had been wrestling with some personal problems. He had grown up in Mankato, Minnesota, a small town north of Minneapolis. His father, a cold, tough, and extremely quiet man, hardly had time for his kids, believing that child care was his wife's duty. When appropriate, he would discipline the children, review their report cards, and teach them responsibility.

Simon yearned for a closer relationship with his father and went out of his way to become involved in his father's favorite activities: fishing and hunting. He preferred football and wrestling, but gave up those sports to spend more time with his father. It didn't help much. They would sit for hours out on the lake, rarely exchanging words. When they went hunting, Simon's father insisted that they never speak; it might scare their prey away.

At forty-two, Simon still could not rely on his own opinions. He was an excellent "soldier," always telling the boss what he wanted to hear. But he had grown afraid of making decisions, asserting his needs, expressing his disagreements. Only when it was very important was he willing to fight for what he believed in. Otherwise, he depended on his colleagues to fight the battles. Even when people got on his nerves, he held back his annoyance, reminding himself to "keep cool." Under duress, he was volatile and prone to sudden fits of temper that seemed unnecessary to others.

At home, he referred to his wife, Michelle, as "the boss." He had married Michelle, a strong, domineering Irish woman, when he was twenty-one. She provided security and comfort for him. So he frequently set his own needs aside on matters that concerned the family. Even his children had their way with him.

THE ROLE PLAY

Everyone in the office knew that Simon was having a problem with Henry, his financial analyst. Henry rarely listened to Simon's directions—not that Simon was particularly direct about them to begin with. Nevertheless, Simon needed to have a heart-to-heart with Henry and hoped to learn some ways to prepare himself for it in this workshop.

I suggested a role play, a technique often used in finding solutions to problems such as Simon's.

SIMON: Henry, how come you don't do the things I tell you to do?

HENRY (played by Mike Webb): But I do.

SIMON (a pregnant pause, then finally the response): Perhaps you do. But then why do I think you aren't carrying out my requests?

HENRY: How come you're bringing this up all of a sudden?

SIMON: I guess it's been on my mind for some time. Maybe I should have said something before.

I interrupted at this point to give some coaching and feedback.

INTERJECTION

Simon, you're still trying to be nice and it's getting you in trouble. Let's examine the reasons your opening got you into a trap that you nicely dug your way out of but could have been avoided to begin with.

1. Your opening question was an indirect accusation, causing Henry to feel defensive.

2. Questions give up control, as is indicated in Henry's answer by denying that he disobeys your orders, leaving you without rebuttal.

3. How come you are asking Henry why you have this impression? Are you expecting him to confirm your opinion?

We went through a few more practice sessions, modifying his statements and reinforcing a new approach. I continued to coach Simon. The two suggestions I made were: state your requests (avoid asking questions), and, if Henry attempts to manipulate you, ignore it. Repeat your statement.

FINAL ROLE PLAY

> SIMON: I prefer to have my requests acted upon and I want to know how come this is not happening.

> HENRY: You've never gotten on me about this before, why now?

> SIMON: You're right, I haven't, but I am asking now.

> HENRY: Well, don't you think I might have good reasons for doing so?

> SIMON: That's a possibility, and I'd like to hear them. I also am confident that the requests I make are justified.

I summarized Simon's strengths both for his benefit and the group's. The primary changes Simon made were:

1. He turned his questions into statements. For example, "I want to know why this is not happening," rather than "Why is this not happening?"
2. He didn't respond to Henry's logical-sounding manipulation about not being told before. He simply agreed, then emphasized that he was asking now.
3. Simon's last response demonstrated what I call the "joint consideration" response. He acknowledged the possibility that Henry might have a valid reason (in reality this was another one of Henry's manipulative responses). Simon reemphasized his point to guard against being manipulated.

INABILITY TO CONFRONT

The next aspect of being Mr. Nice Guy I wanted to discuss was: learning to confront.

Again I asked for a volunteer to provide a situation for us to analyze. Ken Johnson, vice president of administration, raised his hand. He explained his situation as follows: "I have to give our benefits manager a piece of my mind, but I keep avoiding him. We have become sort of buddy-buddy. He hasn't taken care of a problem with our policy and he really needs to get on it. I haven't wanted to bother him 'cause I'm hot and that's when I usually lose my temper. Life is like a game and he's got the ball. I don't know how to get it back.''

Ken had given me another metaphor for "giving up your power." The benefits manager had the ball (power) and Ken didn't know how to get it back.

"Ken, I want you to describe for me in a sentence or two why you think that you avoid confronting people," I said.

Silence fell as we waited for Ken's answer. He picked up his head and scanned the room, carefully looking at his peers before he answered, "I believe if I argue with my peers or fight for my ideas, that means I am not getting along with people."

I then asked Ken to describe his weaknesses in resolving situations. "It's sort of typical of me to think that problems will go away if you don't talk about them. Oh, I know they don't, but I can't help myself from thinking that way. I guess it is kind of hoping for something that you know won't happen. I avoid dealing with others if there is a potential conflict, or if they are sensitive I'm afraid of hurting their feelings. I procrastinate about telling people what I think. I don't like to give them orders. It's even more difficult for me to point out what they're doing wrong. I'm scared they'll be hurt."

"Ken, your reasons are shared by many," I began. Then I told the group, "Five out of seven managers I interviewed said they would rather lie to their employees than give them constructive criticism. They had many reasons for this. 'I'm afraid they might not like me.' 'I don't want to hurt anyone's feelings.' 'I don't want to be thought of as a tough s.o.b.' ''

Then I asked, "If 71 percent of the men I interviewed feel they are in a popularity contest, then who is getting the work done, making the tough decisions, and developing the people moving up? If almost three-quarters of the managers I spoke with avoid giving constructive criticism to people, how many incompetents are being bred?''

Tempering my stand, I continued, "When I say this, it is my intention to be dramatic because I want you all to think about it. If the need for approval runs this deep in the American business psyche and, as a result, many dedicated and hard-working employees are deprived of being the best they can be by lack of direction, aren't managers failing in one of their major responsibilities?

"When you don't speak honestly with your peers, you are avoiding an opportunity to make a contribution to a colleague and to your organization. By withholding the truth, you are indirectly responsible if anything goes wrong."

True, I was being moralistic. However, this was one of the most important revelations to come from my study. It repeated itself time after time in the management training sessions I have conducted for more than ten thousand managers and executives. The vast majority admit this is a problem in their companies and in themselves.

"Okay, I got it," said Ken. "I agree I'm not doing my company or this guy any good by avoiding this problem. But what do I do about it?"

Rather than role play at that moment I decided to give Ken's peers a chance to encourage his efforts to confront the benefits manager. So I broke the group into teams of three and asked each of them to spend ten minutes writing new values for everyone in the organization to operate from. The values were to center around "The Values of Confrontation." By doing this, they would not only be helping Ken but would also help themselves find new ways to work together as a team.

This turned out to be an important exercise. It was the catalyst that changed the corporate culture of this company and freed each individual from the constricting values that prohibited him from speaking his mind. The following statements resulted from the exercise:

1. The truth might hurt in the short term but it helps in the long term.
2. Constructive honesty about someone's weaknesses helps him improve.
3. Leave your ego at home. Then you won't have to worry about anyone else's.
4. Make a contribution to your peers and subordinates by saying what you think.
5. Realize that you can't always be nice; sometimes toughness or directness is more appropriate.

6. Confronting the real problem is better than avoiding the inevitable.
7. Be respected for your courage rather than liked for being agreeable.
8. Pass the scorecard out to yourself.
9. Consider others' opinions, but fight for what you believe in.
10. Face your problems. They can only be solved when you tackle them head on.

After concluding this exercise Ken asked if we could begin his role play. He was eager to try out the new value code.

EXCERPTS FROM THE ROLE PLAY

The cast: Ken—V.P. of Administration; Bob Thompson—Benefits Manager (played by me).

The group described Bob as a nice guy, but one who had excuses for everything. Ken opened with lots of small talk, but finally he got down to the point of the discussion.

Ken: Bob, I know you've been busy but have you had any time to correct the problem with our insurance policy?

Bob: Not yet, but I'll get on it. I've been busy getting insurance for the film that's to begin shooting next week.

Ken: That makes sense, but don't you think a lot of time has gone by since the problem came to our attention?

Bob: Don't sweat it, Ken, I'll handle it. You can trust me.

ANALYSIS

I decided not to give Ken direct criticism. Instead I opted to use one of my own mistakes as a way to pass on the information to Ken and the others. I began by telling him, "I learned a very important lesson about the difference between being kind and giving people excuses to not perform well. One day I was walking out of my office with a colleague who overheard me tell my secretary that I would understand if she didn't get all of her work done before she left the office. After we left, my colleague said to me, 'I know you were trying to be considerate, but you have given her her excuse to leave her work unfinished.' My colleague was right. The work was not completed. I pass this lesson learned on to you, Ken. By saying 'I know you've been busy,' this gives 'Bob' an immediate out. Naturally he answered that he hasn't had time.

"Second, 'don't you think' questions are manipulative. They are an indirect way of saying 'I think.' Let's replace the 'you' with 'I' and your sentence reads, 'But don't I think a lot of time has gone by since the problem came to my attention?' "

Ken responded, "I do that all the time, hoping the other person will see my viewpoint. When you restate it like that I see what you mean."

I don't believe changing behavior is mysterious. Nor do I think one always needs a psychologist to do it. I often teach my clients a quick way to analyze themselves. This time I wrote the following equation on the board:

$$\text{THOUGHT} + \text{FEELINGS} = \text{BEHAVIOR}$$
$$\text{T} + \text{F} = \text{B}$$

Then I told them, "Ask yourself three questions: What am I thinking? How am I feeling? What are my actions?"

My next point of concern was what thoughts or feelings Ken experienced during the role play. I turned to Ken and asked him to answer the three questions for us. He responded, "It was important to keep my temper in check and not to let on that Bob was upsetting me."

I asked, "Is it possible you are upset with yourself because you are not getting this situation handled to your liking? Is it possible that you are angry or frustrated because Bob won't do what you want?

"Bob has no power to upset you," I continued. "Taking responsibility for our feelings is what puts us in control. Every time you make a statement about the other person, replace the 'you' with 'me' or 'I.' This will tell you exactly how you think, feel, or behave."

Feedback is valuable in helping us gain perspective on how our behavior affects others. So I asked the group for their impressions. The comments included: "If I were Bob, I'd know I could pull the wool over your eyes anytime.'' ''You're so nice that I could get you to feel sorry for me because of the heavy workload *you* are giving me.'' "Ken, you'll take the blame for anything.''

We were ready to role play again. To prepare Ken for the role play I told him, ''From now on, think about how you feel, what you want or expect. Don't ask. Suggest, recommend, tell. Be direct and definitive. In fact, during this next role play I want you to go to the extreme: be tough and inflexible.''

EXCERPTS FROM ''TOUGH'' ROLE PLAY:

> *Ken*: Bob, I've been waiting three weeks for an answer on the problems with our insurance policy, and my patience is gone.
>
> *Bob*: Ken, be cool. No need to get heated up about this. It's getting handled.
>
> *Ken*: I'm not getting heated up, I'm hot.
>
> *Bob*: I don't know what's gotten into you.
>
> *Ken*: Bob, I like you, but your excuses have got to stop. Please take care of this matter now and get back to me before the end of the day with a progress report. I don't want another excuse.
>
> *Bob*: Hey, look, I'm sorry. Didn't mean to get you so upset.
>
> *Ken*: Bob, we've been getting along real well, and I don't want there to be tension between us, so I put off pressuring you on this. But the matter can't be put off anymore. We have a job to do, and our friendship can't get in the way.

The group applauded, and Ken turned around in disbelief. He asked, ''Why do you all think that was good? Wasn't I being too tough?''

It was my turn to speak. ''Not at all. You were appropriately tough. I purposely asked you to be 'tough' because, as often happens, the nice, polite part of you still came through, but this time with a sense of what you stand for. That's the only ingredient missing from your previous role play. Life is not 'either/or.' It's not a matter of whether he has the ball or I have the ball. You both have control over how you want to play the game. The goal is not getting control away from the other person or holding it over his head. The goal is to find a way to join your efforts together to produce the necessary results. The goal is to have power over yourself.''

I summarized the key points from the role play:

1. Make statements rather than ask questions.
2. Don't make excuses for people when they haven't done what you want. You may think you are being considerate but you are not.
3. Say what you think first. Then ask the other person for his thoughts. Now, I only tell this to those of you who give up your power. This would not apply to the aggressive person.
4. Be appropriately firm.
5. Express your frustrations early on in the situation. Anger is the result of frustration caused by avoidance of the situation.

LISTEN TO ME

My favorite exercise to do with managers is called *Listen to Me*. It is always risky doing this exercise with a group of people who work together all the time. I briefly described the exercise to my film company group and had them vote anonymously on whether they wanted to do it. They voted to go for it.

Here's how the exercise works: The group members draw numbers to determine the order of participation. I then role play with each individual in front of the group. It is not your typical role play, however. For this exercise, I stand with my back to the participant, and he is instructed to command, but not demand, that I listen to him. When I feel that he has accomplished this, I turn around. Normally, I work with the first three or four people without asking the group to help me. After everyone has an understanding of how the exercise works, I ask the group to help me give feedback to whoever is in the ''hot seat.''

I never explain the purpose of the exercise until the ''experience'' is over. Doing so prevents participants from acting naturally. Instead, they try to imitate the successful participants who preceded them. The goal is that each person learn that completing the exercise successfully depends solely on expressing his own power style.

During the first minute or two of each role play, I say nothing to the participant. If he repeats communication patterns that relinquish control over himself, I stop the exercise, turn around, point out what he has done, and suggest what he might do differently. I then turn my back to him again and we continue the exercise until I sense that the participant is comfortable about commanding me to listen.

What gives this exercise its impact?

First, when no one responds to him, there is no cause and effect. The objectivity is forced to surface. I act as a video camera with instant replay capabilities.

Second, the group members instantly see the impact of their feedback. They learn to make constructive statements that can help someone change without producing defensive reactions.

Third, participants realize how to be powerful without being domineering or overly aggressive. They walk away from the exercise knowing what it means to be in control of themselves and responsible for their own feelings. They see that no one truly has power over them. Telling them that psychological edict means nothing. Showing them how they are in control can stay with them forever.

Fourth, they develop belief in themselves that their own power style is right for them and they stop trying to be like someone else. A genuine security evolves while insecurities dissipate before their eyes.

Simon Tyler was the first to take the hot set. Here are the first five statements he made before I offered some feedback:

OPENING

1. Jan, listen to me.
2. Jan, I want you to listen to me (*a little pleading*).
3. Jan, will you turn around and listen to me?
4. Jan, I said listen to me (*some annoyance*).
5. Jan, when are you going to turn around and listen to me?

I stopped the exercise here to point out the pattern that was evolving.

ANALYSIS

Statement 1 was fine. By statement 2 he was already questioning his effectiveness. Using a question in statement 3 indicates that he has relinquished his power. By statement 4, he is starting to get upset. This tells us he has little patience, and one can seize control of a situation quickly and easily with him. By statement 5, asking when I will turn around, he lets me know that I have control, and he is dependent on my turning around to let him know that he has succeeded. Who is to say I hadn't been listening to him the entire time?

Simon's reaction to my analysis was interesting. "When you didn't turn around after the second time I thought I should try another approach. It seemed like I was begging you to do something you didn't want to do. After the third time, I was sort of annoyed that you didn't turn around, after my being nice and all. As it got to the end I thought about how I have to sometimes talk firmly with my kids before I can get their attention. The last time, before you stopped the exercise, I was ready to give up."

"How did you know that I wasn't listening and ready to turn around after the second time?" I asked. "I was waiting to hear if you would hold firm to your position. When I heard you wavering, I knew that all I had to do was hold out a little longer and you'd give up.

"This time I want you to stay firm and consistent. Don't change how you are saying it. And don't worry about my response. Your success is not dependent on whether I turn around or not. The goal is for you to feel comfortable commanding me to turn around."

We went through a few more attempts. I continued to give him the same feedback until he broke through the idea that his success depended on my turning around. I wanted him to learn to judge himself from his own self-awareness rather than from my responses. There is no guarantee that my response is a measure. I could say one thing (or nothing at all) and think something different.

We progressed to the next point of the exercise: realizing that acknowledging one's feelings puts one in control. Most men think feelings make them weak. The opposite is normally true. This time, the group could hear the anger and frustration in Simon's voice. I turned around and suggested that each time he felt something, he should describe it. Say, "I'm angry, and I want you to listen to me.'' ''I'm frustrated, and I want you to listen to me.'' ''I'm uncomfortable, and I want you to listen to me.''

As Simon expressed his feeling and then his command, he gradually became calmer, firmer, and more in control. This was not surprising. It happens with most people who do this exercise.

I asked the group members to tell Simon their impressions of how he came across during his last attempt. Responses included: ''Your voice dropped.'' ''You seemed so matter-of-fact even while you were saying how angry you were.'' ''It was the first time I wanted to listen to you because you stopped pleading and trying to be so polite.'' ''It was like you were in control for the first time.''

''Simon,'' I said, ''I think we are ready for the last go at this. This time simply say the *listen to me* part.'' After Simon calmly repeated the same statement eight times, I decided to turn around. The group shrieked. It had been tense for all of us. We know what it is like to go through these feelings, and we all wanted him to succeed. And he did. We were ready to move on to the next person and do it again.

COMFORTABLY POWERFUL

I don't know if the above heading is an oxymoron for you. If it is, then here are some exercises you can do:

1. Write down all the ''messages'' you received growing up that told you how to behave with others. For example, ''Be considerate.'' ''Put others' needs before your own.'' ''It's important to be nice.'' ''If you don't have anything nice to say, then don't say anything at all.''

2. Challenge each of those messages. Decide if they are appropriate in your life today. Then write down the opposite of the message and see if that fits into how you might want to behave. For example, ''I can consider my needs as well as others'.'' ''I can express my feelings without being critical or judgmental.''

3. Do this same exercise (comparing messages) with the people who work with you. See how alike and unalike you all are. Use it as a discussion tool. Brainstorming

works better as a group activity, so gather people in teams rather than have them work individually. Consolidate your answers.

4. Notice if you use questions when you are hesitant or worried about how people respond. The compromise position is to first make a statement and follow it with a question, soliciting a response. For example, "I'm not in complete agreement. Would you please elaborate on your viewpoint?"

5. Tell the truth even if it might hurt.

6. Give yourself the scorecard first, always, and forever.

7. Develop self-awareness. Ask others for feedback.

8. Discuss your feelings and impressions with a trusted friend.

9. Observe yourself in meetings and social situations. Pinpoint when and to whom you give up your control.

10. Find a role model. Pick someone you admire whose behavior is opposite yours. Learn how that person handles situations by trying to imitate him or her. Over time, that behavior will meld with your own style.

CHAPTER 10

WE DO IT MY WAY AROUND HERE

As I reviewed the interviews and experiences that would serve as the foundation for this chapter, I was overcome with anger. Going back over the data, I relived many consulting assignments in which the executives I worked with did more harm than good to the people who worked for them. I thought of the self-aggrandizing executives who acted out their need for power, domination, and control, using others as pawns to win at the game of success. These were men who thought nothing of damaging others' lives. I was reminded of the mistreatment and anguish endured by others as a result.

Those thoughts in turn caused me to recall how one man committed suicide because he felt so humiliated by his boss. This man never let on how much emotional torment he held inside as his boss harassed, nagged, and humiliated him. When I asked him why he tolerated his boss's antics, he said he had a large family to support and an ailing mother to care for. I had often wondered how he withstood his anger and humiliation. When the news came of his suicide, I knew that he had turned his feelings inward.

I remembered the time I testified in a wrongful discharge case. Three people had been unjustly fired from the sales force of a major consumer products company. The reason: the new director of sales didn't like them. Granted, none of the three were exceptional at their job, but all were good, adequate, and eager. With the right direction and coaching, they would do a very good job.

But the director of sales didn't know how to develop people, nor did he want to know. He believed it was good to motivate people with fear and coercion. So he harassed and threatened the three employees for months. These employees only needed him to do what managers are supposed to do: supervise, direct, and develop. But his inability to do the job well only compelled him to find ways to be rid of these three people whom he viewed as burdensome.

That is only one example of how an executive can abuse his positional power. Misguided motivations are often well hidden. For instance, on the surface, the executives I interviewed who worked for large, bureaucratic companies appeared to be well adapted. But some were not. Some were obsessed with irrational desires to dominate and humiliate others.

Normally men who misuse their positional power are company men who could not survive without the security of the corporate environment. They are martinets, valuing policies and procedures above people. They are petty bureaucrats concerned about telling others what to do and how to do it. "You will get this report to me on 4/19." "You must follow the company policies." "You will do it because I said so." They believe that by this they are showing everyone they are in charge.

As one such executive explained, "Sometimes I imagine getting back at those I hated for humiliating me. I earned my stripes by being kicked around. So I set up tests to make others endure the struggles I went through. The only way my subordinates will get tough is if I put them through the same grueling tests. If they withstand this treatment, they will have a future in the company."

Another hostile manager said, "Part of the initiation rites to making it in the corporate world is taking the blows that come your way. It pissed me off to carry my tail between my legs and put up with some dumb s.o.b. I've been hurt by some of them along the way, but I'm tough. I manage the same way I was managed. These young kids with their heads in the clouds need some toughening up early on in their careers."

While some managers lust after power, others are afflicted with self-aggrandizing illusions and have no realistic perspective. Self-aggrandizement can often be disguised in expressions of overgoodness or overconcern. The vice president of marketing for a pet food company told me, "I am entitled to tell my subordinates what to do because I make sacrifices for them. I take care of those who report to me. I shield them from the corporate battles. They never know all I am burdened with. They owe me their obedience."

Still, some are merely grandiose with no concern for those they rule. Such was the case with the president of a well-known Fortune 500 company. "I made it into this position because I know how to play the games," he explained. "Obviously I am better than the rest of the guys, because look where I am and where they are on the corporate ladder. Until they are more qualified than I am, they are to serve me. I have no tolerance for disobedience."

I remember asking Ken Leonard, a financial manager, how he got things done. He responded, "I tell them [his subordinates] what to do. That means they should do it without question." And then he admitted with great pride, "I never take the time to listen to people. I have a job to do and I do it. So do they. If they have any questions, let them refer to the policy and procedure manual."

Ken told me this was the attitude any successful manager should possess. He thought he was doing his job well, that his attitude was one to be proud of.

When I asked Ken if he ever encountered problems in dealing with people, he told me vehemently, "I don't have any problems because of my position. I report to the division's president, so people don't challenge my decisions. If they do, I make it clear that I don't like people giving me any trouble. Sometimes they threaten to go over my head. I tell them, 'Do it. The boss is right next door to my office. Do you want to tell him or shall I?' They know I'll probably get my side in first. That shuts them up."

A few weeks before I finished this book, one of Ken's former employees called me. He told me that Ken had retired. The president gave him a retirement party—no one came.

This financial manager is merely an example of many misguided executives who make their employees' work life quite miserable. These people don't care who they step on in the name of "getting the job done."

Not all controlling or domineering bosses wish to step on others to get ahead. And not all are completely unaware of their interactions with those who work for them.

Some are overbearing because they think if others need them then they are important. Twenty-eight percent admitted that they liked being needed and questioned their worth and position when people used their own initiative. Eleven percent enjoyed rescuing people and felt they weren't doing their job if they didn't bail people out. Sixty-two and one-half percent confessed that they were extremely uncomfortable watching employees making mistakes while learning because they felt responsible for everyone's results. Therefore, they interpreted an employee's error as a reflection on themselves.

Fifty-seven percent of the managers I interviewed admitted that they did not delegate authority because doing so meant giving up control. That is to say that four of every seven managers ran their departments by giving orders rather than by letting people think for themselves. When they did delegate some responsibility, they found themselves checking up on their employees to make sure every step was done to perfection.

I often encounter these controlling executives when I am called in to companies to help motivate their employees. These executives can't understand why the employees aren't more committed to doing things the way they should be done. Management complains that the employees are not motivated to do a good job. "Fix this poor morale. Do something to them," they tell me.

I have always found "poor morale" to be a vague term. Normally, it is overused and wrongly applied. For our purposes, let's define poor morale as the condition of no longer caring, with the emphasis on *no longer*. Management forgets that if people have stopped caring it means that they cared at one time. More times than not, it is management's controlling attitude that causes employees to pull back their commitment and concern.

So often management asks the wrong questions. Instead of asking, "What should we do to our employees to get them motivated?" they should be evaluating their own actions. They need to ask themselves, "What have we decided, implemented, or communicated that has caused our employees to lose their motivation?"

But they don't examine their own actions because they believe the boss is always right, or at least should put on the appearance of being so. These men think they are leaders, but they are not. They are dictators. These men don't guide people with their sense of vision and purpose; they intimidate, manipulate, and coerce people into obeying them. As they moved up the corporate ladder, they blindly obeyed the men they reported to. As a result, they believe people should unquestioningly and unthinkingly obey them.

Underneath their strong façade is often a wobbly backbone. These men are masses of extreme contradictions, often giving mixed messages to the people who work for and with them. They are dictatorial, but they can be swayed. They are dogmatic yet indecisive. They are doers but also avoiders of problems. It is impossible for them to admit this, however, because their domineering façade often hides a scared, insecure little boy. They seek power to assuage their panic. They put others down to feel important. Sadly, they are often the ones who most need to change.

They refuse to acknowledge how destructive their attitude is to the well-being of their employees, their company, and eventually themselves. They are unable to value others because they don't value themselves, and those who work for them must tolerate their insecurity and power plays. Or must they?

It is the people who work for these men that I am most concerned about helping. So the intention of this chapter is to help those affected by the power-seeker's actions to understand why and accept that this type of man rarely changes, and to realize the best way to beat the power-seeker at his own game is *not* to play.

To these ends, I have highlighted two men who deal with their need to control others quite differently. In the first situation, Steve Richards is the man who pounded his fist on the table and screamed at me, "We do it my way around here." Insecure, unaware, inconsiderate, Steve ruined many careers over the five years I knew him. Most frustrating was Steve's unwillingness to examine his own actions. Reading about Steve, I hope you will learn what to do when confronted with such a person.

For all the frustrating situations I must work with, there is always the person who makes my work worthwhile. Josh Roberts intuitively knew his controlling management style was ineffective. And he hired me to help him change his ways and make his department a better place for his employees to work. Through his example, you will learn how to change your own controlling tendencies and understand what caused them to begin with.

STRONG FAÇADE, WEAK SPINE

The type of individual who won't look at himself and acts out his distorted motivations on others is exemplified by Steve Richards. Steve adored General George Patton. He owned every book about the legendary general and frequently developed marketing strategies and managed his people by imitating his interpretation of Patton's style.

Steve Richards was management's fair-haired boy. At age forty, he was made vice president of the consumer products division for a major food company. One day he had thirty people reporting to him and was responsible for a tiny division that generated twenty million dollars in revenue. The next day he was responsible for a division that generated revenue in excess of a billion dollars and had five hundred employees.

Reporting to Steve were his assistant, the director of administration, the director of regional operations, the training director, the division accountant, and the six directors of sales. Steve's assistant had worked with him for years and was a yes-man of the first order. The director of administration was old, loyal, and incompetent. No one over the years had ever been honest with him about his shortcomings, and management felt obliged to keep him on in a "put 'em aside job" until he retired. Steve inherited the director of regional operations, the accountant, and the training director, and he treated them with contempt. In response, they feared for their jobs. They were yes-men of the second order.

Yes-men are so busy being loyal, and so conditioned not to think for themselves, that when they are put into a leadership position they respond in one of two ways. Either they become dictatorial, expecting blind obedience, or they refuse to take a stand, make a decision, or express an opinion. Steve was surrounded by the latter type.

His preference for yes-men stemmed from his fear of being disagreed with or challenged. Of course he wouldn't admit this. Instead he insisted that people support his efforts and ideas. Should anyone disagree with him, he would condemn that person for being disloyal, manipulating him into feeling as if he had committed a mortal sin. Steve surrounded himself with yes-men because, in truth, he was one himself. Steve thought he was acting tough, strong, secure. He didn't realize that any secure person not only tolerates disagreement, but often welcomes differing opinions.

The sales directors were a different breed of men, men who didn't understand how to be yes-men. Steve was clearly bothered and intimidated by them. He didn't know how to control them. They didn't respond to his manipulations. And he didn't know how to deal with his people based on their abilities and talents.

Because Steve assumed being in charge meant he had to be omniscient, he was unable to value the knowledge and experience his sales directors brought to their job. In his distorted way, he interpreted their expertise as a threat. I tried for months to encourage Steve to ask for their help, for their ideas and input. He told me, "If I asked them for their ideas, they might get the impression that I didn't know what I was doing. You don't ask your soldiers where to go when you're leading the troops." In reality Steve was in over his head and didn't know the first thing about leading his troops.

Steve had no sales experience while the directors cumulatively had nearly a hundred years' worth. In the first month on the job, Steve succeeded in alienating them. He hired a consultant to design a new organizational structure, at a fee of two hundred thousand dollars. The sales directors could have done the job better and obviously without the exorbitant cost.

Steve Richards made all attempts to appear outwardly secure and capable. Inwardly he was insecure and inept. Men like Steve are often unsure of who they are or how they want to be. As a result, their behavior goes in extremes from dogmatic to indecisive. Their thinking becomes erratic and irrational.

I had consulted with Steve's company for five years before he was promoted to the consumer products division. I regularly facilitated Steve's staff meetings as I had done for his predecessor. In one such meeting the five directors of sales attempted to resolve some administrative problems that affected their field sales managers. Since Steve had implemented his reorganization plan, the sales directors no longer had control over the administrative aspects of their job. These controls now fell under the charge of the director of regional operations, causing numerous problems for field sales.

The problem stemmed from the operations director's failure to give his fifty regional operations managers specific directives. As a result, the stores were not receiving credits and refunds. In the past, sales personnel handled this efficiently. When one of the sales directors asked the operations director why he hadn't issued specific directives on the subject, he responded by throwing his hands up and saying, "I thought I'd wait to see where things fall before I tell them how to do their job." I thought to myself, a typical yes-man's response.

Unfortunately for the sales directors their operational counterpart avoided responsibility. To counteract this, the sales directors took charge, making necessary or risky decisions. The operations director's attitude frustrated them. The appropriate solution to this situation was for Steve to exercise some leadership. He had two problems to deal with: the conflict between the sales directors and the operations director, and the fact that his reorganization plan wasn't working and needed adjustment.

Instead of addressing both the problem at hand and the developing hostility between the sales directors and the operations director, Steve walked out of the room. If it were another executive, one might assume that he wanted his people to resolve this themselves. But not Steve Richards. When he returned, Steve dressed down his directors of sales, "You are a bunch of weenies. Don't you realize the battles I am fighting for you? Why are you complaining about something as petty as this? Don't you realize that if you could do my job better, one of you would be in it?"

He went on, "I'm doing everything right. Our market share is up twelve points and everyone is happy. We are doing the best job we can, even with these wimps working for me. I'm tired of how petty you all are."

They weren't being petty. Their frustration was directed at the operations director, but Steve took it personally. Steve's illusion of shielding his troops from the daily battles was simply that—an illusion.

It was also an illusion that his marketing decisions increased market share. His directors' response to this claim was unanimously negative, "We are in a recession and sales always increase on dry dog and cat food. Our sales performance has little to do with the marketing and sales strategies or even our sales people's efforts. In fact, if we keep up this strategy, by the time the recession turns around, we'll be losing business." Steve was feeling threatened, so he used the "bottom-line" argument to attempt to convince himself that he was doing things right.

In truth, men like Steve believe that if a problem exists, it is an indirect criticism of their abilities. If there are no problems, they interpret that to mean everything is going right. Should one problem present itself, they misconstrue reality, thinking everything is going wrong. Rather than accept their own mistakes or weaknesses, they become more forceful, dogmatic, rigid, and dictatorial. In so doing, they refuse to listen or admit to the real issues at hand.

In fact, an executive's unwillingness to hear problems and "only want to hear solutions" often stems from his fear that he might not be able to solve those problems. So the tactic such a man uses is to put the problem back on the subordinates' shoulders and make the subordinates feel inadequate for coming to him with the problem. Steve had used this technique often, but now it was no longer working.

This problem clearly needed to be resolved, and the sales directors weren't going to let up until it was. This wasn't the first time the sales directors had brought the problem to Steve's attention. Each of them had spoken with Steve individually and felt that they were up against a wall. So they decided to join together and press the issue at the staff meeting.

Steve became defensive because he was doing many things wrong, including avoiding the larger problem of his operations director's lack of leadership abilities and decision-making skills. Although the solution was simple in concept—have the operations director establish specific guidelines and ask his regional managers to implement them immediately—it was not going to happen.

The sales directors became more impatient as they realized Steve wasn't listening to them. Steve issued edicts and ignored others' comments because, as he told me confidentially, "If I listen to someone I might change my mind and appear indecisive."

When Steve realized his sales directors would not back off no matter how he attempted to make them feel guilty or wrong he turned to me and asked, "Jan, am I missing the boat regarding this problem?" At that moment I knew that, depending upon my response, I would either be put into the "weenie" category or I could join the "yes-men" order. I opted to join the "weenies." I agreed with the sales directors.

I responded, "Steve, I think the problem is not one that would be important to you, and I can understand why you might think their comments are trite. However, we have Jay's [regional operations director] declaration that he has not given any directives to his fifty managers in the field. You have their counterparts, the fifty sales managers, working at cross purposes rather than in tandem. Therefore, to those in the field and those managing field sales, this is a very critical issue. It might benefit us to address it before this meeting concludes.''

Steve did not like hearing the truth from me or from the sales directors, so in true ''Steve fashion'' we avoided discussing the real issues. Instead he brought the meeting to a close, tabling the issue until the next day.

Steve was not ready to go home, so he asked me to join him for dinner at Anthony's, an exclusive St. Louis restaurant, where he proceeded to down four martinis in less than an hour while wailing that his people didn't appreciate his efforts. ''I don't let them know how many battles I fight for them, and all they do is get on my case. Here I thought I was the fair-haired boy, but nothing is going right. How dare they challenge me?!'' Devastated, Steve lamented his staff's ungratefulness.

I have worked with many executives who are in over their heads. But rather than admitting this to themselves they search for reasons and people to blame for their own inadequacies. Steve was no different. As he continued to complain, I thought to myself, Steve is talking as if his actions and decisions are based on his concern for them. He is fooling no one. Everyone can see his efforts are only self-serving and self-deluding.

Steve talked about how petty and inept his sales directors were. In his mind he had to make them the bad guys because he wasn't going to accept his own inexperience. The Peter Principle, which asserts that a person will always be promoted beyond his level of competency, was in effect and many people were suffering because of it. I have seen this situation many times before, and it bothers me for two reasons: people who are committed, care, and have experience to do the job are prevented from doing their best; and the overall business suffers.

I listened to Steve for more than three hours, waiting for him to pick his scapegoat. However, before the evening came to a close, the poor soul was yet unnamed. But I suspected it would be one of two sales directors who were highly regarded by all employees throughout the company.

The next morning Steve had come up with the perfect solution. He decided to eliminate the sales director he suspected had influenced the others to "push the issue." In his mind, he had convinced himself that this man had created the problem and influenced the others to agree with him. He thought removing the sales director would get rid of the problem.

Of course Steve would believe that the other sales directors had been influenced by one person, because again Steve was projecting his own thoughts, feelings, and behavior onto them. People who project are unable to evaluate others' thoughts or behavior objectively. Rather than admit to himself that he was easily swayed by others, Steve convinced himself that others were the ones who were easily influenced.

The unfortunate victim was Greg Morris, regarded by his peers and the entire sales force as the most outstanding sales director. In this instance, Steve perceived Greg as "the enemy." Steve had always been intimidated by Greg Morris. He didn't like the fact that Greg was the most respected sales director in the company. However, by denying how threatened he felt, Steve deluded himself into believing that if he got rid of Greg, the problem would go away.

Steve wanted to "kill the messenger" who brought the truth, the truth he didn't want to face.

KILL THE MESSENGER

For quite some time Steve carried on as if he was pleased with Greg's work. As much as he grew to detest Greg, he didn't act upon his desire to eliminate the enemy immediately. In a surprise attack, Greg was removed from his position, cast aside with nothing to do. No explanation was offered but a promise was made. Within two weeks a new position would be announced.

I was not happy with the way Greg was coping with Steve's power play. But, I held my peace until a decision came from Steve regarding Greg's new position. Greg developed stomach problems during this time. I worried about Greg because he had never been much of a risk taker. When I advocated speaking out, Greg argued that I shouldn't take life so seriously.

Greg wasn't the only one affected by Steve's machinations. In men who deny their feelings emotional stress often manifests itself physically. Their body takes the brunt of the emotional turmoil.

Many of Greg's peers complained of backaches, headaches, and injuries incurred during simple athletic activities. Some people began having problems with their blood pressure. One man died of a heart attack during Steve's reign.

Three months passed. Greg's health deteriorated. Still no answer came. Finally, I couldn't tolerate it anymore. Exasperated, I said to Greg one day, "You have got to push the issue. If you don't take care of yourself, who is going to do it for you? You have three children all approaching college age and a wife to support. Do something!"

"I want to stay around to get back at him," Greg confessed.

"That should not be your motivation," I rebutted, "because the person who plots revenge is the only one suffering. Vindictiveness does not pay. You are the one in anguish, stewing over what Steve did, feeling victimized and powerless." Then I added, "Steve will get his due. It could take one year, or ten or twenty. It may not be in our time or in a way we might like. So get on with your life and don't think about revenge. People will eventually get wise to Steve's machinations. It bothers me as much as it bothers you that he gets away with this. The time will come when he won't fool anyone. Trust me."

Greg had gone through much of his life holding his feelings inside, giving outward signs of having things under control. But when he put on his mask of being "in control," it was because he really felt out of control. He saw himself as a victim. His anger festered inside.

Greg continued, "But I can't walk away. Then he will have won."

Greg's thinking was misguided. While he should have been contemplating ways to confront Steve, forcing a decision about his future, instead Greg plotted ways to get back at Steve. Greg needed to learn how to confront situations like this directly and he needed to redefine "winning."

So often people think that winning means someone else has to be a loser. This is true in sports, but need not be true in personal interactions. A win-win philosophy has been touted in management and negotiation philosophy in recent years. In human relations it is better if all parties can win. But when you work for a man similar to Steve Richards, winning needs to be thought of in terms of saving yourself. The Steve Richardses of the world only want to get you. The minute you stoop so low to play their game and "get them back" you have started upon a losing course, for they are devious, manipulative, and unpredictable.

The only objective when dealing with a Steve Richards is to walk away with your head held high. It is by walking away, refusing to play the game on his terms, and starting a new game with a different set of rules, that you retain your self-esteem. Don't respond to his actions. Set your own limits. Don't try to compromise. Hold your ground. Don't play for long. Think of a way out as quickly as possible. In this type of situation, your self-esteem is the real measure of win or loss.

As I explained it to Greg, "Imagine you are in a karate match. In karate you don't meet the force head on because even though you may damage it, you will damage yourself in the process. If you are hit by it, you absorb it. To win in karate you redirect the attack. Redirecting Steve's power play could mean walking away. By staying around and waiting for his answer, your inaction is telling him that he has won. Think of responding to his actions in a way he might never expect."

Many men feel as Greg did: to walk away is to admit defeat. And many men deal with the problem as Greg did. They allow the problem to fester inside, plotting ways they will eventually get even. The more time they spend in vindictive thoughts, the more time they spend suffering. They forget that the other person has moved on to his next victim or strategy.

I wanted Greg to change his perspective and stop playing the defensive position. If I could get him to think offensively he could start an entirely new game that would put Steve on the defensive. Greg spent the next month thinking about his "offensive strategy."

Finally the day came. Greg called to say he had decided to file a lawsuit charging discrimination. Once he made the decision, he wasted no time following through. Less than a month later, I received a subpoena to testify as an expert witness. I explained to Greg that my responsibility was to the company because it was my client. My respect and loyalty to him would be measured by my telling the truth. Although I didn't tell him, I thought he had nothing to worry about.

When Steve received notice of the lawsuit, he knew the company was in grave trouble because of his unnecessary power plays.

I later found out that upon receiving the claim Steve called Greg to admit how wrong he had been. Greg was shocked. "I never tested his strength. I backed off from him because he talked tough. Steve really is a weakling." For Steve it was too late. Greg had been humiliated. Moreover, he was ready to fight, honestly and directly, two ways Steve did not know how to play. Greg had Steve at a disadvantage without even playing Steve's game.

Fortunately I never needed to testify. And Greg won big. He had always dreamed of running his own ma 'n' pa grocery store in the country. After receiving the hefty settlement, he moved to Oregon where he purchased the O'Brien country store, and he also returned to painting, a hobby he loved.

A year later, I drove up to visit Greg and his family. Over dinner, we laughed about old times. I asked him, "Looking back, what have you learned from this experience?"

After a long pause, he spoke, "I know that we could lose everything and I could start over with no problems. I have confidence in myself that I didn't have when I was beholden to the corporation."

After a pensive moment, he added, "It's funny how I didn't want to walk away from the situation, but at the same time that's exactly what I was doing by avoiding the conflict directly. But it's just not worth it playing the game that way. I always tried to get even while pretending that nothing was bothering me. And guess who ended up losing? It cuts out so much bullshit when you tackle it head on. And it saves time. Even my marriage is better. If something bothers me I say something. And so does my wife. I thought that would always push us apart. But that's not so. It's when I hold things inside, playing good old easygoing Greg, that we grow more distant. Talking about things helps us stay close."

As time passed Greg became more proficient at recognizing when he was avoiding problems that needed his attention and when it was okay for him to walk away.

And just as Greg learned how his style of handling problems was not always productive, I, too, realized the good side of being easygoing.

Greg and I have kept in touch, constantly discussing our reactions and thoughts about situations we must deal with. On the surface we acted differently, but the way we dealt with these situations had a common thread. It is ingrained in his personality to look at situations and not take them so seriously, as it is ingrained

in mine to stand up for what I believe in. But as the pendulum
swings from one extreme to another before finding its center balance,
Greg and I have successfully searched for our own balance point.
He is less likely to ignore a situation or diminish its importance. I
am less likely to give all situations equal importance. In so doing
we have incorporated aspects of one another's personality into our
own, rounding out our approach to life.

SHOULD I WALK AWAY?

Deciding to "give up" is always a tough decision for people.
We don't want to be thought of as quitters, cowards, or losers.
However, "giving up" can be the healthiest thing you can do for
yourself.

We will all encounter situations that are not the best for us:
for our self-esteem, for our emotional well-being, for our happiness.
And we will all find ourselves enmeshed in them one time or another,
personally or professionally.

Once you are convinced that you have made all efforts to
resolve a problem, then you are ready to walk away. So when you
find yourself dealing with a person who has a need to be cruel or
disrespectful to you, here are some questions to answer for yourself:

1. How do I feel about myself when I am dealing with
   this person? Do I have a need to be right? Do I try
   to get back at people? Do I try to catch them by
   surprise?
2. What power am I giving to this person? Am I intimidated by him or her? Do I think this person is better
   than I am? What criteria am I using to make this
   evaluation?
3. What are my fears about confronting this person?
4. Am I trying to get this person to recognize my good
   qualities? Am I hoping this situation will pass if I
   ignore it?
5. How do I define winning when dealing with people?
6. Who in my past does this person remind me of?
7. What judgments am I making about myself in this

situation? What judgments am I making about the other person?

8. What messages did I get about being a "quitter"? Do they apply to this situation?

9. What am I afraid people will think about me if I walk away from this situation?

10. How can I regain my self-esteem and feel like I have won without playing his or her games?

Just keep in mind that people who walk away from the Steve Richardses of the world are healthier and more secure than most. They value themselves and others. They are courageous and willing to take risks to grow as a person. And above all, remember that no person or situation is worth your being unhappy. Life is too short. There is always a way out, and often the choice you make will be better for you, if not in the short run, then definitely in the long run.

SOME DO WANT TO CHANGE

Occasionally I meet an executive who is willing to admit that his management style isn't effective. Josh Roberts was having some problems with a few of the people who reported to him and wondered if he should be doing things differently.

Josh said his problem was that his people disobeyed him. "The more I tell them what to do, the more they do what they want," he began. "I don't know if it's my imagination, but it seems that they patronize me on occasion, operating from the old adage, 'Tell the boss what he wants to hear.' I have a very clear idea about how things should be done, and I expect to see those ideas carried out."

Then he asked, "Could you come to one of our staff meetings and help me identify what the problem is?"

I declined the invitation, explaining to Josh, "Without any of your employees having a chance to meet me individually, they would assume I was a spy for you. Or to introduce me as an observer would put them on guard unnecessarily.

"I think it is more important that you let them know you are concerned about your management style and specifically how you are treating them," I continued. "Ask them to be candid with you. Explain that you are considering the possibility of hiring me and ask if they would like to talk with me. It has to be their choice."

Josh's discussions with most of his subordinates proved painfully enlightening. When we met a few weeks later he summed up the problem for me. "I had no idea I was so caught up with myself," Josh began. "All I worried about was making sure everything was right according to my standards and ways. I didn't give anyone room to breathe. I would hate working for me.

"Underneath it all, I knew I was the problem," he confided. "I don't know how to change myself, so I just think about changing other people. I don't know why I decide things for people when they can decide things for themselves. It would infuriate me if my boss determined my agenda and priorities, but that's what I do to them. I know they're capable, but even though I know it, I find myself reminding them about things. There's even a part of me that believes I'm doing it for them."

I responded, "It's typical of the controlling manager to focus on others. They think about changing someone else rather than changing themselves. I believe that those who want to control everything and everyone feel in their heart that they really aren't in control and they aren't happy with themselves. It is the desire to change others, to make them as you want them rather than accept them for who they are that gives you the illusion of being in control. But that's all it is—an illusion."

"But it's not an illusion when things go wrong," Josh retorted. "I have to check up on them, because if I don't they won't get it right."

"Let's look at this problem logically," I continued. "What if you are not around one day and something important needs to be handled? If you have never allowed your staff to risk making mistakes that come with the learning process, they are likely to let things fall through the cracks, ignore the importance of the moment, and wait for you to do it. That's what happens when you act like the rescuer. People are not dumb. They watch how you respond. They know you'll panic if things aren't going the way you want them to. I wouldn't be surprised if the lazy ones around here purposely do things to have you jump in and take charge."

"That's true," Josh answered. "I have two people on my staff who I'm always yelling at because they wait for me to pick up the pieces. They act as if they don't care and they know I do. I've never said anything, but I've thought to myself that they act this way on purpose.''

"Controlling people always need someone to 'rescue,' '' I started to explain. "They do act that way on purpose because they can count on you to think for them. If you try to solve their problems for them, they never have to take responsibility for themselves or for their decisions and the consequences of their actions. And if your advice does not work out, they have every right to blame you.''

I paused before emphasizing, "More important, not thinking for them means giving up your need to control. It means assuming that they are equally as capable as you are. Controlling by rescuing leads to a false sense of importance, and people will end up resenting you for it. No one likes to be dependent forever.''

"It's a depressing thought to think people won't need me any-more,'' Josh responded.

"Oh, but you're wrong,'' I said. "People will need to learn from you rather than have you do for them. You simply have to redefine the way you help your employees. There is a major distinction between taking care of someone and caring about another person. When you take care of people you deprive them of experiencing themselves. When you care about people you give them the acceptance and support to be who they are.''

And then I suggested, "Instead of laying out the steps for people, you can guide them and educate them so they can learn to do for themselves. It is true that providing people with the knowledge to do for themselves means they no longer need you. But there's a joy in watching people become self-reliant. It becomes a burden to have people dependent on you. You are doing a disservice to yourself and to them in the long run.''

On that note, Josh asked the inevitable question, "So how do I change?''

"Most controlling individuals think change is replacing one action with another one,'' I began. "In this case, it's not that easy. To give up a controlling style means changing your attitude. It means looking at why you need to control others. This you have begun to do. It means understanding that, in your case, you like people to need you and you want things done your way.''

I went on to define for Josh how a controlling manager acts. "A boss who is controlling decides for another what he can decide for himself, determines his subordinate's agenda and priorities when he should leave the details up to his subordinate. He patronizes, reminds, advises, or cautions a peer who is equally as capable. He uses compliments and praise to guide behavior rather than expressing appreciation for the good qualities of his co-workers.''

Josh and I continued to discuss his reactions. ''As a manager, you are powerless to change someone else. You can only change yourself. Changing your own actions causes the person to respond to you differently. Focusing on changing the other person is merely manipulation. It doesn't have lasting results, so why waste your time and energy?''

Josh responded, ''To stop controlling or rescuing people I have to be more realistic and less idealistic. I feel like a wimp admitting that I panic when things don't go according to my plan.''

''You mean, according to your fantasy,'' I interjected.

It is not uncommon for powerful men to have the illusion that their way is the only right way to do things. They live in a world where their authority is rarely questioned and few people give them honest feedback. For Josh, giving up control meant relinquishing his fantasy that life existed only on his terms. And this was a tough fantasy to give up, because it had some components of reality. Josh had been successful thus far, so why should he change? He also felt that if he did not maintain strict control, things would go wrong, and he was, after all, responsible for the results.

But to focus only on the results means a manager or executive is shortsighted. He needs to focus on the development, the learning of those creating the results. So what if someone makes a mistake, as long as it serves as a learning situation. Mistakes can be corrected.

''Could it be right that I judge my own worth on actions of those who work for me? I'm beginning to think that I take their failure as my own, their mistakes as my failings,'' Josh confessed.

I assured Josh that his reaction was not uncommon. Many executives judge their worth by those who work for them. But one must detach himself from those who carry out his orders. Once executives I have worked with accept that they are truly powerless over others, they feel more secure about who they are.

So we set out with a simple plan to help Josh break out of the controlling mode. We met once a week to discuss how he would delegate the projects at hand. In the course of our discussions we explored his unwillingness to trust others and other feelings that arose. This helped Josh recognize that his actions were guided by many feelings he had been unaware of previously. As he looked upon his work with me as a learning experience, he was able to translate this to his management responsibilities.

"I don't have to be in charge. I have to give them direction," he said with amazement.

We struggled together for almost a year. Each week it was a little easier to learn how to trust the people who worked for him. And each week Josh got better at letting his expectations and ideas be known.

"I hadn't been communicating as clearly as I thought," he informed me. "I have a lot going on in my head. I see how things need to be done and I expect others to do it that way. When they don't I get upset. But I've been giving orders instead of explanations."

Josh worked hard examining his thoughts and feelings. It is important to first change your attitude. Changes in your behavior inevitably will follow. To feel one way and act another only causes one to feel like a fraud. At the same time it causes others to perceive one as insincere. Eventually Josh began to feel secure in providing direction and guidance; and as he understood himself better he accepted that his need to do for others rather than let them do for themselves was really self-serving. To genuinely give and support others' growth Josh learned to stand back and watch them find their own way to express themselves. His good feelings and reinforcement came from watching the success of his subordinates' efforts.

One of his last comments to me was, "It wasn't easy at first to let the people working for me deal with the consequences of their own actions. But I know if I don't, I am taking away opportunities for them to learn, grow, and discover things about themselves that they might not have known. They will learn how to make good decisions. I might have a few heart attacks and develop an ulcer or two in the meantime. But they will know what they can do on their own and when to ask for my help. They might even develop an appreciation for the genuine contributions they make to the company, if I stand back. They might discover self-pride. And 'saving' people is really the worst thing I could do for them. I was depriving them of valuable learning experiences."

Those executives who wield power through fear and coercion often decrease productivity and morale in the long run. They force their employees' energy to be directed away from their work and into worrying about dealing with their boss. I continually try to impress upon the executives I coach that the more they can create an environment in which employees feel accepted and safe, where people have fun and can be creative, where people can make mistakes, explore different avenues of thought, and make their own decisions, the better and more productive the results will be.

So if you are like the Joshes of the world, here are some suggestions that might help you change your management style and give up your need to control:

1. *Accept others as they are.* The opposite of control is acceptance. Although it is very difficult to practice, it is a wonderful goal to concentrate on accepting an individual as he is, rather than trying to change him through coercion or manipulation. Underneath our desire to change others lies a selfish motive.

2. *Stop seeking people who let you control them.* It takes two to play a game. Those who have a desire to control others seek out malleable individuals. They look for others who are less secure, less educated, less experienced than themselves so as to have the upper hand. Surround yourself with people who have something to offer you as well. In the beginning you might feel intimidated or unsure of your role in the relationship, but take the risk to discover a new side of yourself and to enjoy a relationship based on equality.

3. *Encourage your subordinates to be independent.* Watch out for using praise as a form of control. Don't set up a situation where your employees are dependent on you for approval. Being an approval-giver is another form of control. Instead encourage the people who work for you to think for themselves, to feel free to challenge your ideas, to take initiative.

4. *Allow people to make mistakes.* You don't have to save someone from learning through experience. And someone else's failure is not your own. To let people make mistakes means you must learn to say and do nothing. It means you can't jump in and keep a mistake from

happening. But you can help someone understand what went wrong and why. Then you can encourage that person to think about ways to resolve the problem.

5. *Face your own fears.* We are manipulative and coercive because we are afraid. We might be afraid of speaking honestly. We might be afraid of looking bad. We might be afraid of someone's ideas or actions. When you focus on how you might want to change someone, you are not accepting your fear about how this person is behaving. Whatever your fears might be, it helps to accept that you are out of control when it comes to dealing with others. You can only be in control of yourself. If you accept your fears and set about resolving them, then the need to change the other person becomes nonexistent. You focus on how you want to handle it. Your thoughts come from security rather than panic.

EXECUTIVES WHO ARE CHANGING

For years, men were raised to view the workplace as a battlefield; compassion was to be left at home. However, a new value is now permeating the workplace: concern for the individual.

I am happy to see that many popular management books have helped to create an awareness in managers and employees about the value and benefits of giving people greater authority and responsibility.

The Steve Richardses of the corporate world are no longer in fashion. Autocratic executives are threatened as they see how the superior-subordinate reporting relationship is on the verge of extinction. They are rapidly being replaced by leaders who care about others and who look at their power as a responsibility to be exercised with caution and concern.

Still, some men are hesitant to change their ways, while others are confused about how to integrate this new attitude into their own management style. Today many executives feel the pressure to adopt a participative management style. They are discovering that their employees are less willing to put up with authoritarian bosses. The majority of employees want more control over their jobs; they want to be respected and trusted. They no longer want to follow along mindlessly.

However, I am concerned because quite a few of these executives, after reading the latest popular management books, think they have changed. They are talking the right language, which I call "The New Language of Management," but their behavior still conveys old management language and practices.

In the next chapter, we meet many executives who are examples of the new management philosophy—a philosophy based on values rather than motivations. These executives are growing in numbers. Rather than sacrificing their personal life for career success, they are running their businesses better, managing their people better, and enjoying their personal relationships and endeavors more.

I am particularly inspired by these men because they are creating work environments in which people can take risks and push themselves to their personal limits. I am amazed by their ability to converse about emotional issues openly and freely. They do not have to act macho or be in control. And they are not perfect. They are aware of their feelings and actions—and that awareness leads to continual growth and change.

CHAPTER 11

I HAVE NO AMBITION TO CONTROL OTHERS

In many businessmen's minds, controlling has been synonymous with leading. But as more employees, at all levels, are turned off by the people they see at the top, rejecting them as examples of leadership, a new style of leadership is emerging.

Emerging leaders have no desire to be the authoritarian boss. They don't sacrifice their beliefs and ideas to gain approval or to fit in. They don't use others as pawns in their own career game. However, rather than looking at what they don't do, I reviewed the case histories of such men and found what they *do* that makes them today's leaders.

Contrary to the autocratic leaders, who create policies to control and harness the creativities of others, the emerging leaders view policies as the guides rather than as the rules for making decisions. Void of the ambition to control others, these new leaders want people to feel they have the freedom to innovate, to experiment, and to take risks.

Their motivation to lead comes from the dream of creating a work environment that gives people the opportunity to contribute. Their own contribution comes from helping people grow, giving employees freedom and control to make appropriate decisions.

The men who will successfully lead us through the next decade are guided by a purpose greater than themselves and operate from values and principles that contribute to unfaltering consistency in their thoughts and actions. They value having power over themselves rather than having control over others. They care about satisfying employees' and customers' needs. They manage by trusting rather than supervising employees and by depending on and valuing others' expertise and abilities. They trust both their logic and intuition to guide their decisions and are ever concerned about developing themselves personally and professionally.

In the following pages we'll be looking at four different ways the new leadership is implemented: John Rollwagen, who articulates the new thinking; Robert Mondavi, who shows us it is never too late to change; Dave Webb, who demonstrates the use of power without position; and the Guild executives, who exemplify the new leadership in teamwork.

THE PHILOSOPHY ARTICULATED

John Rollwagen, the chairman of Cray Research, whom you met in Chapter 8, best articulates the emerging leaders' viewpoint, "I am classically disinterested in power. Anyone who thinks he has a real sense of power has got to be kidding himself.

"People do tell me I'm a very powerful person. But I think that comes across because I have very strong feelings about things. In that respect, if I'm influential because I express my ideas or my feelings, well, I'm happy with that. And I do say what I think and I say it early," he continued.

I responded, "I'm glad to hear you let people know what you're thinking early on, because so often people will discuss various approaches to a problem, for instance, and the boss sits back and listens. When he finally speaks, it often does come across in a forceful way, so people tend to back off. They think if the boss just expressed his idea everyone should go with it."

"That's exactly why I do it. I don't like it if someone backs off," John responded.

As he explains, "I have to be careful how I use my influence. It's not that I believe in consensus. I don't. But I do believe in a shared direction, in a common understanding." Men like Rollwagen know that people will follow the leader rather than think for themselves. These men are so secure with themselves that they don't need people to blindly obey. They like being challenged.

"How have you let people know you're not caught up in your positional power?" I asked.

John answered by telling me a story. "When I became president, my phone stopped ringing. I was in the men's room one day and overheard one employee say to the other, 'You can't bother John with that, he's too busy.'

"So I began letting everyone know that I have nothing to do. When I say this to our people, they laugh nervously. My only job was to make sure the mission was intact. But we have a very simple business mission—to make the world's most powerful computer.

"It's also important for me to guide the management philosophy at Cray. I encourage the other managers to trust people rather than supervise them. Of course we occasionally have a few martinets. We tolerate them, but they don't last long. I'm known for walking around the company and if I see a particular manager has made an unreasonable request, I'll tell his subordinate to ignore his boss's orders.

"Now, some executives would think I'm usurping my subordinates' power. I'm not, and few people at Cray would think of it that way. They're relieved we don't get bogged down in bureaucratic details. I want people to feel it's their decision. We hold people accountable. We let them decide the way. We've found it breeds honesty."

At the same time the pressure to be "the" example exists. But these executives don't succumb to it. They don't believe they have to know about or how to do all the jobs they manage. Rollwagen talks about the time he met with forty interns who participated in the summer program at Cray Research. "I had asked all forty interns to tell me about themselves and what projects they were working on. After they finished I told them I didn't hear one job I could do. And that it was important that they finish the job before they left because each project was highly important." He went on, "That meeting only helped to reinforce how CEOs are not in the position to call the shots. You have to give people the freedom to decide and create for themselves.

"I offer discipline without blame. It's important that the people at Cray know they can explore any idea that supports our mission. But sometimes those ideas don't pan out. You can't shift gears without pain. Of course you feel a twinge of pain as you leave the old course. But when you get on the new course it feels so good. My role is to encourage people to take the necessary risks and not worry about making mistakes."

"Has anyone changed his own way of managing because of your management style?" I inquired.

"No question," John replied emphatically. "I've given people a sense of the freedom they have here. One person in particular changed dramatically. Les Davis is a tough, good engineer and good communicator with a dry, expressionless sense of humor. He was tough and autocratic. Over time he's relaxed more. Now he commands more respect than anyone else in the company. He knows more about what's going on."

John was not in the least bit threatened that Les commands more respect than he. He's a man who has the position but doesn't care to misuse his power. Instead he wants others to be as happy as he is and love their personal and professional life as he does. He wants them to have power over themselves as he has power over himself.

"I do what I want and I want others to feel free enough to do the same," he concluded.

IT'S NEVER TOO LATE TO CHANGE

I decided to write about Robert Mondavi because, at seventy-four, he is an inspiration to all. He started Mondavi Winery in 1966. His family had been in the wine business in the Napa Valley since 1919. From across the room the first thing you notice about Bob are his smiling blue eyes, sparkling with enthusiasm and zest. His presence comes not from his stature but from the warmth he conveys to one and all.

If you were to meet Bob Mondavi, you would be surprised by his unpretentiousness. Bob has no desire to be the center of attention. In fact, frequently his attention is on others, learning about them, praising them, understanding them.

We all know the Mondavi name, but until I interviewed Bob, I had no idea that his company never advertised on TV or in print. Their advertising and public-relations philosophy has always been "people-to-people" introductions, meeting the customer, the retailer, the restaurateur. I met Bob through his wonderful wife, Margrit Biever, who is credited with bringing international recognition to not only Mondavi wines, but to the wine industry of Napa Valley, a point Bob makes sure that one and all know.

But that is only one of the many ways Mondavi Winery has been the leader in marketing California wines. Mondavi sets the pace and the other wineries follow. For instance, they recently began selling futures on wine, and four other wineries followed suit. Bob Mondavi decided to rename two wines: Sauvignon Blanc and White Pinot, which we know as Fumé Blanc and Chenin Blanc. This brilliant marketing decision started the new trend of renaming wines in the industry.

One trait that clearly sets the Mondavi Winery apart from the other Napa Valley giants is their desire to share their success and recognition with their industry colleagues in the Napa Valley. The Mondavis created the Napa Valley Wine Auction, which is a charity event raising in excess of three hundred thousand dollars annually for the hospitals in the valley. Yet you won't see them taking credit for it. There is a wine expo in Bordeaux, France, that Mondavi wines were asked to participate in. In true spirit, the Mondavis felt sharing their exposure with other Napa Valley wineries would be of benefit to all. So they asked twenty-one other wineries to participate in the expo with them. And they are currently working on ways to communicate to the public that wine, in moderation, can benefit one's health, and they are working with those who treat alcoholism.

Charity begins at home. Bob Mondavi believes taking care of others begins with his employees. Each year, between eighteen and twenty-five employees are selected to tour the wine country of France so they will have a better understanding of winemaking, a process that is centuries old.

Employee involvement and input is important to Bob. When a new wine, White Zinfandel, was to be released everyone was given a case. Bob wanted every employee to not only be familiar with the new product, but to offer his or her comments on the wine.

However, Bob didn't always believe in the value of delegating responsibility or taking the time to understand others. One of Bob's opening comments was, ''Over the past four or five years my values have changed. I care about communicating with people. I have developed a greater understanding of people, which has made me more accepting of them. I find people really give me an inner satisfaction as I watch them take control of the business.''

Two situations caused him to reevaluate his management philosophy and style. The first had to do with addressing a problem of sibling rivalry. The second had to do with realizing no one was communicating with anyone else, mainly because Bob kept holding on to the reins.

Bob's two sons and his daughter work in the business. Mike, eight years older than his brother Tim, handles the marketing and sales, while Tim is the winemaker, in charge of production. Marcy represents the winery in New York and Europe, so she is not caught in the crossfire between her brothers on a regular basis. After his sons were in the business for a while, Bob began to notice that their intense competitiveness with one another was adversely affecting the company.

Coupled with this sibling rivalry Bob was faced with a management team that was afraid to make decisions. For seventeen years he had run the show at Mondavi Winery and before that he and his brother had been in control of another family winery. His managers had learned to depend on Bob for direction. As both sons were vying for control, Bob became an even more important person to depend upon.

One meeting in particular brought this problem to Bob's attention. He described it to me, ''We had always been the leaders in introducing new wines or in our marketing strategies. But one of our competitors' moves made me realize we weren't on the leading edge. When I suggested to the head of sales that we introduce a new product to the sales force in a certain way, I had *expected* him to go along with me. Instead he told me we wouldn't be able to do it because of some problems none of us were aware of. It was at that moment I looked around the room and realized no one was communicating with anyone else. And it didn't help to have my sons competing with one another or for me to always be in charge.''

Suddenly at seventy years old, Bob had to determine why his management team was not communicating with one another. And coming to the answer meant looking honestly at his own actions. Bob concluded that he needed to step away from the business and give others the decision-making authority they needed to get the job done; that he needed to step out of a controlling position in order to get others to change. Or, as his son Mike puts it, "He stopped 'barking orders' and he became everyone's mentor."

Although it is often unarticulated, emerging leaders instinctively know they are the ones who must change rather than looking for ways to get others to change. As long as they continue behaving in the same vein, others will respond as they have in the past. However, if you focus on changing others, they will only succumb to your pressure temporarily, frequently reverting to their old ways because you are still acting as you did in the past. In other words, if you change your own actions, then others will change accordingly.

Bob explained the changes he made in his management philosophy and approach. "I decided to establish a management council, rotating the chairmanship amongst six corporate officers. Now, not everyone thought this was such a good idea because they had all grown accustomed to looking to me for the answers. But I had to change the way *we* were operating, which meant I had to change my role. My chief financial person argued with me. He disagreed with this concept of shared power so vehemently that he resigned. Others didn't resign, but they entered the arrangement half-heartedly. But I thought no one should have too much control or been in a power position for too long."

"How long ago was this implemented?" I asked.

"Four years ago and it works great," Bob began. "Our former financial guy stayed on as a consultant. Over this time he has also consulted with other wineries, so he has a basis of comparison. A few months ago he told me that he never believed my idea would work, but I've made a believer out of him.

"It solved the problem between my sons. But more importantly, it got everyone talking with one another. There isn't one person who makes a unilateral decision. Everyone works together. And everyone has a sense of contributing to our success. I enjoy watching them learn from one another."

Although Bob didn't say so, I sensed that these changes were extreme deviations from how he had acted previously. I inquired, "Did you always appreciate others' efforts and derive pleasure from them?"

"Oh, no," Bob replied as he shook his head. "It's not that I don't expect the best from people. I still do. But I've revised my expectations of them. I've stopped condemning people when they don't do things the way I expect."

"So you are a reformed perfectionist?" I responded.

"Most definitely. And I'm happier because of it. So are the people around me. I've stopped being disappointed because I've learned to understand people. I factor in the fact that they will make mistakes, they won't do things my way or when I want it. I no longer focus on how they reach their goals. Instead I encourage them or teach them how to get 'there.' Now I'm able to appreciate people. It doesn't pay to criticize them."

There were many times as I spoke with Bob that I wished other executives, often twenty, thirty, or forty years his junior, had the ability to look at themselves realistically, and admit they needed to change. I wondered what it was in Bob that gave him the ability to do so. Through a circuitous route the answer came. As I was searching for the reason that Mondavi Winery was the industry trendsetter, I realized there was a common thread in all of Bob's accomplishments.

"I've never been satisfied with what I accomplished. By this I mean, once I reached a goal, I always looked at how I could improve upon what I did. I never rested on my laurels," Bob started to explain.

"So that's what causes you to always think of the next marketing niche, to admit you are wrong about how you have handled a situation, to know that you must constantly change if you want to stay successful," I reflected.

"Exactly."

These changes have extended to the way his family interacts. In the late 1970s, at sixty-seven, Bob got divorced. For months his children wouldn't speak to him. But Bob did not think this would be good for the business or for his family. So to ensure communication flows smoothly among his family members, Bob Mondavi, his two sons, his daughter, and his ex-wife, who still owns a major portion of the company, meet twice annually. They go on a company and personal retreat where they discuss the issues bothering them, find solutions, and plan their future activities.

Any corporate executive or middle manager who was raised on outdated management philosophies and practices, but believes it's too late to change, need only look at Robert Mondavi. He is proof that emerging leaders are not defined by age, but values. They have a desire to grow, personally and professionally; they care about others; and they know understanding themselves leads to a greater understanding of their employees and family members.

POWER WITHOUT POSITION

As organizational structures are being flattened, eliminating superior-subordinate relationships and removing hierarchical reporting systems, the ability to influence others without using positional power becomes more important in today's work world.

When I worked with Jim Garrick, the director of the Center for Sports Medicine, I first met and interviewed Dave Webb. Dave was one of the primary care physicians at the center. As I was writing up my notes one day, I realized that he had a gift that many other men could learn from—a sense of feeling comfortable with how powerful he is.

At first glance, Dave's goatee makes him look stern. But when you hear him speak, you know he isn't at all. He is unassuming, talks in a slow, deliberate manner, and exudes a quiet strength. His penetrating wisdom coupled with a matter-of-fact pragmatism comes as a surprise.

Dave described himself for me. "I'm not charismatic. I don't stop a room when I walk in. In fact, if I'm quiet for a while, people sometimes think I'm an idiot. When I do speak, suddenly they act as if I am a sage. I'm neither," he said nonchalantly.

I became aware of Dave's innate abilities when Jim told me how Dave resolved the problems of how the partners at the center should be given surgical assists. Since Jim was the center's only orthopedic surgeon, the other five primary care physicians' income was greatly influenced by the number of surgeries they assisted with Jim. It seemed the staff meeting got a little heated when one of the doctors complained about the newest partner's proportion of surgical assists. According to Jim, Dave jumped in and resolved the matter.

As he explains, "Frankly, I thought a couple of them were making a bigger deal than necessary, and I wasn't going to let their complaints drag on indefinitely. So I tried to work out what was fair. One of the doctors, Al, did have a point.

"Over the year Al and Bill hadn't assisted on as many surgeries as the rest of us. So, even though the policy has been for us to assist on our own patients, Marie, Mark, and I offered to give up assisting on our own patients' surgeries so they could get caught up. But Al wasn't happy with our offer.''

Over the time I interviewed Dave, I consistently saw how his values and principles influenced his thoughts and actions. In turn, this contributed to the consistency in his answers and the examples he gave me. Dave knows who he is and never pretends to be something he is not. He is a man you can take at face value. Men of quiet strength are guided by intention.

Dave continued to recount for me what occurred, ''The discussion continued as we debated some other possibilities. By then it was apparent to me that one of the doctors was trying to pull the wool over our eyes.

''When I told this particular doctor that I was absolutely opposed to not getting back onto a schedule, he accused me of being harsh.''

I wondered if Dave took this personally or saw the manipulativeness implied in the criticism. ''How did you react to that?'' I asked.

He leaned forward and shrugged his shoulders as he said, ''It didn't bother me. He accused me of that because I wasn't going along with what he wanted.'' At that point I learned Dave abhorred duplicity and was not easily threatened by attempts to manipulate him.

''How do you deal with a person when he attempts to manipulate you?'' I asked.

He said with a smile, ''I check my pockets every time he leaves the room, to make sure the snake hasn't ripped me off.'' Then, quickly reverting to his pensive, serious manner, he explained, ''People who are manipulative forfeit their chance for good feelings from me,'' he replied simply. ''I'll continue to be direct. That's all.''

''Did you realize you were being manipulated when it was happening or did it come to you later?'' I inquired.

''After the meeting when I was riding home, I realized exactly how I was being manipulated. I knew if I had challenged him in the meeting, he'd make too big a deal denying what he was doing. When I got home, I wrote up a plan sorting out what was fair, putting the new procedures in writing. The next day I gave a copy to everyone so they could vote on it. It was logistically straight-forward."

After a pause, he added, "To my mind, this was a way to distribute the surgical assists in a fair and equitable manner. Each doctor received equal treatment in surgical rotations, an equal number of rotations, and frequent rotations. We all had equal opportunity, not necessarily equal results."

What intrigued me most is that Dave did not have to assume this responsibility. He is not the associate director of the center. He and his peers are equal partners. While most people avoid potential conflicts, Dave seemed compelled to jump into the middle of them. I wanted to know why.

As Dave explained it, "I had a strong motivation to help Jim. I perceived the problem worsening and thought Jim could use a hit. He has helped me so much. I did it out of loyalty to him."

This is not the loyalty of a yes-man. This is the loyalty of a man who knows he balances the strengths and weaknesses in his boss, but remains his own man. Where Dave differs from the people-pleasers or the power-seekers is that he is willing to confront people because he genuinely wants people to be the best they can be. The "nice guys" never say anything because they are too worried people will not like them. And the power-seekers use information as a weapon to confront others. Dave Webb recognizes and believes in people's ability to do things well. He gets frustrated when people are not producing as well as they can because to him, "people are wasting themselves."

Dave is also quite receptive to feedback. When I mentioned some of his co-workers were concerned about how he was exercising his power, he wanted to know who felt that way, only because, "If I don't understand them, then I won't be doing my job well." Then he added, "I have no ambition to be in control of other people. So it's important that I'm sensitive to their needs, to the way they need to be managed or spoken with."

Dave doesn't expect himself to be all things to all people. He knows when to apply his strengths and when to let someone else offer his or hers. That is the source of his power.

In the following section, we will see how this same strength is demonstrated in a management team.

TEAMWORK IN MODERN TIMES

I am often asked, "Do you think a strong leader needs weaker people below him?"

And I answer, "No, only the weak look for weaker links so they can appear strong. Those who are genuinely strong and secure in their power don't need to impose it on anyone. To the contrary, they seek out other strong people to challenge them."

Meet the leaders of Guild Winery. Gerry is the president, Chris is the chief financial officer, Ron is the marketing director, and Doug is the sales director. They call themselves the Ball brothers. Gerry is Mr. Highball, Chris is Mr. Hardball, Ron and Doug exchange the titles of Mr. Lowball and Mr. Snowball.

When I conducted a two-day marketing strategy meeting for them, I had the opportunity to see how four strong personalities could work well together. This team took an almost bankrupt winery and within eighteen months turned a profit. Not one person has any desire to lay claim to his success. They think of the outcome as a "shared success."

Unlike Steve Richards, whom we met in the preceding chapter, the Guild executives illustrate how secure they are in their own areas of expertise, yet simultaneously dependent on their peers for input and constructive criticism. Rather than each of these men expecting the others to be like him, they value their differences. As Chris said to me, "Our differences only enhance the quality of our work."

For example, during one marketing strategy meeting Ron expressed his dissatisfaction with the direction of the discussion. Later that evening Gerry and Chris reminded Ron of his comment and felt it was important they resolve this issue before the next day's session. The next morning, the issue was brought up again, but this time Ron and Chris both summarized the differences in their thinking and working styles. This helped everyone understand the root of Ron's displeasure, without taking it personally. It also opened the way for others to express their ideas on how the remainder of the meeting should proceed.

In this example, the Guild executives demonstrate what most emerging leaders are good at: they are able to discuss process and content and be aware of both at the same time. Think about process and content this way. The process is how people work together.

The content is the work they are doing. How often have you sat in a meeting where nothing was accomplished? Managers who don't pay attention to process lead ineffective meetings because they ignore the dynamics that take place, believing that the lack of attention will help the problems go away.

The same values and principles bind the Guild executives together: the desire to succeed, the challenge of solving tough situations, the concern and respect for other individuals, the dependence on others. Yet as similar as they are in the values they hold, they are dissimilar in approach. For instance, Gerry shoots from the hip, making quick decisions that don't depend on market studies. He has a track record of successes in the industry. On the other hand, Ron comes from a Procter and Gamble background, which means he plans before he acts. He studies the marketplace. He develops rationales and strategies to support his viewpoint. Doug is a good mixture of both, while Chris goes over things with a fine-tooth comb.

Gerry deserves much of the credit for setting the corporate culture. As he tells everyone to leave their ego back at home, he has done the same. No one is afraid to disagree with or criticize the boss. Gerry wants the atmosphere to be one where each person's territory is fair game for the others to comment on. And he has created this culture by example rather than by words.

Chris is not your typical financial person. From the beginning of his career, he has been concerned about developing his "people" skills. When working with Chris he doesn't emphasize the bottom line. He evaluates the business plan and weighs the impact the decision will have on the employees. And, unlike most financial people I know, life is not black and white to him. He has an uncanny ability to perceive how he and how others need to improve.

Ron and Doug, the marketing and sales vice presidents, respectively, are examples for others. Contrary to most marketing and sales executives, who battle for power and control, Ron and Doug interact as a team rather than as two opposing forces. At times it is hard to determine who's making the marketing decisions and who's making the sales ones. Some people might view Ron as a paradox. On one hand, he is extremely logical and factual. On the other, he delights in discussing people, their motivations and their needs. Doug has worked in the field and in the corporate offices. He is both sympathetic to the needs of his people and able to balance them with strategic decisions. Secure within himself, Doug welcomes Ron's opinions, as Ron similarly solicits his.

I strongly believe in the competitive spirit, but I don't believe competition should be cultivated between peers. In the end it is unproductive. When I asked Ron and Doug why they didn't feel competitive with one another they both gave the same answer, "Our competitors are the other brands in the marketplace. Not one another." Their focus is on getting the job done and doing it together.

During our two-day strategy session, Gerry invited the two advertising executives working on the Guild product line. "It's better if they hear the decisions we make firsthand rather than have any one of us attempt to re-create two days of thinking," Gerry told me. This, too, is thinking uncharacteristic to many executives. Although the advertising agency is working for them, many brand managers feel a need to guard their decisions, only disseminating the bare minimum in information needed for one to do his job.

The Guild executives shared in their play as well. Ron was the new kid on the block. The other three had endured many turbulent moments and had already started Guild on its successful recovery. They didn't know how Ron weathered storms. So they set up a test. One night after working late, Gerry, Chris, and Doug were sitting around thinking about competitive strategies. Chris looked at a competitor's poster of a bikini-clad woman, who, in Chris's words, "looked like a Dawn, to me." So Chris took a pen and wrote on the top: *Dear Ron*, then signed it, *Love Dawn*. Gerry chimed in, "Let's send it to his home." And Doug said, "If we do that we have to write *Personal and Confidential*, signed with a heart on the outside."

At the time of this prank Ron was in New York on business. It seems his wife had opened the package and a cold thaw was felt across the phone lines when he called home one night. The next day a secretary, who knew about the prank, alerted the boys that Ron had called asking if a Dawn had called him at work. Upon hearing this the boys chuckled with glee.

During the meeting Ron was the one who told me this story and they all laughed together. Months later Chris and I analyzed the reason they all did this. In true male fashion they tested Ron and they were happy with how well he passed their test. "The three of us had weathered many months of the bad time, leading the company out of bankruptcy. Ron joined the team late and hadn't endured many of the pressures the rest of us faced. We needed to see how well he withstood pressures,'' Chris remarked.

The Guild executives are an example of a business team that works together, concerned about winning rather than beating one another. They value the quality of their relationship collectively. Consensus on their strategy and action must be there for them to work together, while at the same time they are tolerant of each other's differences.

BECOMING AN EMERGING LEADER

I am sympathetic to those executives and managers who want to change, but are unsure about what to do. I think it is important for men who want to change to adopt an attitude whereby they are no longer interested in asserting power over others. They need to stop measuring their effectiveness in terms of how well they are obeyed. When many men tell me, ''My people don't listen to me'' or ''I can't understand why people nowadays need to question every decision,'' I respond, ''If you define respect as blind obedience, you will never know who respects your ideas. Executives need to earn people's respect based on what they do, how they think, and how they implement their ideas, not by the position they hold. And, to be even more pointed, stop feeling powerless or out of control if one does not obey you on first command. People need to be involved in making the decisions they are to implement.''

The crux of the issue is POWER. In the past, one set of values defined leadership. When most business environments were more bureaucratic, stable, and predictable, rules and policies were adequate tools to manage with. However, in a rapidly changing business world, where few things are predictable, it is important that employees feel free to respond to customers' needs by making the necessary and immediate decisions.

Currently entrepreneurial leadership is chic. Visionary leaders are admired, written about, and in demand. People are fashioning themselves after the charismatic evangelist or the entrepreneurial maverick. But we need to move away from these labels and look at what skills and values make someone successful in today's marketplace.

Men like John Rollwagen, who is ''classically uninterested'' in power; Bob Mondavi, who feels it is never too late to change; Dave Webb, who is guided by his values and principles; or the Guild executives, who value the differences each peer brings to the party, demonstrate for us the thinking and the actions required for the new leadership. None is concerned with what worked in the past, only with what works today, that in turn will take us to the future.

These men believe in their own judgment. They think in terms of how "we" are going to accomplish the company's goals and objectives. They dispel the myth that a strong leader has to have a strong ego. They are guided by their concern and belief in others, by contributing to others' development. They are willing to assume the role of leader when necessary, but avoid usurping anyone else's power or control. And they look at their business from a strategic viewpoint, taking calculated risks and building on their already well-respected track record.

So if you want to change, but are not sure how to begin, I have developed some questions for you to ask yourself. You can also ask others to answer these questions, offering their perspective on your management style. Based on your answers (and others' input) you will be able to develop your own personal road map, charting your course and becoming an example of the new leadership.

ASSESSING MY MANAGEMENT PHILOSOPHY AND STYLE

1. What values would currently define my leadership or management style?
2. How important is it for me to feel in control?
3. Would I like to have "me" for a boss? If yes, why? If no, why not?
4. Can I accept it when others disagree with me? How do I demonstrate this?
5. Do I accept others' differences in style and philosophy, or do I expect people to be like me?
6. What three qualities do I share with the men profiled in this chapter?

7. How do I demonstrate to others that I value them? their input? their honesty?

8. In what ways do I empower others?

9. What values would I like to incorporate into my philosophy and actions?

10. What attitudes and values would I like to change?

11. How well do I listen to others? Do I always try to control situations?

12. Do I think about how I want others to change, rather than focusing on how I need to change?

13. Whom do I consider a good role model to learn from?

14. Whom do I work with that I can ask for some constructive criticism and honest assessment of how I manage others?

15. What is the first step I want to take in making these changes? How and when will I begin?

I am amazed at the increasing numbers of executives who are concerned about the power and control they wield in organizations. They are destroying the bureaucratic structures they have helped to create and enforce. As more executives see that a global economy and global competition is no longer a theoretical concept but a reality to contend with, they are realizing that one of the ways to cope with the problems presented in our rapidly changing business environment is by focusing on the way they and their managers lead the organization and its people. Although the men in this chapter might be a minority today, they will soon be recognized as the role models for many other executives who are finally ready to relinquish their control over others for the sake of their company, its people and our economy.

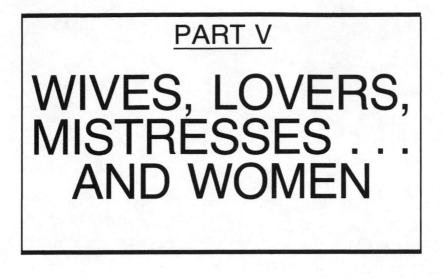

PART V

WIVES, LOVERS, MISTRESSES . . . AND WOMEN

CHAPTER 12

AN ENEMY HAS INVADED MY SANCTUARY

Anyone who thinks it's been easy for men to accept the changing roles of women is mistaken. Men are not supposed to attest to this, for that would, of course, be an unmanly thing to do. Some might even consider it chauvinistic if they voiced their complaints.

But it's the truth.

The difficulties men have had to endure as women have made changes in their roles, at home and at work, have been unappreciated, even ignored. As one executive said to me, "One day you wake up to see your sanctuaries have been destroyed because women decided they didn't like the way the game was being played. They were angry at us for being the men we were taught to be. They blamed us for their plight and unhappiness in their roles—the roles they were brought up to assume. I don't know who my wife is anymore. And I don't understand these angry women at the office. You wonder, Who is this enemy in my sanctuary?"

In the course of being groomed for their careers, men were taught to view the workplace as a sanctuary where they could act out their aggressions, work and play with the boys, and strive to achieve their dreams. And their home was to be a sanctuary of a different kind—a refuge where they could have their wounds healed from the battles fought every day. Instead these retreats have become disputed territories.

Men were prepared for a world where women were supposed to take care of their needs both at home and at work. The rules were simple and understood by both sexes: Women would always be there to support and nurture men. They would be a man's appendage, slave, mother, nursemaid, and lover.

In many men's minds, these changes (women's rejection of these roles) were, and possibly still are, unwanted and undesirable. Men had not asked women to change, and yet men were expected overnight to view women differently. If they didn't, they were accused of being insensitive male chauvinists.

Modern man felt an added pressure if his wife entered the business world. He was expected not to be threatened by her attention to her career, but when she seemed to be paying less attention to his needs, he would sulk, pout, and complain, hoping she would get the hint that he felt slighted. If she completely ignored his feelings, he would finally rebel by telling her she had to quit her job and pay more attention to the family. None of this seemed to work. In extreme cases, his failure to accept the new conditions brought his marriage to an end.

Most women want the changes that have been made. Many women want to work outside the home. They don't want to have to hide their intelligence in order to "get a man." They don't want to be controlled by another person. Women deserve the first-class status they are fighting for. At the same time men deserve credit for how they have learned to accept the unsolicited changes.

It's confusing out there, at best. A woman is sometimes a man's lover, caretaker, or friend. Other times she is his competitor, boss, or mentor. Many men are unsure about how to deal with the "liberated woman" because they don't know how to respond to the mixed messages that are often given. One moment men are supposed to be liberated; the next moment they are to be gentlemen. It's okay to pay for dinner, but don't make the mistake of opening the car door afterward.

Some men are ashamed for being competitive, for feeling threatened or acting chauvinistically. Further, societal pressure has shamed them into keeping their feelings to themselves. The problem is that they never learned to cope with feelings of envy over a woman's success.

One man said to me, "I have three daughters and I want them to be able to do anything they want. I'd rather they aren't dependent on a man. I know my wife's not happy with counting on me for the bread and butter. But that's how it was for us. I tell my girls they'd better think about how they are going to support themselves. Yet at the office I don't encourage any of the women to go for it. If they do, they might get a position or project that *should* have been mine. It's crazy for me to think about it this way, but I do."

This man admits to the ambivalence many men often feel about women becoming financially and emotionally independent. Men have defined themselves in relation to others. More specifically, many men define their masculinity by the degree of a woman's dependence and subservience. They equate being loved with being needed. As women need men less, men question their own worth.

In a man's mind, when a woman makes her own decisions, earns her own living, he has lost control. Losing control is equal to castration.

The changes in women's roles are unlikely to reverse themselves. Current indications are that two-career couples will be the norm by the late 1990s. The "liberated" woman is here to stay, and the chauvinistic man is therefore likely to become extinct. If men are to survive emotionally and have healthy, productive relationships with the women they live and work with, they will have to adopt new attitudes.

In this chapter we will examine the issues surrounding men's confusion, anger, and ambivalence regarding the new roles women are assuming. We will look at their sexual attitudes, their need to be needed, and their fear of "smart women."

SEX IN THE EXECUTIVE SUITE

"We prefer to promote unattractive women. It's too disturbing to have a good-looking broad in the boardroom. I've watched men lose their concentration, often ignoring more important matters," said the young chairman of a leading financial institution.

Men's clubs have refused to admit women. The Bohemian Club, which counts among its members George Shultz, Ronald Reagan, and Henry Kissinger from the political world as well as A. W. Clausen, president of Bank of America; Frank Borman, former chairman of Eastern Airlines; and David Packard, chairman of Hewlett-Packard, has a national reputation for refusing to admit women. The club claims it's because it wouldn't want a woman to see men peeing on trees.

A friend of mine who is a member confided the real reason why men are resistant to women joining. "The only reason men won't let women into the Bohemian Club," he said, "is because instead of taking care of business and socializing as we do, everyone will enter into competition over who's going to be your date for the weekend at the grove, whether you have a wife or not."

A favorite client and good friend, Gary Moore, explained it this way, "Men judge themselves by the women who want them. There are enough ways men compete in business without adding the 'Get the Beautiful Woman' game. It only forces us to compete in yet another way, a way we would like relief from. In our company your power position increases based on whose secretary you are screwing. But we also have to maintain the façade of being happily married so the boss thinks we are stable."

My confusion was dissolved after reading Warren Farrell's book *Why Men Are the Way They Are*. There the author tells us, "For decades marketing researchers studying men have found that the only common denominator that can appeal to men of all classes is their desire to achieve acceptance by the culture's most 'beautiful' women."

He goes on to say, "It hurts a lot less to be rejected by a sex object than it does to be rejected by a full human being, so if a male can turn women into objects and sex into a game (and call it 'scoring'), he is able to treat rejection less seriously. He will hurt less."[1]

At first I had a hard time understanding this kind of thinking. The mistake I made was assuming the opposite of unattractive is attractive. To most men the opposite of unattractive ranges from beautiful to sexually appealing. Men believe that women are important determinants of their desirability. As one man said to me, "If a beautiful woman wants me, I must be okay."

What Gary Moore, Warren Farrell, and my anonymous Bohemian Club friend say is true. The problem men have with women giving mixed messages ("It's okay to pay for dinner, but it's not okay to open my car door") reflects men's confusion about their sexual roles. They haven't been taught to interact with women in a way that isn't sexual or based on sexual roles. I began to appreciate that men don't want women in business because the games men have been taught to play with women are forced to surface. Suddenly it is the man asking himself, "Do I act like a man or do I act like an executive?"

This question brings up another important aspect, which is: men have not been taught to take responsibility for their own feelings. Instead, men are taught to externalize most things. They attribute the origin of their feelings to someone or something else. They don't believe their feelings originate in their own psyche. As a result, when many men say, "She turned me on," they believe the woman has the power to do this and that they have no power around such a woman.

I learned men feel this way in 1981 when I was teaching a course at Fordham University with Dr. Carl Rogers and twenty other staff members. We led a ten-day program called "Men and Women Together," which was intended to explore the issues men and women were facing at that time.

For nine months prior to the summer workshop, the entire staff met one day a month to explore the issues in ourselves. Philosophically we believed that unless we were aware of our own prejudices and fears, resentments and disappointments, we would not be able to guide the workshop properly.

Each month we explored different aspects of relationships between men and women. The month we dealt with sexual power proved to be enlightening. Zachary Paulson, a thirty-six-year-old university administrator, aired his resentments about women entering the enclaves of management by saying, "Women bring sex into the workplace. They turn men on and we are powerless to do anything about it."

Stan Halstead, a thirty-eight-year-old psychologist, challenged Zachary, saying, "You believe a woman gives you a hard-on without touching you." Then he looked around the room at the other men and said, "That's the problem with most of us [men]. We don't take responsibility for our own sexual or emotional feelings. That's why we end up dependent on women or at least thinking that we are. When I realized that no woman makes my dick hard, that I get it up because of how I'm looking at her or because of what

I'm thinking about her, my whole attitude about women changed. Specifically, I stopped being afraid of them. They didn't have the power I thought they did.''

Nearly 67 percent of the men I interviewed believed their sexual response was not in their control, that it was something that happened to them. But as more men begin to realize they are in control of themselves, that no woman has power over them, there will be less fear of women in the boardroom and in the bedroom. This will only come when men are willing to explain their feelings to the women they love and the women they befriend. As women come to understand men's fear of being powerless, that understanding will create a peacefulness and supportiveness in the workplace. Women will be less angry and men will be less afraid.

SHE NEEDS TO BE IN CHARGE, BUT I NEED TO BE NEEDED

''She doesn't rely on me for the things she wants out of life. It catches me by surprise when I find myself wondering if she loves me because she doesn't need me to earn money or make decisions. It's either she loves me because she needs me or she won't love me because she doesn't need me,'' said Tom Pritikin, corporate counsel for a major packaged goods firm.

Tom is in a bind that many men are experiencing today. He thought he liked the idea of a dual-career marriage. He and his wife Jennifer were married for three years when he encouraged her to go to law school. She hadn't seemed happy in her job as a buyer at Bloomingdale's. She had a good, analytical mind and had been on her high-school debate team. She had always talked about being a lawyer, and since she hadn't initially become one she decided to marry one.

I met them after Jenny had been practicing law for five years. She had established a practice for herself that was very lucrative. In fact, she made more money than Tom.

Tom continued, ''My father was always the breadwinner. With that came the responsibility for making the decisions that were best for my mother and the kids. I sometimes think I'm being a sissy when I ask Jenny what she thinks. We make joint decisions. Rarely will she defer to me. She says I shouldn't worry about this. She loves me because I'm her best friend. I understand her. But I don't think she can appreciate how difficult it is for me to say, 'I feel important when you ask for my opinion and do what I say, so stop acting like you can get along fine without me.' As women learn how to take control, we are supposed to learn how to give it up. It doesn't seem fair that one side gains and the other side loses.''

With respect to control, Tom is right. It isn't fair. Men are being asked to change a major aspect of their personality. Most men grew up watching their fathers act as permission givers, ordering their mothers around. Their mothers subserviently acquiesced to their fathers' demands. Men felt important when people listened to them. They grew up believing it was a sign of weakness to listen to anyone else. At the extreme, some men only feel manly if a woman is dependent on them.

But women today are no longer asking for permission. They are making their own decisions, making decisions for others, and jointly making decisions with their husbands. As a result, some men are searching for new ways to define their importance in a woman's life.

Someone listening to Tom might think he is worrying over nothing, wanting to improve things that are already working very well. But how one externally responds to a situation can be different from how he internalizes it. Some people, including myself, think that life has been unfair for women under the old rules. And the way men have had control needs changing. But it is important that these necessary societal changes bring people closer together.

To Tom's credit, he is willing to explore his discomfort with the roles he and Jenny are assuming. He has both the emotional courage to admit how and why he *feels* inadequate and the presence of mind to know in truth he is not.

Tom and Jenny openly discuss the power struggles that arise before they get out of hand. Tom is able to learn how women view the ''control'' issue. As Jenny explained her feelings to him, ''It's not that I need you less. I need you differently. I need you to think *with* me, to help me analyze the problems I encounter with my clients. Because I'm not subservient doesn't mean I don't love you. I love you because I don't have to fight for my right to be in control of my life. I like being in charge of me. And I love you because you don't force me to be dependent even though you might want me to be.''

It took a few years before Tom realized that subservience and dependence are not love. Love is separateness rather than dependence. Tom is learning new ways of loving and being loved. He and Jenny encourage each other's emotional and professional growth. They aren't threatened if they don't think or feel alike. They have learned to revel in the differences, each having a separate identity. And they are comfortable with their identity as a couple.

Jenny and Tom are continually finding solutions to working together as they give up their psychological and sexual role conditioning. They realize that they were taught to behave and feel "like a man" or "like a woman" should. But those old rules are not working. They still don't have everything worked out and new issues constantly surface. However, with compassion and determination they resolve them.

TAKING THE BACK SEAT

Another reason men are resentful of women's independence is that it means they get less attention.

An IBM executive, whose kids were in college and whose wife was beginning to make a career for herself, told me, "I don't like the idea that she no longer pays the same amount of attention to me. I'm happy she has found some work she likes, but her newfound happiness means my newfound unhappiness. She's too exhausted to wait on me. She's preoccupied with her own work when I want to talk about mine. Her independence makes me realize my own dependence."

Men are led to believe that they aren't supposed to admit that they are dependent upon women. But unless they are willing to face the fact that they *are*, they will be unable to free themselves from this emotional bind. As women build lives for themselves separate from their spouses, men have to learn to adjust to being first fiddle sometimes but second fiddle other times. Above all, men must learn that although a wife might pay attention to her career, this does not make her husband less lovable.

In their emotional dependence men have placed too much significance on a woman's actions as the measure of their lovableness. As men learn to depend on themselves for some of the emotional support previously garnered from their wives, they will become more emotionally available to the woman in their life. And as people are more emotionally available for one another the issue of attention becomes one of quality rather than quantity.

Another man, Chuck, confessed, "I'm jealous of the time my wife spends at the office. When I was growing up, Mom was always there for my dad and us. I don't like having to do the laundry because she hasn't had time to get me clean socks. We fight over the socks, but that's not really what's eating me up. I don't know how to tell her I need to know she still loves me. When all her energy is going into her job, I wonder if she still loves me. I can't tell her I need to be reassured because I'm supposed to be the strong one in this relationship. Fuck this strong trip. I want some attention. I want to know I still matter."

I asked Chuck what he does when he doesn't get the attention he wants. "I withdraw. I don't tell her she looks nice. I don't ask her about her day. I wait until she gets upset enough to yell at me and then I let her have it. She's got to learn what it feels like to be ignored. It hurts like hell and I'm not going to let any woman hurt me."

Chuck dealt with his anger and hurt as many men do, by withholding his love. This indirect form of communicating causes relationships to degenerate. To inflict pain on another because you feel hurt by his or her actions only destroys the trust and intimacy that exists.

Chuck thought he was punishing his wife for hurting him. As much as he wanted her in his life, he was pushing her away. Yet actions speak louder than words. In his wife's mind, she was being rejected but she wasn't sure why. She thought he was taking his problems at work out on her.

Men need to learn how to express their needs and expectations more clearly. But, like Chuck, many men told me they felt it was a sign of weakness to have to ask the woman in their life to satisfy their emotional needs. One man even said, "I thought women's intuition meant she sensed my needs before I did." I came to understand that quite a few men operated from this same myth. And a myth it is. It is difficult enough for us to understand our own needs let alone be a mind-reader about someone else's. Honesty and expressed expectations create mutually satisfying relationships.

Good communication is the single most important factor for working out these issues and making the battle of the sexes become a meeting between our hearts and minds.

SMART WOMEN IN THE WORKPLACE

At work the desire to be "in control" exists in both men and women. Few employees wish to succumb to blind obedience. As mentioned earlier, men continually ask me, "I never questioned my boss, so why do my employees question me?"

"Playing follow the leader is no longer a popular game," I answered. "People want to think for themselves. Everyone wants control over his or her own work life. They want to be responsible and involved. Commitment comes from making decisions and having a sense of ownership."

Men don't particularly like other men challenging their decisions, but they have learned to accept it because they themselves have jockeyed for control at times and they understand male motivations. On the other hand, they find it difficult to accept a woman's desire for control. The worst situation is when she *does* get legitimate control, when she is the boss. Many men have come to believe the myth that women are not capable of leadership positions. Fortunately for women this myth is being destroyed. But the process for men is painful.

As a product manager at Procter and Gamble confided, "I never listened to any girls when I was young. You thought it was an abnormality if they were smart in school, so I hardly paid attention to them in college. I married someone who is bright but definitely not a challenge. But I work with women whose intelligence scares me. It is an insult reporting to a woman when you were told they are less capable and not as smart as you. You grow up believing you are superior to half the human race. But someone sold us men the wrong bill of goods because many women are damn smart."

Other men told me how frightened they were by smart women. One of the top financial consultants in the country confided, "I had a meeting with the vice president of International Harvester. She's a woman, bright and attractive. She's so smart it's scary. She not only understands what you say but she is two steps ahead of you.

She grasps everything so quickly. With many women you can get away with things or take advantage of them, but not smart women.''

Women, in the past, were taught to play dumb and helpless. They were raised to fool men into believing they aren't as smart as they are. (And some women haven't given up this game.) And men learned to ''misuse'' women by taking advantage of those who weren't smart. As more women are giving up this game, men are confused. When the myth about ''dumb women'' is contradicted by reality, men have trouble recovering. It has to do with the good old control issue. If a woman is smart, men feel out of control. And, as we've seen, control is often a man's measure of masculinity.

On the other hand, not all men are threatened by smart women nor do they define themselves by being in control. I was at a conference where I met Dr. Doug Carmichael, coauthor of *The Gamesmen*. Doug, two other women, and I critiqued the day's activities over a nightcap.

Doug listened to our comments about the panel discussion. Without warning he challenged us, ''I'm surprised you never brought up these points during the discussion section. You all have excellent insights that other participants could have benefited from.''

As we talked, Doug told me, ''Smart women are more fun to talk with; they're sexier. They catch on to nuances. They are more helpful and God knows we all need more help. I actually think men who aren't very smart, who always have to be 'right,' are the ones who are threatened by smart women. I've never had a particular stake in being smart. My ego's never been into proving I know more than anyone else.''

Gary Moore is another man who is not threatened by intelligent women. He said, ''One's I.Q. has no sex rating. A brain is a brain. Some people are smart and some aren't. I want to learn from the best person, whether it's a man or a woman. I know I'm not as quick as some of the men or women who work for me. But I bring other skills to the party. I don't have time for people who want all the credit or think they can do everything on their own. We are in this together to create an idea that is bigger than all of us.''

Gary's comments are representative of how other secure men feel about smart women. The common denominator I found in men who aren't threatened by smart women is that secure men realistically know their own strengths and weaknesses, which means they know when to depend on others. To let themselves be dependent means they have to trust. To trust they have to give up control. And giving up control does not mean giving up their identity because they know their identity is comprised of many components, the least of which is controlling another person.

NEW EXPECTATIONS

As men and women change their expectations of one another, the fighting will stop and ways to work and live together will be found. As men and women redefine loving and being loved they will be less threatened by one another's career or ideas and more secure in themselves and with each other. As we learn to encourage another's growth, rather than be intimidated by it, we, too, will grow.

The four chapters that follow will discuss how some men have resolved these dilemmas for themselves. We will look at why men marry, why they have affairs, and what prompts them to get divorced. We hear, too, from the women in their lives, talking frankly about why they are frustrated with their husbands and lovers. And, we learn from the happily married couples what makes their marriages work.

CHAPTER 13

MONOGAMY IS NOT A NATURAL STATE

"Fidelity is a woman's word," said one of the men in my study.

"How could fidelity be a woman's word?" I retorted, unable to believe what I had just heard.

Nonetheless, this notion is a fact—in the mind of many men, that is. And that is where the problem for many women begins.

I did argue this point with one of the men who was part of the in-depth study. In the course of our discussion I realized how my "femaleness" prevented me from understanding what men were saying to me. He pointed out to me that I simply was not understanding an aspect of male sexuality. And he was right.

Here's what happened: I gave the original of this chapter on "Lovers" to him. After he read it he told me that it left him cold, that I had missed the point. "Many men are with other women because it's the same as wanting two nice cars. Nothing more and nothing less. Stop being so psychological," he bellowed.

I was stunned by his comments. Not because I had never heard his words uttered by anyone else, but because there was some truth in what he was saying to me. As a woman, I had been raised with fantasies of romance, love, and fidelity. As a corporate psychologist, I've worked closely with men for over sixteen years and I know that it's unrealistic to expect them to be faithful. As a woman I feel

203

that is "wrong." As a psychologist I know what these men are telling me is "right."

This man helped me see that I had disregarded a major factor in why men have extramarital relations. I didn't understand the biological drive men experience. With blinders on I looked at the situation from only a psychological standpoint.

So, back to the research I went. Which meant I went back to speak with the men. I called an Apollo astronaut, a famous film producer, a couple of millionaires, three senators, seven moguls, twenty-three chairmen of Fortune 500 companies. Then I called a handful of more normal, regular types: men who were happily married, men who were financially comfortable, men who were emotionally secure, and men who were moderately successful.

I asked some of the same questions about affairs and fidelity. I heard the same answers, but this time I listened without my female screening device. I turned off the internal mechanism that tried to find some deep reason for their infidelity. In some instances there were none. They all (monogamous and polygamous men) told me the same thing. They didn't believe it is the nature of the beast to be monogamous. They claimed to be naturally polygamous. "Fidelity is a choice," said many men.

My astronaut friend told me, "Men may choose to be monogamous but that doesn't make it natural. We tone [our sex drive] down. Think about male animals and how they handle quite a number of females. Men have the desire for more than one female. It is that simple."

I responded, "Are you telling me that when I want pumpkin, vanilla, and chocolate frozen yogurt because I like all the flavors and don't want to decide, that is the same as the way you men think about wanting a woman?"

My astronaut friend said, "You've got it!"

According to the men in my study, women force upon them the notion of fidelity. It is our nesting instinct and our desire for exclusivity that cause men to feel guilty when they desire other women.

Almost thirty years ago, in the age of "togetherness," when Kinsey published his landmark findings on sexual behavior in men and women, he and his co-workers found that extramarital experiences were not uncommon. At the time the statistics on adultery took people by surprise. A full 50 percent of the married males surveyed had engaged in sex with an outside partner before the age of forty. As Maggie Scarf writes in her book *Intimate Partners*,

> All estimates of extramarital sexual activity tend, moreover, to be on the conservative side. For statistics on marital infidelity are notoriously difficult to gather, given the secretive nature of the adulterous behaviors. Most experts do, however, consider the "educated guess" of sex researchers G. D. Nass, R. W. Libby and M. P. Fisher—that at the present time some 50 to 65 percent of husbands and 45 to 55 percent of wives become extramaritally involved by the age of forty—to be a relatively sound and reasonable one.
>
> Reviewing all the statistics over the past thirty years one could assume that extramarital experiences are the "norm" rather than the exception, and anticipate such encounters occurring in their own relationship. But that is not the case. Most people don't. They are viewed as totally unexpected, catastrophic events. Affairs are looked upon as dishonorable and shameful behavior. Despite the widespread feelings that affairs are awful, the statistics tell us "many spouses seemed to go ahead and get involved extramaritally anyway."[1]

For our purposes an affair is defined as an extended relationship with a woman, other than a mate, that includes sex and a degree of emotional involvement. One-night stands or brief business-trip encounters that may last for one night or for a few days are often engaged in for pure sexual pleasure, excitement, or recreational sex, but they are not here considered to be affairs.

More than 66 percent of the men I interviewed admitted to having had at least one affair. Only 18 percent of the men I spoke with claimed uninterrupted fidelity. That means 82 percent of the men in this study had engaged in at least one one-night stand or a brief business-trip encounter. Only a small group, roughly 3 percent, admitted they enjoyed the chase-and-conquer game, using one-night stands as a vehicle for proving to themselves that they were still attractive and could perform well.

It was clear to me that I had to write these men's stories. I could anticipate some of my female colleagues' disgust with me, but if I didn't tell these stories I would betray the men who had spoken so honestly with me and taught me about some of the ways men *are* different from women.

I don't mean to imply here that *all* extramarital liaisons are biological. That is not true. In fact, although affairs definitely have a biological side and men may engage in one solely for sexual reasons, emotional factors play a significant role in ongoing affairs. As I reviewed the case histories of the men who had one or more prolonged affairs, I could not ignore the psychological components. I could accept that men don't place as much meaning on casual sexual encounters as women do. Men enjoy these liaisons for the mere physicality. Men, however, are not mere animals. If they were, I could embrace this biological viewpoint wholeheartedly. Men might possess animalistic qualities, but they are human beings with intellectual and emotional drives.

When the need for emotional intimacy became part of the equation, that's when I stopped accepting one of the men's "two nice cars" theory and returned to looking at the psychological needs that drive men to the arms and beds of other women.

I have come to the conclusion that the majority of men marry for the wrong reasons. And they are beginning to realize this. Therefore, although it is worth noting, in this chapter, why men do marry, it is even more interesting to examine what causes them to stray.

I GOT MARRIED BECAUSE . . .

Only 10 percent of the men I interviewed claimed to have married for love. Ninety percent married for practical or selfish reasons or out of insecurity. Or looking at it another way, 47 percent married for practical reasons, 36 percent married out of insecurity, and 7 percent married for selfish reasons. Two out of three have had affairs and only a third would select the same wife.

Of the 47 percent who married for practical reasons, the specific reasons they did so include: marrying for prestige, picking a woman who would be a good career facilitator, thinking it was time to get married.

The 36 percent whose decision to marry "stemmed from insecurity" stated one of two reasons: because they thought their spouse was a "good catch" and feared another one might not come along or because they married to fill a void in themselves.

Although they sound similar, the following examples differentiate the two. We are all haunted by insecurities and it is not uncommon for men and women to pick someone because that person fills a void in themselves. As one senior vice president of finance told me, "I've always been the introverted type. Ethel was bubbly and cute, so outgoing. She made me feel alive. I wasn't very social but I knew I had to be for the job. Ethel filled that gap in me. I figured we would make a great team, so I proposed."

Some men define themselves by the woman they are with. Their worth as a man is dependent on how the woman they marry looks and acts: "I married Nancy because she was pretty. All the other guys thought she was a great catch. I wasn't sure another pretty girl would come along so I thought I better snatch her up before she had second thoughts about me."

As people mature, they usually outgrow many of their insecurities. When one lives with someone for a long time, one also learns from that person and incorporates some of his or her behaviors. So some of the reasons a man originally needed his spouse may no longer exist. As a result, he may begin to question why he is staying in the relationship. A man may find himself resenting the dependence he once cherished. Or he may have an affair with someone at work who appreciates him for who he is, while his wife still sees him as the "needy" or insecure man she married.

The 10 percent who married for love place a higher priority on relationships than on success. They cherish their family life and believe they must give more than 50 percent to make sure their marriage continues to be a fulfilling relationship.

ROMANTIC VERSUS PRACTICAL MARRIAGES

After thirty-three years of marriage, Carl Levinson, the president of a major equipment manufacturer, loves his wife more than the day he married her. He has always placed his family before his career. I have sat for hours listening to Carl tell me stories about his relationship with his wife. One time while we were flying from Los Angeles to Atlanta together, I asked him what had held his marriage together over the years. He answered, "I look at those fools around me ignoring their wives and children, thinking that people in the business world care about them. Everyone is out for himself. The only place you have for shelter and comfort is with your loved ones at home. And unless you nurture them just as you would a rose garden, they won't be there to bring beauty and pleasure into your life. I knew what support my family gave me and I never abused it."

He continued, "Marriage is a two-sided proposition. No matter how much you start out loving one another both people have to make it grow. My wife always made sure we had time together at night. We split the duties with the kids when they were young. The quicker we got them to bed the more time we had together. We enjoyed sharing the duties. If we had both been busy, she'd feed the kids separately so we could catch up. She's taught me a lot and I love her for it."

Until I conducted this study I was a victim of the "romantic myths" that tell us the happiest marriages are unions of true love. I have come to believe *some* marriages based on practical reasons can be fulfilling to the individuals.

Jack Greggins, a prominent lawyer for one of the country's leading firms, married his second wife, Robin, because of "what an asset she could be to my career and social life." Jack told me his wife taught him how to dress, whom to cultivate as business contacts, and what social gatherings would further his career. As a result, they have achieved a social status many people would envy. They fly in friends' private jets, attend benefits with high society, and own homes in prestigious parts of the world. Jack's Rolodex is categorized by country rather than by last name. On the coffee table in his office lies a scrapbook with various social columns from around the world mentioning him and his wife. No matter which wall you look at you will find pictures of Jack with celebrities and politicians.

Jack invited me to their home along New York City's Central Park South. As I exited the elevator that opened directly into their condominium I gasped at the décor and the breathtaking view. His wife greeted me, taking my coat and offering me a tour. As I stepped into the living room Robin waved her arm around the room and told me, "Michael Taylor did the apartment." At the time I didn't want to hurt her feelings by admitting I didn't know who Michael Taylor was, but I later learned he was an extremely well-known decorator.

After I had received a verbal dissertation on the best material things in life, Robin, Jack, and I spoke about what brought them together. Robin explained their reasons to me: "Love was not a consideration. We respected one another and saw what marriage could do for our lives together and apart. Our reasons were mutually beneficial although selfish and practical."

Before I bit my tongue, the next question slipped out of my mouth. "But, your sex life, well, do you care for one another sexually? Is there passion between you?"

I wasn't sure who was answering me because one would start the thought and the other would finish it. Robin began, "No, there isn't much passion in our lives, but we aren't passionate people. We both are heading in the same direction, and that keeps us together."

Jack elaborated, "Sometimes we question if there is something wrong with us because we aren't 'hungry' for each other the way other couples seem to be. Weighing both sides and evaluating the history of our friends' relationships, we seem to be better off. We're still together and they aren't. I think that speaks for itself."

And Robin concluded, "We've decided it is unimportant that our sex and emotional life is sometimes barren. We've each had a fling or two, but that only made us happy to have one another. Those emotional deviations only take energy away from our path together. Besides, they endanger our relationship. It's not worth risking what we have together to find mad, passionate love with someone else. I think we have a quiet love for one another born out of respect."

But not all practical marriages work out as well as Jack and Robin's. Often these marriages fall apart when their heart eventually overrules their head.

Ken Broderick epitomizes the executive who married for practical reasons that gradually became irrelevant, making it difficult to sustain the relationship. He told me when he married it was for all the right reasons: "In wanting to climb the corporate ladder, I knew I needed the right trappings. My pedigrees came from Harvard and Yale. I had gone to Exeter prep school. I needed to have the 'right' wife. So I took Angela to be my corporate wedded wife. She looked the part: not too attractive, not too bright, not too outspoken. Not too anything; so she was just right. Over the years she dedicated her life to my career. Each time we moved she never complained. She entertained for me, impressed my clients and boss, and raised my children. Above all she never threatened another corporate wife. I've never loved her, but she is the perfect wife.''

Ken continued, "I feel guilty when I think about how boring she is. Maybe if she hadn't sacrificed herself for my career she'd be more interesting. I have even attempted to talk myself into loving her. That strategy hasn't worked. When I evaluate the pros and cons of leaving her, the pros win out. At this point, I want to find someone with whom I can be passionate, who I can love.''

There is so much societal pressure for men to be successful in all their endeavors, and for them to admit that their marriage is less than fulfilling is the equivalent to admitting failure. I think we need to move away from judging whether a relationship is successful or not. Instead, it is important to understand the needs of men that are not being met by marriage.

AFFAIRS FULFILL UNFULFILLED NEEDS

Affairs or brief liaisons sometimes fulfill men's needs. These unmet needs and dreams include: to find a compatible sexual partner, to be appreciated for their abilities and achievements at work, to be admired rather than criticized, to pretend they are still single and free, to enjoy recreational sex, to add some excitement to their life, and to escape from a miserable marriage.

In a retrospective study of 750 case histories, clinicians Bernard L. Greene, Ronald R. Lee, and Noel Lustig found sexual frustration, curiosity, revenge, boredom, and the need to be accepted and recognized were the ''reasons for the affair'' most frequently given.[2]

Many men believe that affairs can help, or, at least, do not harm their marriage. An affair satisfies their immediate emotional needs, postpones having to face their marital problems, or serves as total escape from their unhappiness. An affair can be a respite that helps men avoid the guilt of contemplating abandoning their marital roles and responsibilities altogether.

Affairs can relieve some emotional pressure that builds in the marriage. As men learn to avoid putting all their emotional expectations on their wife, they become far less demanding and far more accepting of their spouse's limitations. For many men, an extramarital liaison doesn't mean they love their wife any more or any less. In fact, an affair often helps them appreciate the contributions their wife has made to their life and their success. If they have outgrown their wife but want to stay in the marriage for the children's sake, an affair often meets their emotional and sexual needs, while allowing them to honor their familial responsibilities.

More than 68 percent of the men in this study said they felt women have a difficult time responding to a man's vulnerabilities. Women are raised to expect a man to be strong all the time. The burden this places on men is often impossible to bear. Men often say that their marriage began to fall apart when they let their "weaknesses" show. Men and women need to take heed of this problem.

As women have become aware of their dissatisfaction about the roles society has imposed upon them, and as they have voiced these concerns and made changes in their personal and professional lives, men have been forced to reevaluate their own roles. As women have demanded that men be "more in touch" with their feelings and men have made the efforts to do so, this inner search has produced some unexpected responses. As a result, men are no longer accepting, without question, the roles expected of them simply because they are male nor the expectations that come with marriage.

In recent years I have heard more men complain that women aren't ready to accept "the sensitive, liberated man." I have watched marriages fall apart as men have revealed their inner secrets. But no one has addressed the role women play in this problem. The absence of comments can lead one to believe that men are the culprits and women are the victims. In some cases, the opposite is true.

Although many women I knew were encouraging men to understand their feelings or even teaching them how to do so, from the men's comments this percentage of women was small. In short, men found women weren't willing to emotionally "be there" for them. The president of a major motion picture company summed it up for me, "You women think you want us to be more open, to show our feelings and be sensitive, but that's not the case. Women clam up when we act that way. They don't really want us to show our feelings. They merely want us to understand theirs."

As much as I hate to admit it, I was one of those women. When I wore my professional hat, I had no problem accepting—in fact, encouraging—men to be aware of their feelings, to let their tenderness and their vulnerabilities show. But when I took that hat off and had to be a woman who interacted with men on a personal or social level, I was uncomfortable. It took me a while to accept the new ways men were behaving, even though these were actions I desired. The problem was that I didn't know how to respond to men who were, in some respects, more liberated than I. I had to break out of the stereotypical behaviors I had embraced and learn to react spontaneously, without prejudice or expectation.

Put another way, women are discouraging intimacy from occurring when they do not accept their spouse's feelings. As I spoke with my women friends about my feelings, they began to see this problem in their own lives. It was a factor contributing to the problems in our relationships. We hadn't given up our fantasy of being captured and cared for by Prince Charming, we had merely displaced it. Now that many of us no longer needed a man to provide for us financially, we seemed to put all-out dependency needs in the emotional basket. We wanted men to understand us like our women friends did. We wanted to connect on a deeper level. We wanted to be dependent emotionally, yet independent financially. And in the early years of liberation, I think many of us saw it as a battle to be won rather than as a responsibility to be held.

So men have had as hard a time dealing with us as we have had with them. And I think it's time men felt freer to articulate the difficulties they have endured, without fear of being called a ''male chauvinist pig.'' Anyone would feel rejected under these conditions and look for acceptance elsewhere. A man has enough internal pressure preventing him from admitting how rotten or defeated he might feel at any given moment. He needs a place to be heard, to be who he is, to say what he thinks and needs. That is what intimacy is all about.

It is a mistake to think men aren't concerned about finding ways to make relationships work. They simply are not as experienced at this job as women are. Where normally men have depended on the women in their life to take care of the maintenance work in a relationship, many men are acknowledging that they need to take a more active role in defining their needs and desires and in communicating them to the special person in their life. So more men are taking workshops, going to counseling, or talking with men and women friends; they are exploring what they want from a relationship.

An affair has often been the easy place to go, the place for a man to take his mask off and let his needs, dreams, and desires be known and met while still fulfilling the marital roles, duties, and responsibilities he has taken on.

The story is quite different when fear of intimacy is the problem. In these instances men use affairs to avoid feeling committed to their marriage. Being involved in two (or three) different relationships stretches their emotions in many directions and keeps the relationships superficial and "light." No single relationship fulfills their needs.

If these men are so unhappy, why don't they get divorced?

Nearly 80 percent of the men who have had affairs told me the reason they stay in the marriage is because they are afraid no one else would tolerate them the way their wife does. They are dependent on her. They appreciate her because of all the inconsideration she puts up with. They have fun with their lovers, but it is their wives who stick by them, whom they fall back on for security. Perhaps they don't realize that the reason they are rarely confronted by their wife is that her fears also prevent her from facing the truth about their relationship. Much as there is an unspoken agreement between the boys that they all stay married, there is an unspoken agreement that neither husband nor wife will threaten the status quo.

If a man got divorced to be with his lover, his once ideal relationship would be saddled with all the burdens and obligations he deals with regularly and has affairs to escape from. Besides, just because a part of him is unfulfilled, there are many aspects of his marriage and family life that he is unwilling to relinquish because they satisfy his needs.

Noted psychologist Abraham Maslow stated, "A satisfied need is no longer a motivator." When an affair satisfies their needs they return to their marriages a happier person. Unfortunately for the lovers, the benefits of their love, effort, and hard work are reaped by the wife, for these men often return to their marriage with their self-esteem restored.

So let's look at what the needs and conflicts are that motivate men to engage in affairs and more often than not return to their marriage.

SHE DOES THINGS MY WIFE WON'T DO

For many men the sexual act is symbolic of the anxiety they feel to perform each and every day, each and every moment. But sex is a measurable, short-term, tangible act. They know whether they succeeded or failed, whether they were good or bad, whether they were accepted or rejected.

Sex is also very important to men because it is a way for them to express their feelings. Men who are uncomfortable expressing themselves verbally speak with their body. Some of these men are married to women who don't particularly like sex. One man confessed that his wife suggested he find a girlfriend so she wouldn't have to make love with him. He thought his reasons for not enjoying sex were all his fault until he had an affair.

Mike, an attractive though slightly overweight man, told me, "My wife hates sex. It's amazing that we have four kids. I got tired of being rejected all the time. One night I was at a company party and this cute girl came over to talk to me. After a while I told her I had to get home, my family was waiting for me. I felt compelled to announce that I was married. Her response floored me. She told me if I were happily married, I wouldn't be at this party. And, if I were married to her I'd want to get home as early as possible.

"The next thing I know is that I'm staying at the party to talk with her. After a while we left, went to her place. I was afraid I wouldn't be able to get it up—it had been so long. But no problem. And boy, did I enjoy it. I never knew sex could be so good."

Another man told me that his wife didn't like oral sex. He decided to stop demanding that she do something she considered repulsive. "My lover will do sexual things my wife won't do," he said. "I was constantly demanding things from my wife and she was constantly rejecting me. I've eliminated a problem by demanding less things at home, and my lover satisfies me in every other way possible."

The "sexual lover" provides the physical release that so many men require. She obeys, she experiments, she satisfies. If needed, she patiently teaches the man what makes her feel good. He comes back because their intimate interludes take the pressure off the problems at home, help him gain a perspective on his sexual needs, and develop sexual self-confidence.

SHE ADMIRES ME FOR WHO I AM TODAY

Men who marry between the ages of eighteen and twenty-two often fall into this category. When we marry young, our personality is not fully formed, we are unsure of ourselves. Yet, as the years go by and the experiences accumulate we grow and change. The problem so many of these men expressed was that their wife still treated them like the boy they married.

When I asked them what an affair added to their lives, the responses included:

"Having an affair offers me another version of myself."

"When I try to tell my wife what goes on in my world, she doesn't seem interested."

"My wife won't see changes in me. She treats me in the same old way."

"I gave up trying to impress my wife. She doesn't understand me. My lover works with me and admires everything about me that I want to be noticed for."

Given that men are raised to believe that being a breadwinner and provider are important roles offering meaning and purpose to their lives, many men define themselves by what they do. They tend to believe their "lovableness" comes from how well they perform in their work world. They look to their spouse for appreciation and recognition. When they don't receive the admiration from their wife and they do from another woman, this can often lead to an affair.

Thomas Doyle married his high-school sweetheart, Roxanne. Their eight-year courtship developed into marriage after they both completed college. The first few years of marriage were absolute bliss. Then they began to develop different interests. After a while, Thomas began questioning whether he had made the right decision.

For years, he would occasionally "pick up" a woman while away on business. No big deal, he thought. Then Thomas had two intimate affairs, one with a close friend of Roxanne's, the other with his secretary. Roxanne found out about both of them and they severely threatened their marriage.

After the second affair, Roxanne insisted they see a marriage counselor to get to the root of the problem. Thomas complained to the counselor, "When I try to tell Roxanne what goes on at work, she's not interested. She still wants to treat me like she did when we were in college. But, we're grownups now. Life's different. I'm different, but she doesn't understand that. Once she told me she wished we were as close as the days back at Michigan State. I'm tired of reminiscing about the past. That's gone."

Then he asked, "Is it so wrong for me to want her to admire me for what I do? Each time I had an affair, it was because I gave up trying to get her to see me for who I am today. It's not that I don't love Roxanne. I do. But I don't feel that she loves me for how I am. I know my lovers did. They admired me. They appreciated things about me that I didn't even realize existed. They helped me learn more about who I am today."

As we grow up we each learn different ways to define being loved and being loving. We expect our needs to be satisfied without articulating them. And then when our needs are not met, we get angry. Thomas and Roxanne spent over a year in therapy learning about the unspoken expectations they had imposed on one another. They slowly began to confide in each other about what their needs were. Moreover, they each set their resentment aside about not having the other live up to their hidden expectations and began reaching out and satisfying the other's needs.

I remember one meeting with Roxanne where she told me the biggest lesson she learned while they were in counseling was, "Thomas needed me to appreciate him for being the breadwinner. So when I started appreciating what he did rather than complaining about how I expected him to be, we got closer than ever. We women don't appreciate how important the roles that our men assume are to their self-image. They fight battles and we never think to appreciate them for that. Instead I would complain that he had come home late. It seemed I would focus on how he didn't bring me flowers, how he wasn't romantic, how he hadn't said I love you. It took a lot of pain on both our parts for me to see that his way of saying I love you was to work hard and provide a nice home for us. He said I love you by asking me to go on business trips with him."

And Thomas told me, "I always thought I was supposed to avoid bringing home my work problems. So I'd never discuss anything with Roxanne. But then I'd get madder than hell at her for not showing more concern. The problem was I never told her what was troubling me or what latest battle I had conquered. I stopped communicating with her about my world, but I still expected her to understand the nuances and situations that would arise.''

There are many couples like Thomas and Roxanne, who met during high school or college, ''hung around'' together, shared the same activities and friends, were inseparable by day and by night. Then came entry to the grown-up world. One person (usually the wife) stayed at home to set up their personal life, while the other went out to ''the jungle'' to provide for the family. In the work world, the pressures were different, and perhaps greater. The couple grew apart. Often the wife had nothing to hold on to but memories from the days when they did have things in common, whereas the husband had created a new kind of life for himself.

The attentive-and-admiring lover often shared his work world with him, acknowledged parts of him that his wife never knew. The lover fulfilled the desire to share meaningful, important aspects of his life. She stimulated and challenged him. She helped him discover himself. As long as she continued to admire and challenge him, he kept coming back.

I KNOW BY THE WAY SHE LOOKS AT ME THAT SHE THINKS I'M WONDERFUL

A woman who nags, criticizes, and tears down her husband does nothing more than chip away any trust he might have had in her. Beyond that, such treatment may cause a man to be fearful of his wife. Here is a sample of some quotes from men who married critical, demanding women:

> ''I feel like I have to walk on eggshells with my wife.''

> ''Nothing I do is ever good enough. Even when she's not around, I feel like she is peering over my shoulder, waiting to inject her acerbic opinion regarding what I've done or said.''

> ''I hate to admit it, but I am pussy-whipped and I don't know how to get free.''

What compels one to stay with someone who nags and criticizes him? Although it might sound like an oversimplification or gross generalization, we often pick someone very similar to one or both of our parents to marry. And since we learn how to love from our parents, we usually look for love similar to that which we experienced while young.

In the case of a person who grows up to marry someone who constantly criticizes him, the reason often has its roots in his upbringing. He may well have grown up with a critical parent, who rarely gave the love, reassurance, and approval needed by the child. So he grows accustomed to being criticized, accepting any kind of attention. But underneath the hurt and rejection is a child who seeks parental love and approval. When we are raised with a critical parent we grow up with an opinion of ourselves that is generally not very positive. This child feels something must be wrong with him since his parents don't love him. But maybe if he tries a little harder, if he's a little better at school or sports, he will be loved. So unless this issue gets resolved in childhood, the boy becomes a man, acting out the same behavior, only this time with his wife. And such a man with a critical wife would never even think of leaving her, because deep down he feels he deserves her criticisms.

Ross Bertrand was cautious, hesitant, and shy by nature. Since age five, he had to wear thick glasses that made his green eyes beam out. Ross married Patrice, a tiny, elegant woman. While Ross's disposition was accommodating, Patrice had an iron will. She constantly scolded, made demands, and found fault with him.

Ross rarely defended himself, preferring to be like a turtle, pulling his head into his protective shell to avoid unpleasantries. Still, he longed for some approval. He constantly tried to do things that would please Patrice, but they just never seemed to be right. Degraded and demoralized, he retreated from life. He didn't know that his depression was the anger he felt toward Patrice for always tearing him apart. He felt lethargic, withdrawn, and afraid.

In his work as a pharmaceutical salesman, he met a nurse named Chris who was funny and alive and who made him laugh. Their attraction was instantaneous, but he was afraid to make a move. Instead he would gape at her, longing for her to suggest that they meet away from her work. In time she did, and a wonderful romance ensued for almost a year. Chris helped Ross see how charming and sexy he really was. She loved his little-boy quality, an enthusiasm for life that most men rarely showed. He was playful and funny. Chris thought Ross could do no wrong. Over time, Ross regained his self-respect.

The man who is accustomed to being criticized needs an "unconditional lover" who embraces him, making him feel that he is wonderful. She tells him how handsome he is, how smart he is, how funny he is. In the beginning of their affair he will test her love, fearful that she will discover he really isn't worth the positive, warm, and loving thoughts she has about him. Some men run from the unconditional lover, refusing to accept the good part of themselves and afraid to believe they truly are lovable. Others regain their self-esteem and either refuse to take the criticism at home anymore or leave their wife.

IT'S LIKE THE TV IS ON, BUT THERE IS NO SOUND

You married your wife when you were young. She was pretty; you were insecure. She was outgoing; you were shy. It's now ten, fifteen, twenty years later. Each morning you wake up, turn over, and look at a woman you no longer feel close to. Your role is to be the provider. You have succeeded. But you aren't happy and neither is your wife. Your life together has been reduced to petty bickering and sniping at one another's ways. Your marriage is not working and you don't know why. You are afraid to confront the issue because if you discover what's wrong, you might have to do something—like get divorced. It's easier to maintain the status quo.

A former astronaut, who has been married four times (three of his wives being past lovers), claimed, "Most of my friends don't understand my willingness to get divorced. They would rather stay in an unpleasant situation than face the problems. So they augment their marriage with affairs while still trying to win their wife's love. Men don't know how to give up and not consider that failing. But marrying the wrong woman doesn't necessarily mean you failed."

Some men, no matter how unhappy they are, would never consider getting divorced. Yes, they fantasize about it. But they would never do it. Their reasons vary: religion, responsibility/obligation, children, peer pressure. Regardless of the reason, the underlying feelings center around a sense that they have failed, and because they have failed, they feel they really are not lovable.

In reality, these men are extremely dependent on their wife for their sense of self-worth. Women have often been raised to feel like nothing without a man, while men have often thought that without their other half, they are only half a person. "Having a woman makes me feel complete," men exclaim again and again. Their marriage gives them the personal identity that they need. Unfortunately, all too often, men don't see themselves as separate from their wives. They define themselves by how their wife feels about them. They often married the first girl they slept with and have never had sex with another woman. They never had the opportunity and experience to realize that what one person dislikes about you, another can love. They never learned to form their own opinions about who they are. Instead, they judge themselves by how their wife reacts to them.

Or they judge themselves by the physical qualities of the woman they date or marry. A man's dependence on his wife, on her looks and personality for his own sense of self, is not only unrealistic, it's dangerous. These men often believe that their wife's feelings represent those of the entire female species. Only when they find that another woman is attracted to them do they begin to question their self-perceptions.

One man, who married his wife because she was adorable and popular, told me, "If my wife, who is overweight and not the cute girl I married, rejects me, why would anyone else want me? I'm ashamed to take her to company parties. She looks ten years older than me. I'm always afraid of what other people will think about me when they see me with her."

Because such a man is extremely insecure and hesitant, he needs a "seductive" lover who will make the first moves, who will encourage, who will find the ways for them to be together. Only after he is sure of her feelings for him will he respond. Yet, even if he falls in love, he will not leave his wife. Fear, insecurity, and dependence bind him to her.

I DON'T HAVE TO ANSWER TO ANYONE

The demanding man views himself as the keeper of power, able to dictate when his wife can do as she chooses. He will say, "I give my wife permission to play cards with her friends once in a while." Or "I give my wife permission to go to one of her club meetings and not fix me dinner." Ironically, these same men look to their wives for permission, projecting aspects of their mothers onto their wives. They may say, "I always feel I have to ask my wife if it's okay for me to go out with the guys."

Often they picked a demanding wife who fights with them for control. On the surface these women seem submissive and motherly, but underneath they are struggling to be in charge. The relationship is glued together by the power struggles that constantly arise. They argue over what time they should eat, what movie they should go to, which route they should take to the store, enjoying the struggle more than the impending activity.

When a man in this kind of marriage decides to take a lover, he often picks a demanding woman similar to his wife. She may initially seem subservient, but people like this are often manipulative. Rather than speak out about what they want or don't want, their style is to agree, then complain. Such a woman is obedient on the surface, but her motto is, "Tell him what he wants to hear, but charm or nag him until you get what you want."

Another aspect of this type of affair is that the man who is running away from feeling obligated and responsible but miserable in his marriage and wants a "no strings attached" affair may well find himself suddenly saddled with paying part of his lover's rent, buying her food or clothes, and even giving her money to spend. The cycle is repeated—what he runs from he attracts.

The problem is that our man, desirous of this "pseudofreedom," really likes the demands placed on him. He picks the "subservient-demanding" lover because he thinks that his women don't love him if they are not complaining or being possessive.

I SCREW AROUND BECAUSE THE OTHER GUYS DO

Some men chase women for the excitement that they experienced in their teen years and to prove to themselves that they are still desirable. The "conquest game" is loaded with psychological baggage from years gone by. I do believe these men when they tell me the occasional fling is innocent and has no deep significance in their life. I also think that one-night stands are a way for men to deal with their loneliness and insecurity. An affair brings temporary relief to the emotional pain, the same way a drink helps one relax after a trying day.

One man told me, "I screw around strictly for laughs. I get bored on occasion. So, what the heck. I never do 'it' at home. Only when I'm on the road."

Another spoke of the time he went on a business trip with a few other men from the office and was shocked that the first order of business was lining up women. He went along with them rather than be teased. Each time they traveled, he yielded to his fears that if he didn't go along with the rest of them, he would be thought of as a coward.

Often innocent men, men who don't have the emotional desire to have an extramarital experience, are dragged into the game because they want to be like the other guys. Once introduced to the game, they find it exciting. Part of them sees nothing wrong with having recreational sex. As one man said to me, "I pretend I'm single and free. I forget about the problems at home. Life can get boring, so you've got to make some excitement. No one else will do it for you." And then he added, "I would never think of hurting my wife. She wouldn't understand my need to still play the field. Variety is the spice of life."

It is the men who start out believing that this game is innocent, succumbing to peer pressure, and suddenly find themselves in love with the woman who wasn't supposed to mean anything to them that concern me more. When they "played around," initially it was with innocence. But when they continued to have extramarital liaisons they began sharing less of themselves with the person they live with. By sharing themselves with a stranger, they often divulge secrets that should be shared in their primary relationship. By discussing secrets with an intimate stranger the primary relationship diminishes in importance and intimacy. This can lead to unmet needs and lack of communication. A marriage that might have been okay or even good before this game started can break down by default because the time and sharing is going to the wrong place.

These men think they and their marriages are impervious to

any side effects of their "fly-by-night" encounters. They pick women who quickly jump in the sack, like to be wined and dined on expense accounts, and might or might not be looking for more than a one-night liaison. When these men fall for such a woman, a conflict ensues. The old standard that you should never respect someone who sleeps with you on the first date causes some men to wonder, How can I care for someone I don't respect? This conflict is coupled with the most common conflict that results from any affair, being "torn between two lovers." Rarely are either of these conflicts resolved without any damage.

Often men avoid dealing with the conflicts, simply withdrawing from the affair and guiltily retreating home. This temporary fidelity is short lived and the cycle repeats itself. They have come to depend on the game for excitement and for a way to hang out with the guys. They have not learned how to share themselves with their spouse or work out problems that arise. Instead they still believe that they screw around because the other guys do and nothing is wrong with their marriage. Until they face the fact that their marriage has disintegrated, mostly due to lack of attention, both spouses suffer. These men must stop this self-deceiving game and learn to communicate with their wife.

WHEN AFFAIRS NO LONGER WORK

Affairs help men create a fantasy life, a pretend world where everything is okay. But eventually that game runs its course and stops working. If you don't uncover your reasons for infidelity now you will repeat your intimacy patterns in your next relationship. Look at how the problems you experience in your marriage repeat themselves in your affair(s). We are attracted to people for different reasons—some healthy and some not so healthy. We can never run from our psychological garbage. But we can clean it up.

Jack Robinson, a charismatic thirty-nine-year-old studio vice president, woke up one day and decided he was not going to play around anymore. "I couldn't live with myself. I was lying to everyone, including myself. No one was happy and I was keeping all these people on a string. I decided that I had no right to ruin anyone else's life while I was trying to figure out what I wanted to do.

"It wasn't easy at breakfast that morning. I told my wife I

wanted us to see a marriage counselor. She was devastated. Tears and all. She had been perfectly happy these nineteen years we were together. I crushed her when I told her that I hadn't been. I hate hurting anyone. I feel guilty about that, too. But I'd rather feel guilty about telling the truth than to continue lying to everyone around me.

"My problem all these years is that I ran from conflict. I don't like feeling uncomfortable. I always think that if I can keep everyone happy then I don't risk losing anyone's love. If anyone gets upset with me, and I mean anyone—I want to run and hide. That's what I did with these affairs. Whenever my wife was displeased with me I'd run to someone else. Someone who didn't know me and thought I was wonderful."

Jack and his wife were in counseling for more than a year before he felt they were going to make it. Overall it was rough. He learned quite a few things about himself—pleasant and unpleasant. Jack learned that he got angry and impatient when Margo didn't read his mind about what he wanted. He never felt comfortable asking for what he wanted, so he became demanding instead. Margo finally risked telling him that she felt quite distant from him and wanted to be included in more things. She never asked what was going on in his life because she knew that bothered him. She, too, was afraid of conflict, so she withdrew and refused to give him what he needed.

At the start of their counseling they decided that they would not attempt to determine if their marriage would survive after each counseling session. They made a pact to stay together for one year and at the end of that time they would decide if they wanted to renew their commitment to one another. When the year came to a close Margo and Jack agreed that they had salvaged what had once been a wonderful relationship and they had every intention of making it even better.

Not all men use affairs as the only avenue of escape from an unhappy marriage. Some couples are partners in avoidance. Instead of honestly communicating their dissatisfactions or fears they talk about having a child to bring them closer; they make a decision to move or they use their jobs or outside activities to avoid spending time together.

For instance, one man told me he and his wife moved sixteen times during fourteen years of marriage. He also averaged two affairs a year. Another couple told me that they moved four times in ten years and had five children before they realized this solution was ineffective and the best thing would be for them to divorce. Some men keep the same lover around for years to help them avoid thinking about the unpleasantness at home. Others change their lovers like they change their underwear.

One of my good friends called me one night to tell me he was thinking about separating from his wife. During our two-hour conversation my friend confided how much he wished his wife would be killed in a plane crash or driving to work. It would make life so much easier, he thought. Merely having the thoughts produced overwhelming guilt. How could a good Catholic boy leave his marriage? he asked himself. The good Catholic boy answered, "I can't," while the adult part of him said, "I must." But he didn't know what to do.

Not all men escape from their unhappiness by fantasizing. Instead they "logically" weigh the pros and cons. They rationalize their feelings away with thoughts like: I'll stay until the kids are off to college. Or like: I'll have affairs from time to time to relieve the pressure at home. This mental game can go on for years.

There are less dramatic signs, however, that need to be understood. I have watched men become grouchy, frustrated, and impatient when they are unhappy. They refuse to admit to themselves they are discontented because admitting they are unhappy means they must do something about it.

So whether they are fantasizing or rationalizing their feelings, they are denying the fear of facing the problems in their marriage. I think there is only one option when men find themselves in a relationship that is no longer working for them. That option is to muster the emotional courage to openly discuss feelings and make every effort to work out difficulties. All too often, when marriages fall apart, one or both parties feel like a failure. However, blaming oneself or the other person is not the issue. Understanding what went wrong, though, is. Whether one uses the outside assistance of a clergyman, counselor, or psychologist, the purpose of going through this introspective process is for one reason alone: to salvage one's self-esteem and lessen the chances of repeating the same mistakes.

In doing so the goal can either be to rebuild a marriage or resolve the differences so both parties can leave the marriage with some understanding and good feelings about themselves and each other rather than feeling like failures.

Not all relationships can be salvaged, nor are all worth salvaging. So let's move on to the next chapter and look at how a few different men have dealt with the problems in their marriage.

CHAPTER 14

SHE'S THE PERFECT LITTLE WIFE, BUT . . .

You find yourself thinking:

—We once were right together. Now she's the wrong woman for me, we have nothing in common. Our values and our interests are different.

—My God, she reminds me of my mother. That's who I tried to get away from, and instead I'm living with her. I don't mind being babied, but I do want an equal.

—She's the prettiest thing you've ever seen, but she doesn't challenge me. She's really the perfect wife, does all the right things, but she's bloody boring.

—I was this insecure kid. I couldn't believe it when she paid attention to me. My wife was this cute girl, real popular. I thought I might never find such a good catch again so I proposed. She's always filled a void in me.

—I decided to marry her because she would make a good facilitator for my career. She knew all the right things to do and she was great with people. Besides, she was pretty.

All right, you are willing to admit that the thought has crossed your mind . . . the reasons you and your wife decided to get married might not be the reasons to go on together.

Over 71 percent of the men interviewed expressed some form of dissatisfaction in their relationship with women. Some men have discovered they have outgrown their wives. Some find their wives to be boring, unchallenging, and unstimulating. Others have recognized they are confused about what they want from women. And some even admitted that they never thought about marrying a woman who would be their friend, they just wanted the "perfect wife."

I think there is always a fine line between walking away from (avoiding) a problem and deciding to leave (facing the truth). Problems need to be addressed. But sometimes they cannot be worked out with the other person. Above all, people need to work out their side of the problem, their contribution to making things go haywire. Too many people avoid dealing with the problems in their relationships, instead opting for divorce. They expect a quick fix. They run from one person to the next. This is no solution. At the other extreme, far too many men stay in unhappy marriages for various reasons. Some subscribe to the myth that men are unstable if they divorce. Some are afraid of the stigma associated with divorce.

There are enough books on the market that tell men how to make their marriage work, how to be more romantic, or how to be creatively intimate. None encourage them to look at how they may have married for the wrong reasons or help them make the decision to reconcile or to divorce. To help remedy that lack, I'd like to share with you how some men have dealt, successfully or not so successfully, with their relationships and/or divorces.

SHE WAS WHAT I WAS NOT

Sam Frederick married his wife, Helen James, for qualities he admired but felt he himself lacked. Helen was a fighter, while Sam preferred to take the back seat. Sam was an executive with IBM in upstate New York, and Helen worked as a vice chancellor for the State University at Binghamton.

When they first met, Sam was in the process of getting divorced from his first wife. Wounded and dejected, Sam had no fight in him. When Helen learned the terms of the separation and subsequent divorce agreement, she hit the ceiling. "She's running off with another man and your two children. You are giving her your life savings and the proceeds from the sale of the house. How can you let that woman take so much of what rightfully belongs to you?" she screamed at him. And then she proceeded to draft a new separation agreement that included equal division of assets and joint custody. She knew Sam wanted custody of his oldest son, Robert, and she was going to help him get it.

Sam went to court and won custody of Robert, as well as equal division of assets. But the judge, an old-fashioned man in his sixties, didn't like the idea of Helen and Sam living together. He thought the boy shouldn't be exposed to such immoral behavior. So Helen would not be allowed to stay overnight as long as they were not husband and wife. In Sam's mind the perfect solution would be for them to marry, which they did a few weeks later.

Helen was beautiful, outgoing, and friendly. Sam was shy, very bright, and reticent about talking to people he didn't know. "I would depend on Helen to get a conversation going or to introduce us to people. I couldn't go to a cocktail party without her," he told me. She loved to entertain. He confessed, "Without her I would not have moved up in the company. I depended on her for so many of the qualities I don't have."

I met Sam after he and Helen had separated. Their first three years of marriage were bliss. The last year, however, had become a battle for control. Sam believed in ultimate togetherness and insisted they spend all their time together, even if it meant reading different books in the same room. "She told me that she was going to have dinner with a girlfriend. I told her that no married woman in Binghamton would go out at night without her husband," he recounted with a tone of indignation. "Then she started rebelling," he continued. "She wouldn't be home when I got home from work. She'd spend money we didn't have. But the final straw was when she applied, without telling me, and got accepted to this course for executives at Harvard. That meant she was going to be away from home for six weeks. I put my foot down and told her she couldn't leave me. But she went anyway."

While she was at Harvard, Sam had an affair with one of his subordinates. He confessed, "I wanted someone who wouldn't be a challenge to me. I had noticed this cute young girl who had come to work in our department. She'd smile at me. We got to talking one day and she had me laughing like I hadn't laughed in months. I needed someone to get me out of my doldrums. Since Helen didn't seem to care about our marriage as much as her career, why should I? So I started spending time with Leslee.''

But Sam was not discreet. In fact, he was so angry at Helen that he wanted her to know what he had been doing while she was gone. So he made sure to take Leslee to restaurants his friends frequented. He left trails of signs for Helen to find when she came home.

Helen, however, was not one to put up with games like this. She felt it was one more way Sam was trying to control her. She told Sam she was leaving because she felt smothered, unable to be her own person, to have a life separate from his. She enjoyed being ''Sam's wife,'' but she wanted to be ''Helen'' as well.

Sam had too much pride to tell Helen how much he needed her, and besides, he had Leslee to make him laugh, so he let her go. Helen filed for divorce.

One night Sam was home alone. A wave of loneliness and remorse swept over him. He called his sister, Eileen, to say Helen had left him and they were getting divorced. Eileen, at thirty-seven, was on her third marriage. Sam was only four years younger, but he now had two marriages under his belt. Eileen couldn't bear to see her younger brother repeat her patterns. Eileen had a way of rescuing Sam whenever he was in trouble, and she insisted he come down to New York City and meet with her therapist.

As soon as his divorce was final, Sam married Leslee. But before the cycle of looking to women to fill a void in himself could begin again, Sam entered counseling to understand what propelled him to do so.

THE WAY IT WAS IN THE PAST

As Sam and I explored his past together, he told the story with insights he had acquired as a result of being in counseling.

Sam, according to his therapist, had been scripted to look for women who would rescue him because that was the way his sister treated him. She, in essence, was his mother, as his real mother worked and was rarely home for the kids. His sister filled the initial void.

"All my life I have looked for women who want to fix my life for me. It's a miracle I have gotten anywhere in my career," he said wistfully. And then, looking off, Sam sadly pondered, "I guess I use them at work too. It seems my life is filled with women who can't do enough for me. Some guys might think I'm nuts for complaining. But this game doesn't seem to be working anymore."

I asked, "Have you explored the reasons you smothered Helen, and as a result drove her away?"

Sam responded, "Of all the truths about myself that I have had to face, that one was most difficult. My therapist [a woman] helped me see how threatened I felt by any of Helen's outside activities. I wanted her to have a part-time job so she wouldn't get bored. But I wanted her to be my full-time companion, always there for me like my sister was. I took each of her accomplishments as a threat, as a way of saying to me that I wasn't lovable or as important. Helen's love of her career reminded me of how my mother didn't have time for us kids."

I can understand Sam's emotional outbursts and demands, for they were the only way he saw to regain some control over his life. Many men married to career-involved women believe that they are not as important as their wife's career or outside interests. These are often men who are dependent on women—mothers, sisters, or wives—for a sense of self or lovableness. Though I spoke with many men who feel this way, this observation contradicts how we normally view relationships, that is, with women as the dependent parties.

Sam explained it to me this way: "I only mattered when I needed someone. My sister was off playing with her friends or out on her dates having a good time. She'd forget about me. So I learned to be a troublemaker, to be forgetful and careless. Even though she'd get upset, I never had to fix anything I messed up. She always put everything back together for me."

Many relationships exist because one person assumes the caretaker role and the other that of the needy person. But these relationships fall apart when one of the individuals no longer needs to play his role in the psychological game or when the caretaker begins to resent being the rescuer.

The worst thing another person can do for someone is deprive him of the responsibility of negotiating through life, of learning to handle problems and correcting mistakes. By taking care of and taking responsibility for Sam, the women in his life were finding ways to control him. Or at least it helped them maintain the illusion of being in control. Often the person who plays needy and wounded rarely assumes responsibility; instead he externalizes blame and finds fault with the way others are acting. He doesn't see himself bearing any guilt at all.

Sam's sister Eileen, Helen, and Leslee all might have meant well; but they were fulfilling their own need to be needed and important at the expense of Sam's emotional independence and self-esteem.

Sam and Leslee spent the first two years of their marriage in counseling learning what they wanted from the marriage and from the other person. They also thought it would help them to catch their mistakes early in the game so as not to destroy a love they wanted to build.

It is important for all of us to examine the love patterns we bring to our relationships. We see how our parents acted toward one another and toward us and from them we learn or don't learn how to love other people. To move beyond behaviors learned in childhood, we must understand what we contribute to a relationship and what we want out of it.

EXAMINING YOUR MOTIVES AND NEEDS

As women have questioned what they want from their marriages and relationships, men have begun to do the same. They are questioning their own needs and expectations about what a relationship should fulfill in their life and admitting the conflicts they feel. These conflicts include those between the desire to be cared for and depended upon and the desire to find a woman who will be an equal companion and who shares their values and goals; between tolerating an unsatisfying relationship or abandoning one's familial and societal responsibilities; between considering one's own needs and well-being or thinking about the needs and well-being of others.

I have a few suggestions to get you going in your own exploration.

    1. *Be aware of your own needs in the relationship.*

Spend some time alone, thinking about what initially attracted you to this person. Reflect on times you felt satisfied. Ask your mate to do the same. Then select a quiet time to discuss the insights you have arrived at. Take turns. Have one person talk, while the other person listens. Then switch.

2. *Discuss your expectations of one another.*

Think about the needs, hopes, and expectations you brought to the relationship. How are they no longer being met? What expectations do you have that you haven't communicated? What dreams have you kept to yourself that need to be aired?

3. *List your appreciations and resentments.*

On one piece of paper write down all the qualities you appreciate. Each sentence should begin "I appreciate . . ." On the second sheet of paper turn each of the "I appreciate" statements into "I resent" statements. For instance, you might appreciate how compassionate and nurturing your mate has been. At the same time you might feel her to be intrusive and smothering. Often we look at the same qualities through different filters at different moments. As strange as it may seem, the aspects we initially appreciated in the other person can become qualities we resent.

4. *Evaluate how you have depended on one another.*

How have you used one another to fill the voids? For instance, a man who does not like to get angry but prefers to act easygoing will frequently marry a woman who is aggressive and expresses her anger.

What roles do you play in the relationship? What roles does your wife play? Discuss this with each other.

5. *Learn to disclose your feelings, not accuse others.*

When expressing your feelings avoid all "you" language. Whenever you start a sentence with a "you" it points a finger. Instead disclose your feelings by using "I" statements. *I feel hurt* vs. *You hurt me*. The former accepts responsibility while the latter places blame and frequently causes defensiveness, anger, and pain.

6. *List the assets and liabilities of staying together or getting divorced.*

As you would in a financial situation, list your assets and liabilities. Use four pieces of paper. On the first one write: *Assets of staying married.* On the second: *Liabilities of staying married.* On the third: *Assets of being single.* And on the fourth: *Liabilities of being single.*

The purpose of this exercise is to look objectively at your relationship without pinning dissatisfactions on your mate. You will be able to ascertain what importance you place on marriage and/or on being single. And you will be able to make a decision with confidence by objectively distancing yourself from a very subjective, intimate situation.

Performing this exercise will help you to avoid the mistakes that many of the men in my study have made. Moreover, it will help you to be honest with yourself, to identify your own truths, and to avoid fooling yourself.

I WAS ONLY FOOLING MYSELF

Peter Dart, a man of privileged background, married his high-school sweetheart, Gayle. They had both grown up in Bloomfield Hills, Michigan. She went to Vassar, while he went to Harvard. They both went to Stanford for graduate work. She got her master's degree in secondary education and he got his M.B.A. in business administration. By the time he was forty, Peter was president of a major semiconductor company. They had three beautiful kids and the ideal life. Gayle went on to get her Ph.D. She later became superintendent of schools. Peter was proud of her career and regarded her as an excellent mother and wife.

Peter lived according to a prescribed set of rules that had worked for years but were suddenly not working anymore. After fifteen years of marriage, Peter knew he wanted out. But like many of the men I spoke with, he was paralyzed from acting because, as he put it, "I hate hurting people."

Instead, Peter thought of himself as the martyr, placing others' security and happiness above his own. Rather than get divorced, he endured his miserable life for another two years to save his wife and children from any pain. The only problem was that this rationalization didn't work.

Peter learned this in a very painful manner. One day he and his youngest son were playing badminton in the backyard. Peter wasn't in a very good mood and seemed unenthusiastic about playing. His son got mad and shouted at him, "Just 'cause you're miserable with Mom, doesn't mean you have to act like you don't care about me. We know you and Mom don't like one another anymore. Does that mean you don't like us kids?"

"I sat down and cried," Peter said. "I never wanted to hurt the kids and that's exactly what I was doing. At that moment I knew it was not whether I was going to leave the family or not. It was rather, How do I leave?"

All too often couples such as Peter and Gayle think they are putting on a good front for family, friends, and strangers—but people know. Everyone sees through their charade but the couples themselves. There are many telltale signs. Suppressed hostility and dissatisfaction surface in the strangest ways: snide comments about your partner in front of others, anger with the children when you are really angry with yourself, or absence from the home because "work is so demanding."

The fact is, divorce is often painful, guilt producing, and scary. Many people are injured. Children of divorce do suffer. But couples who stay together for the sake of the children are doing their children a great disservice. Children need to be raised by people who love one another rather than by those who merely tolerate each other. Is it fair for a child to be raised by an emotionally absent father? Many men go to work before their children awake and come home, eat dinner, and go to sleep. They are there in body, fulfilling their role of breadwinner, but not of husband or father.

Parents who think their children are unaware need only guess again. Many children resent growing up in an emotionally vacant home. When they are young they can't articulate these feelings. I have spoken with many men between the ages of twenty-three and thirty-five who wish their parents had divorced or faced their problems because they might have had better examples to learn from. Instead these men are in counseling learning how to undo the patterns they acquired from watching their parents interact.

To get divorced, in fact to even consider divorce, takes emotional strength and courage that few men are willing to demonstrate. The "responsibility ethic" permeates their heart and soul so strongly that should they think of leaving their marriage and family, many men are immediately overcome with guilt for even considering it. Such a man may be afraid others will perceive him, should he divorce, as a "responsibility rejector," an unstable man who has abandoned his obligations and therefore cannot be trusted with any authority on the job. Since the majority of men are raised to believe divorce is a sign of weakness and/or failure, the peer pressure—both spoken and unspoken—prevents many men from making a necessary change in life-style.

I often encourage men to ask themselves these questions: Do you prolong the pain by withdrawing from and rejecting those people you live with or do you address the problem and let everyone get on with rebuilding his or her life? And . . . will the pain your children suffer from your leaving be less than the pain they will feel from living in a house with two parents who don't love one another?

Arriving at answers to these questions is not an easy process. It requires facing the guilt and pain that surfaces when a relationship doesn't meet the needs of both parties. Some men believe that if they avoid thinking about the problems in their relationship, time will resolve the difficulties. But time isn't the solution. Conflicts must be tackled head on and compromises must be made to resolve incompatibilities. In the remainder of the chapter we will look at how men answer the question "Do I leave or do I stay?"

DO I LEAVE OR DO I STAY?

This is the question that plagues the married man who juggles family life and an affair. It is painful for him to part with his lover, returning home to the reality he is trying to escape, and painful for him to be at home with his family, for he feels the emptiness and longing to be with someone he loves.

Bill O'Dell knows this conflict all too well. He is one of the five most gorgeous men in my study. Tall, with black wavy hair, deep aqua eyes, and a strong Irish jaw, his extreme good looks intimidate many women. He enjoys the benefits of his looks, and it might even be said he exploits them to the maximum.

When he was younger, Bill never considered falling in love with any of the women who came his way. He enjoyed being a playboy. His attitude was that in time he would find a ''nice'' girl to settle down with but while he was in his prime he should play the field. Unfortunately the best of plans don't always work out according to our fantasies. When Bill was twenty-two he met Peggy, a nice Catholic girl who was more sophisticated than the other girls he had dated. He liked her independence. Reminiscing, he told me, ''In looking back she was playing hard to get. That was the first time a girl had ever treated me like I didn't matter. I couldn't stand it. Peggy became a challenge.''

They dated for four months before Bill moved into Peggy's apartment. A month later Peggy was pregnant. Bill, religiously devout, knew he had to marry Peggy. The Church would never forgive them. Bill's Catholicism prevented him from even considering an abortion. Besides, in 1964 abortions weren't even legal. So they got married.

Bill resented his newly acquired obligations from the beginning. ''Hell if I was going to let that little inconvenience stop me. I went out on the town the night before I got married. I fooled around the day after we got married. I've been having affairs for the past seventeen years that we have been married.''

Bill was a salesman for Sperry-Univac, a computer company. His job required that he travel three or four days a week. No one heard any complaints from Bill because this allowed him to continue his womanizing while managing to cope with the obligations at home. Peggy was a good little wife, producing babies every two years. By their seventh anniversary they had four boys running around the house.

Bill's pattern was to jump from one woman to another. He looked at women as objects who were there to satisfy his ego and his sexual needs. After years of playing this game Bill told me, ''I don't remember when it hit me, but I realized that these women looked at me as an ego-booster, they were using me just like I was using them. I began to feel like a good-looking piece of ass, an arm piece. They would talk about how jealous their girlfriends were because they had landed such a 'hunk.' They never spent any time finding out about me.''

That all changed when he met a woman who was not impressed with him at all. Bonnie Bedford, medium height, slightly overweight, suddenly caught Bill's eye. They were in a business meeting. He flirted but Bonnie would not flirt back. In fact, she seemed indifferent. This only sparked the challenge. Bill continued to pursue her. Still no bite.

One night Bonnie, her boss, and Bill went to an elegant and romantic restaurant. Her boss begged off early, leaving Bonnie to finish her dessert with Bill. Bonnie was unaware that Bill had asked her boss to cut out early. He told me, ''I was not going to give up. She was single, strong, interesting. And I wanted her. I needed to stack the deck and I knew her boss played around on the side. He understood. I wasn't going to lose this round.''

Bonnie eventually succumbed to Bill's ways and found herself in a romantic affair. Bill told me, ''We'd been seeing one another for about five months when I realized that I suddenly felt weird, different about this girl. I didn't ever remember feeling this way before.'' ''This way'' turned out to be ''in love.'' Bill had been swept off his feet.

Bonnie's attitude drove Bill crazy. She was rather nonchalant about the relationship. She told Bill, ''You are a good Catholic boy and you married your wife because your religion told you that you should, so I doubt you'll ever get divorced for me. Let's take the relationship day by day and enjoy our time together.''

Bill didn't quite handle it with such calm. He loved Bonnie and wanted to be with her all the time. Their affair lasted for four years. During that time Bill learned that falling in love with someone and having a mutually satisfying relationship could eliminate your desire to be with anyone else. He was quite surprised when he realized that he had, over time, become oblivious to other women. For the first time in his life he considered monogamy.

At one point Bill even considered getting divorced to be with Bonnie. ''I wanted to leave my family to be with her. But the guys discouraged me. Maybe they felt they would lose me. As the saying goes, 'Misery loves company.' We were a group of unhappily married men and we fooled around together.

''I hated myself because I wasn't strong enough to be different from the boys. I hated myself because I listened to the priest rather than to what made me happy. All the guys knew that Bonnie had me and they teased me about it. I'd try to prove they were wrong by scoring the best-looking chick. Only when I'd get her to bed I couldn't get it up. Thank God they never knew. I didn't want to be with anyone other than Bonnie. It even became difficult to continue to 'service' Peggy. I did that because I felt it was my duty to keep her happy.

"Whenever I wasn't with Bonnie I felt so lonely. I needed the guys I worked with to like me. Then the worst possible thing happened. I became the marketing director. I was their boss. Overnight we were no longer equals. I often continued to pursue women with them because that was the only way we were still peers. I needed them.

"But we weren't the same anymore. Once I fell in love with Bonnie, I didn't want to hustle women anymore—except when I was on the road with the guys. I did anything that I could to make sure they still accepted me as one of them. I couldn't betray them. We were a bunch of unhappily married men competing for the crown of king stud. We didn't care who we scored with. I don't think any one of us cared to sleep in an empty bed. Being on the road makes you so lonely. Sometimes it's better having a warm body to cuddle with than to get bombed and forget your troubles.

"During those years I felt like a split personality. I was one person with my family, another person at work, and a third person with Bonnie. Behaving this way was driving me crazy. Sometimes I'd spend three or four nights a week at Bonnie's. I'd tell Peggy I was traveling when I wasn't. Or, instead of leaving for a trip the night before, I'd stay overnight with Bonnie and take a seven A.M. plane. It got to the point that no one could count on me. I couldn't stand the guilt I was living with. I hated myself for acting out this charade. I'd promise to be home for dinner and instead drive over to Bonnie's so we could have dinner together. Peggy managed the house, raised the kids. I'd promise to fix the faucet but was too exhausted, so I'd make Peggy call the plumber. Even my kids began to say they could never count on me.

"It wasn't that I didn't love my kids. I did. After our oldest son, Tommy, was born I started to think Peggy was excluding me. She had always been so attentive before we were married. It was horrendously painful because she'd spend all the time with the kid instead of me. Now we have four kids and Peggy has no time or energy for me.

"I tried to find all sorts of reasons that my relationship with Bonnie wouldn't work. I put a list together of all the things wrong with her: fat ass, not very glamorous, too short, not pretty enough. Nothing worked. Anytime she threatened to break off with me I ran back to her like a puppy dog. I couldn't let go of her. I never loved anyone like I loved Bonnie nor have I loved anyone since.

"Bonnie had been in love once before. I couldn't let go of her no matter how much I knew I'd never get divorced. I had to hold on to her. I didn't want her to deprive me of this feeling and I was afraid if I gave her up I would never feel this way again. Yet, as much as I wanted to be with her, my guilt kept me returning to Peggy and the kids.

"On one trip, Bonnie got into a jealous fit. She had this illusion that Peggy had life better than her. I couldn't convince her that she had the best of me. In Bonnie's rage she called Peggy. I was paralyzed while she dialed the number. I sat there while she threatened Peggy's life. I sat there while she said, 'I wish you were dead.' I sat there thinking that I wished Peggy were dead. My life would have been so simple.

"I was very insecure back then. I was afraid of my buddies' disapproval. Sometimes I wondered if Bonnie would wake up one morning and discover that I really was an ass. I stayed with Peggy because she knew the worst of me and put up with it. For years I have dreamed of the days when the kids are grown and I could leave. Then I catch myself. Maybe Peggy and I will grow old together, our resentment and pain binding us together."

I ran into Bill five years after he and Bonnie broke up. We spoke for a long time. Life's circumstances had humbled him. He had started his own business and failed. He was a little overweight and had not aged as gracefully as I had expected. Bill had never faced his feelings or his needs. From our conversation I got the sense that these failures had forced him to look at the man in the mirror and be honest. Peggy had since left him and he was involved with another woman like Bonnie. He also had three other lovers in different cities.

Unfortunately for Bill he made his decision by default. Had he faced his problems rather than used successive affairs to forget them, his marriage might still be intact. More important, Bill might have found a way to prevent his problems from repeating themselves.

EMOTIONAL BLACKMAIL

Mark Sullivan is a nice Catholic boy from Ohio. He married his high-school sweetheart, Kathy. She is pretty, wholesome, and smart. They had known one another since junior high school. Mark and Kathy got married at eighteen and divorced at thirty-six, after spending more than half of their life together.

It was painful to watch Mark agonize over his dissolving marriage. Reality surfaced when he suddenly had time on his hands. He had always been able to run from his problems by running to his career. Without the numerous distractions he previously counted on, Mark's unhappiness would not go away.

Mark's company was having financial problems so they offered employees money to leave. Given Mark had more than fifteen years in the company his buy-out package would be considerable. For years he and another colleague had put together real-estate partnerships, making considerable money for themselves during the California real-estate boom. He had always dreamed of having his own business and the opportunity seemed to present itself. Within months he opened up his own tax accounting firm and a real-estate company.

As Mark and I both realized many months later, his marriage had been over years before. But Mark and Kathy went through the normal phases most couples go through before conceding to this truth. They talked about having another child but vetoed that idea because their only daughter, Katie, was already ten years old. They thought the age difference would be too great. Then they talked about moving, which they finally did, and so setting up house delayed reality a little longer. Besides, Kathy's career was on the rise as she had just been named controller of a Fortune 500 company. They threw themselves into their careers, leaving little time to be together. This made things more palatable. The only option they didn't discuss was having an affair, although they thought about it.

Mark began divorce proceedings. Given that he had amassed a large real-estate fortune, he knew the state's communal property laws dictated they would have to split things fifty-fifty. Mark, like

other men, agonized over this factor. Since many men define themselves by what they do and what they acquire, giving up half of
their fortune is equivalent to giving up half of themselves. But a
combination of guilt and compassion made Mark refuse his attor-
ney's suggestion that they fight for a greater percentage of the
property settlement. I admired Mark's decision.

Kathy, for her part, was completely destroyed by Mark's ad-
mittance that their problem was simply that they had outgrown one
another. He had remorsefully accepted that, but Kathy was unwilling
to let go. She threatened suicide; she attempted to turn their daughter
against Mark; and she convinced Mark's mother, who lived with
them, that he was "killing" her with this decision. When they finally
separated, his mother moved in with Kathy and wouldn't speak to
her son for almost two years.

During the first year Mark was separated we spoke frequently.
Kathy had not let up with her emotional machinations and Mark
was guilt-ridden. Time passed and Mark still felt responsible for
the pain she convinced him he caused. The property settlement had
not been reached and his guilt was getting the best of him. So he
accepted Kathy's argument that he wasn't being fair.

Fast forward. They had been separated for nearly three years.
Two days before one of the property settlement meetings Mark and
I met for lunch. Mark looked like he had been dragging for weeks.
"Getting any sleep?" I inquired.

"Not much," he began. "Kathy seems to be so miserable,
and it's all my fault. She's still threatening to kill herself. She keeps
telling me I'm an irresponsible louse for abandoning my responsibilities. It seems Katie cries all night because I've abandoned the
family. She tells me I have no appreciation for the years she sacrificed her career so I could move up in the company. She's turned
Katie against me and my mother won't even talk to me."

I responded, "There's some truth in what she says about the
sacrifices she made, right?" Mark nodded.

"Good, we both agree," I continued. "I am assuming you
didn't hold a gun to her head or threaten her if she didn't move
with you. So stop taking all the blame. Too often women try to
make their husbands feel guilty for the sacrifices they have made
when fifty percent of the choice was theirs. Don't buy this manipulation. Weren't there sacrifices you made for her at different points
in your marriage?"

I saw a spark in his eye. It seemed I had made a logical point he could accept. "You're right," he began. "I did make quite a few sacrifices. I worked full time and went to college. When it was Kathy's turn to go to school I told her I would support her entirely. I hated having to balance work and school and I didn't see any reason for her to do so. Then when she decided to get her M.B.A. I put her through school again. And I passed up a promotion so she could finish rather than transferring to another school.''

"I'm glad you are beginning to see that you both made sacrifices to keep your marriage together for as long as you did. You've decided this time around the sacrifice—your happiness—is too great, but she still wants you to play by the old rules. You have every right not to. All marriages are built on trade-offs, and you both seem to have made them." I paused to watch Mark's reaction. He again nodded in agreement.

"Stop me if I'm throwing too much at you," I began again, "but your guilt is right at the surface, so let's see if we can deal with it."

"No, go on. I'm beginning to see how she has intimidated me," responded Mark.

"Okay. I want to address this issue of blame. You are not responsible for her misery and pain. I don't even believe you were ever responsible, but I know you won't buy that theory so let's skip it. Let's both agree you are no longer responsible. And I shall present my black-and-white argument for you financial types. Don't worry. No gray area in this one."

I continued, "One, you didn't decide to get involved with Majorie because you wanted to make Kathy miserable. You have been without a woman for almost a year. Your own wounds have healed. It's not that you left Kathy for someone else. You were both without partners during the first year. You obviously have chosen to deal with your breakup differently."

I barely paused before I went on to the second reason. "Two, you have been separated for almost three years. If she is still suffering it is her problem and no longer yours. The action that caused her initial pain was three years ago. You have done nothing since but try to settle this case, giving her one of the houses your partnership owns outright. She is bringing on her own suffering. If she wants to live in misery that is her choice. Your guilt and compassion have caused you to bend over backwards. She turned your daughter against you for almost two of those years. How come you aren't telling me about all the suffering she has caused you, how you lost sleep for months on end because Katie believed all the lies Kathy told her about you? Don't you think it is awful she used your daughter as a pawn to get at you, bringing on unnecessary pain to an innocent thirteen-year-old?

"Now I'd like to deal with the final manipulation she has been using on you for years—abandonment. You didn't abandon either one of them. You have provided for them and established a relationship that has a different form. You, like all men, have been raised to be a responsible breadwinner, husband, and father. Should you choose to discard one responsibility and take on another you are accused of irresponsibility, and if people are hurt you are guilty of abandonment. No way. One of the most difficult aspects men experience in the divorce process is accepting the fact that responsibility and choice don't have to be mutually exclusive. You can accept and reject different responsibilities. And when you reject a responsibility such as your role of husband and father, you do have a responsibility to be fair, compassionate, and honest with those involved. You have provided financially. You have repaired the relationship with your daughter and your mother. And doesn't it mean something that your mother finally got fed up with all of Kathy's manipulations?"

I sat back and waited in silence. After a long pause Mark looked up. "I think I'm getting angry," he said, smiling.

I threw my arms in the air and shouted, "Hallelujah, it only took three years. It's about time we considered your rights, your sacrifices, your hurts in this whole mess."

Mark called me the next week to say he had handled the property settlement meeting better than those in the past. "I know you've been trying to get it through my stubborn, logical mind that I didn't need to feel guilty for so long. Just wanted you to know I finally heard what you've been telling me since I decided to leave her. It made sense to me that I wasn't doing anything anymore to cause her pain. But now that I'm angry I'm not willing to be such a nice guy. The more she resists, trying to intimidate me and play on my guilt, the more I'm taking back." After a long pause, Mark added, "If she wants to accuse me of causing her pain, let her."

Mark's situation is only one of many I've been privy to. I strongly believe women shouldn't be cheated out of material belongings or monetary settlements. At the same time men who are emotionally preyed upon shouldn't give up what they have rightfully earned because they will naturally feel guilty in these circumstances. Above all, men need to stop feeling emotionally responsible for others. I hate to break the news to you guys, you just aren't that powerful.

To help you avoid being emotionally blackmailed, here are three not so simple steps to get you to shed the cloak of guilt you automatically assume.

AVOIDING EMOTIONAL BLACKMAIL

1. *You are not responsible for other people's feelings.* People choose how to respond to situations. It is a fallacy that feelings just happen. Think to yourself when someone is trying to make you omnipotent, ''I am not that powerful and I am not guilty.''
2. *Redefine your responsibilities and the roles you are willing to play.* For your own peace of mind it is important to know that you have been fair and have not abandoned your responsibilities. For example, being a father meant being home every night. Once you are separated it might mean calling every other day and visiting once a week. When you give up one way of doing something, you need to establish new criteria to measure your actions.
3. *Give yourself permission to be angry.* That doesn't mean you act on your anger. But you can't let your guilt envelop you. The action you are taking is unpleasant and can be extremely hurtful for all involved, including yourself. You have some emotional rights as well. Your well-being depends on admitting and coming to terms with your feelings. Ask yourself: How am I letting this other person intimidate me? What logical, manipulative things am I being accused of?

NOT DO I OR DON'T I—BUT HOW DO I LEAVE?

Deciding to get separated or divorced is one of the most difficult decisions a person can make. It is painful, guilt producing, and frightening. It brings up feelings of ambivalence, loneliness, and disappointment.

As I mentioned earlier, far too many people take divorce and failed relationships as a personal failure. I tend to have a different view. I am not even inclined to subscribe to the thinking that we make mistakes in picking people, because what initially attracted a person to us was probably the reason we needed to be together. I believe that people unconsciously know what needs the other person will fulfill. The answers might not be obvious at the onset of the relationship, but as time passes the psychological reasons we were drawn to the other person come to light.

Thus it becomes more a matter of learning what caused us to make a decision to pick a particular person and what is it in our past that contributed to our decision. I often recommend to people that before they make a decision to separate or divorce, it is important to thoroughly analyze the reasons they initially came together, the needs that were fulfilled but are no longer, and the disappointments they must accept. Here are some questions well worth considering.

BEING TOGETHER OR BEING APART

1. What was it that made you special to one another?
2. What were the reasons you decided to marry?
3. If you were to marry again, would you pick the same person?
4. In what ways has your mate satisfied you over the years?
5. What do you find most satisfying? least?
6. Do you consider yourself good or best friends?
7. When did your perspective about the other person change?
8. What aspects of life do you disagree about (raising children, money, career, values, religion, shared responsibilities, etc.)?
9. How do you (or do you?) communicate about successes? failures? achievements? interests? ideas? feelings? values? anger? sadness? disappointment?
10. What is holding you together? What is pulling you apart?

CHAPTER 15

WHY DID SHE LEAVE ME?

Men take heed: If you are interested in saving your marriage or relationship, or if you want to understand what women need from men, read on.

HE CAN DO NO WRONG

One night, Gordon returned home after an exhausting business trip to find Carol in the bathtub with her wrists slashed. Carol was rushed to the hospital. She survived.

Before attempting suicide Carol tried everything to get Gordon to realize that their marriage was disintegrating. At first she begged him to go to a marriage counselor. He refused. Then she screamed, cried, and pouted. When that didn't get his attention, she went on strike—refusing to cook, clean, entertain, or take care of herself. The strike backfired. He got angry. Her husband refused to give her her allowance. Carol told me this went on for months.

Finally her suicide attempt got his attention, but it was too late. Carol was bent on finding one way or another out of their marriage.

"I left Gordon because I was tired of prostituting myself. All he gave me was a roof over my head, a nice one, mind you, but so what. And sex, but only when he wanted it. Other than that,

247

forget it. I was supposed to wait on him hand and foot and be grateful I had the benefits of his position,'' said Carol with disgust.

"Even after I tried to kill myself,'' she continued, ''he didn't think any of our problems were his fault. Some psychiatrist told him that I had the problems to work out. He was okay. But when the kids refused to spend any time with him, he began wondering if I had been right to complain.''

When I spoke to Gordon, he informed me, ''I provide nicely for her. I don't know what she is so upset about. I have many pressures at the office. I don't need any at home. I do my job there. Her job is to make life peaceful for me when I get done with my daily battles. Why can't she understand that?''

And then, almost as an afterthought, Gordon said, ''Do you know how many women are waiting in line to be the wife of a bank president? I'll have no problem filling her shoes.''

Gordon, like many successful, powerful men, thinks he is impervious to personal problems. These men live an unrealistic life in which people worship them, tell them what they want to hear, and never challenge their actions. They think they can do no wrong. So when someone does complain about their actions, they believe it is the other person's problem, not theirs.

WHO'S HOLDING DOWN THE FORT?

"She told me she wanted a divorce because she was tired of always being the strong one in the marriage. I didn't know what to say, so I agreed to the divorce. Then she went on to tell me how bored she's been over the past few years. This was the first inkling I had that she wasn't happy. I couldn't believe it. How could she be unhappy, while I was so happy?'' mused Jim Reilly, one of New York's most successful investment bankers.

When I spoke with Jim's wife, Suzanne, successful in her own right as a literary agent, she told me, ''I've told him we have problems and we need to work them out, but he doesn't hear me. Or sometimes he pretends to listen to me, giving lip service to my complaints—'Yes, dear, I can imagine the way I am is frustrating to you. I'll have to work on changing a little.' But he never does. Jim will never tell me what he's thinking. We hardly talk about anything. I need to know more about him. We've been together over eighteen years and I don't know the man I'm living with.''

Suzanne, frustrated by giving warnings that fell upon deaf ears, left Jim. He was devastated. ''I didn't believe she'd really do it. I thought she was being a typical emotional female, so I let her rant and rave, thinking everything would be better in a few days. But I guess I was wrong. Things didn't get better; they got worse,'' he told me as he shook his head in disbelief.

Unfortunately I spoke with many men like Jim, who prefer passive resistance to active surrender. As men realize their placating ways of the past no longer work, they will have to learn how to deal with their own feelings and become more empathetic to their spouse's.

IN THE ARMS OF ANOTHER MAN

Robert Pryor was distraught. He discovered his wife was having an affair with his archenemy. ''It would have been better if he was my best friend. I can't imagine losing to someone I hate. I don't know why she had to look elsewhere, she was getting enough at home,'' he exclaimed.

Robert, at least, had the presence of mind to ask her, ''Why did you stray?''

''Maybe if you acted like you cared about me, I wouldn't have been tempted. But all you think I need is a little pat on the head and some sex. And that's all I get—sex and a couple of pats. You give more affection to the cat,'' Annette told Robert after he confronted her.

As he thought back over their twelve years together, he realized he had taken her for granted, even at times patronized her. Above all, Robert never thought about satisfying Annette sexually. He would satisfy himself, then roll over and go to sleep. Annette told him, ''After you'd start snoring, I'd cry myself to sleep. I was so hurt and angry. I resented being used for your pleasure.''

Robert took her dissatisfactions to heart, but it didn't help. Annette eventually left Robert for his archenemy, the man whom she loved and who loved her.

I was sorry to hear their marriage ended. If only Annette had spoken up sooner, when there was something to build upon, they might still be together today. But at least Annette has moved on to a better relationship and Robert has applied what he learned from this heartbreaking situation.

Months later Robert said to me, "Why didn't anyone ever tell me that women and men are different? Women need to be seduced. I think sex and I get stiff. Worst of all I never thought of pleasing her. I used to think women were getting into this semantic shit, you know, having sex or making love. They were right. We men were having sex and the women wanted to be making love."

He paused, then remorsefully added, "I've changed my ways now. I'm with a woman who tells me what she needs, which helps to remind me when I fall back to my old ways."

Robert Pryor epitomizes the male sexual attitude. As I listened to men describe for me their thoughts about sex, I began wondering if they ever consider partaking in this wonderful activity for pleasure's sake alone. So many turned it into a conquest game, a way to measure their potency, a vehicle for defining themselves. I remember asking one man, "Is it more important for you to reach an orgasm or to enjoy sex?"

He looked down his nose at me and indignantly responded, "Why, the orgasm, of course."

A WOMAN'S REASON FOR UNREST

Suzanne, Carol, and Annette were three of the thirty-six women I had the opportunity to interview. The women willingly spoke with me during scheduled interviews or our conversations developed spontaneously when I called their mate at home. A few wanted nothing to do with me, perceiving the counseling and advice I gave their husband as a threat. The women who did open up with me were delightful and offered great insight into the reasons men and women are having problems getting along today.

I have included here a letter from one of the women I interviewed. Her pain, disappointment, and insightfulness expresses what men and women need to hear, better than I could say it.

Dear Jan,

I'm glad Tim and I had the opportunity to talk with you. I don't think anything is going to help our marriage.

I guess it's because Tim doesn't want to change. He thinks I'm the one who should make the changes to adjust to him. What about him adjusting to me?

I don't want men or women to make the same mistakes we made. They can avoid destroying their own marriages (or relationships) if they would spend some time looking at how their needs are different and making some compromises.

I don't know why Tim never knew how much I loved him, even though I'd tell him all the time. I loved that man so much that I did anything and everything for him. He liked starched shirts and hated them done at the laundry. So I washed and ironed his shirts, just the way he liked them. He hated eating out because that was a hazard of his work. So I cooked his favorite meals.

And I did this along with building my own career. I'm not complaining, mind you. I liked being Tim's wife. And if being Tim's wife meant doing these chores, I'd do them.

I enjoyed coming home to do these things for him. We did have a housekeeper, thank god, because without her I would have gone crazy. But I did all the special and extra things Tim wanted done.

We were together for a long time (in today's terms). Fourteen years together and you can finish one another's sentences. He always knew he could count on me to grant his every wish. Problem was, Tim started taking me for granted and I resented being used.

In the beginning, I never told Tim I was unhappy (first mistake). Instead I'd put on a cheery face and continually try to please him. It seemed better for me to forget about my anger than say something. Instead I thought, "If I make him happy, then we'll be happy." Wrong. That didn't work.

I started complaining to friends. After a while my good friend Elaine told me to tell Tim how I felt or shut up. When I realized I'd have to speak up for myself, I went to an assertiveness training workshop to learn how. (I wanted to do it right, so as not to rock the boat.)

I thought I told Tim, in a nice way, that I wanted us

to change some things in our relationship. I was managing my career and taking care of Tim, Tim's career, and the house. I wanted my duties altered. He didn't like that. He accused me of changing the rules of the game. I thought that's what was supposed to happen between two people: you grow and change together. But Tim wanted things just like they always were.

Not me. Once I let my wishes be known Tim started pouting. He'd come home and wouldn't talk to me for hours. He knew how much this upset me. It took all I could muster to hold back the tears. Then he started going out with the boys for a couple of drinks. But the couple of drinks turned into too many. He knew how much I hated when he was drunk. I would try to assertively tell him how I felt. He didn't care. When my ''assertiveness'' didn't work, I'd scream, sometimes saying things I later regretted.

The final straw happened at one of my company's functions. We sponsored a table at the cystic fibrosis benefit. I had invited clients to join us. My boss was there with his wife. Tim was sure unhappy when people asked him if he was my husband; and it was like adding salt to a wound when they'd tell him how wonderful I was.

Tim got drunk and left the benefit. I was humiliated. Tired of keeping my anger in check, when I got home I let him have it. He wanted to hear nothing of what I had to say. I was trying to be superwoman and it wasn't working.

I tried to talk with Tim. We never really communicated, you know, feelings, thoughts, secrets, and all that stuff. So I thought it was about time we got to know one another after fifteen years together. Tim didn't want to talk. He wanted things back to normal. Normal for him was my working a job, bringing home half of our income, taking care of the house and Tim's needs, and keeping my mouth shut. Well, I'm a person too, and I am tired of being too nice.

We fought all night. The next day I went to see a counselor. Told him about our fight, my trying to change a few roles and duties in our relationship and Tim's resistance. I wanted to do anything to make things better.

You wouldn't believe what this doctor told me. He said I needed to learn to stand up for myself even more. Seems that I've let Tim get away with bullying me for all these years. He also warned me that my standing up for myself might only produce one winner: me. I might lose Tim in the process.

I was determined to prevent that from happening. Tim and I were two mature adults who could work this out. (Guess who's the optimist and who's the pessimist in our relationship?) So I went home and begged Tim to talk with me. Tim thought we should go to bed and make up. That's the way he always tries to deal with our problems.

Why don't men understand that we women need just a little emotional attention? A little goes a long way. I asked him why he didn't tell me he loved me. You won't believe what he said, "I wouldn't have married you if I didn't love you. Why do you need so much reassurance?"

It's the same in bed. I just need a little petting. For him it's all or nothing. Lots of times, I'd rather have nothing at all. Why can't he understand that sometimes I just want some physical attention and I don't want that to mean, Let's get into the missionary position?

I've always thought making love takes two people (kind of an understatement). I think Tim thought it only took one active person and one corpse. I was expected to lie there as he satisfied himself. Once I asked him to warm me up a little bit before he tried to do it because he was hurting me. Instead of warming me up, he blew up. He accused me of criticizing his lovemaking.

"What lovemaking?" I asked (second mistake). "I only thought you wanted to screw anything that didn't move," I added (third mistake).

Let me tell you why I'm complaining. He doesn't even know how to hold hands. All these years of being held by limp fingers and I decided to say something. I don't know how I said it, but it was something to the effect that our hands needed to connect more. Tim responded, ''That only needs to happen when we are in bed.'' And I remember what I said back, ''You're wrong. It needs to happen outside of the bed, so what happens in the bed is better.''

That instance caused me to realize that this man had no physical desire to be close to me. He only wanted me for sexual satisfaction. Oh, if only I could impress upon other men how important kissing and holding hands are to the quality of lovemaking. Tim hardly even kisses while we're ''screwing.'' I think he does it only long enough to get heated up. How do you teach a man to kiss?

Without Tim to talk with I started spending more time with my friends. I needed someone to confide in and my friends were there for me. One of my friends, Tom, understood me so well. I kept wishing Tim and I could talk about things the way I did with Tom. Some of my girlfriends suggested I leave. I wouldn't think of it.

I kept going to this psychiatrist. I didn't like what I was finding out. Tim hasn't cared about me as a person. I've been his mother, dishwasher, housekeeper, nanny, and whore. I got brave enough to confront Tim with this ''insight'' (fourth mistake, or maybe blessing in disguise).

Tim admitted he needed me. But he didn't understand why I needed him to relate to me as a person, not a slave. He told me his father never counted on his mother to discuss things with and therefore, why should he. His mother never made these kinds of demands on his father, so why should I. His father ruled the roost and that's the way it was going to be for him.

I tried explaining how I wanted there to be some trust, some closeness between us, but Tim would have nothing of it. How close could we be if Tim couldn't talk about things he felt were important? I never told you this, but I had an abortion because I knew our marriage wasn't the greatest. We needed to work on it and a child would only postpone that from happening. I wanted us to be happy together before we brought any children into the world.

As I stopped pretending everything was okay between Tim and me, my friends starting telling me how bad things were for them with their husband or boyfriend. It seems we all seem to have the same complaints. One of my women friends told me her husband is the same way.

When you're doing your interviews, do you mind if I give you some advice to pass along to the men and the women?

I hope you don't mind my being presumptuous, but I thought you'd say yes.

First, women and men don't seem to think about love or sex in the same way. The men I know want to be loved for bringing home the bacon. They want us to admire them for how they are at work, but they won't share that part of them with us. They want to be appreciated at home for how they are at work, but it is virtually impossible to appreciate talents you don't have an opportunity to see. Now I know why men have affairs with women at work: these women coo and stroke their feathers.

How am I to tell him he's a wonderful diplomat when he won't even tell me how his day went? How can I say, "Oh, you're so powerful," when he doesn't tell me about his responsibilities or what he accomplished? When men are willing to share the good and bad days with us, then we, too, can marvel at how wonderful they are; but if they don't tell us anything, we have nothing to respond to.

Secondly, whoever told them intimacy means giving up your freedom lied. If they didn't worry so much about being strong and in control, they could let themselves be more open with us. I don't expect to know everything about Tim, but I do want to understand how he thinks and why he feels as he does.

Problem is, he doesn't know so how can he tell me? Men need to spend more time understanding themselves. If they do, they can help *us* understand *them*.

Thirdly, men better stop looking at us as sex objects. Some of my friends will do anything to avoid this marital duty. We want someone to share our ideas and interests with. We want a companion. We want a man who will be our best friend and confidant. They don't have to share everything, but enough so there's a common bond, so we can grow together, in some, not all, ways.

From how my women friends describe their husbands, men need to think about being less rough, insensitive, or hurried. Often what these men need most is for their wife to tell them how they like to be touched and what makes them feel good. But they don't. These men need a woman who will teach them how to sexually meet a woman's needs.

And when they stop looking at us as sex objects and realize we are caring human beings who need warmth, love, and affection and like to give it as well, they might decide to work on being better lovers. By ''better'' we don't mean showing us fifteen positions. We mean more tender, affectionate, slower, interested.

Fourthly, careers are here to stay and men better get over feeling threatened by it. Tim in the early years encouraged me to move up in my company. When I started getting someplace, he felt threatened. I don't know why. He's successful in his own right.

I was everything to Tim. He wouldn't have had it any better had I been home all day long. But he didn't like something else, in addition to him, mattering to me. He would rather have me be needy and dependent. And I was in some ways, but when I started outgrowing my dependence, he got his back up.

I told him time and again I wanted a career because I liked taking care of myself—BIG MISTAKE. He thought my not needing him meant I loved him less. Tim didn't understand it meant I love him more. I only need him less. Need and love are the same thing for men, but it's not that way for more and more women. Men need to look at us as whole people who want to love another whole person.

I don't know how to end this letter. I've needed someone to tell how I feel, but I also needed to believe that I might be able to help men (since I couldn't help Tim) and help other women.

Tell the women, ''Let your needs be known. Speak

up early before a problem gets out of hand, and you can do something about it. Don't let your man intimidate you because you want to change. Tell them it's okay to be angry, but they'll have to get over it.''

And tell the men the greatest disservice we have done to them is playing dumb. In doing so, men have never had to work at being interesting. We always conquer our boredom or dissatisfaction with a smile or a question. We women have fooled them and it isn't fair.

We've accepted them for so long, just as they were, so grateful to get a man that we never let them know how much we really expected from them. Tell them we expect them to be more sexually interesting, more desirous of personal growth, and less needy for us to be dependent on them. What we want instead is for them to be our companion and our friend.

CHAPTER 16

SHE'S THE BEST THING THAT HAPPENED TO MY LIFE

In the previous chapters, we've discussed the problems in relationships. Now it's time to look at relationships that work!

Believe it or not, there are some people who are very happily married. And spending time with these couples was one of the most enjoyable parts of this study. But before I rave about these wonderful couples, let me explain the criteria I used to determine who would be included in this chapter.

First, each couple had to have been married for at least fifteen years, or have lived together and subsequently been married for the same time period. Interestingly, with one exception most of the couples written about in this chapter have been together a minimum of twenty years and some more than thirty-five years. The couple that is the exception to the criterion of fifteen years or more are on their second marriage, and they have been together over ten years. When you are around them there is no doubt that they love one another dearly. When you listen to them, they articulate the same feelings and beliefs about marriage that the other, longer-married couples express.

Second, I spent hours, days, and weeks with every couple profiled. The interviews were often relaxed and informal. On occasion I would tag along to social events so I could see how they interacted with one another. I traveled with one couple for a week. Two live in my hometown, so I was able to spend time at their homes, to see them in many situations, and gather impressions over a few years. Another couple invited me to be a houseguest, partaking in family activities.

With respect to the interviews, each couple answered questions separately and/or together. The questions included: What does marriage mean to you? What is the most important aspect of your relationship? Why did you decide to get married? How do you feel about your spouse? Why do you stay in the marriage? How do you handle problems and conflicts between you? What do you think makes your marriage work?

Let me begin with the answer to this last question. Six common characteristics shared by all the couples seem to be the ingredients of a happy marriage:

1. Being friends
2. Making a commitment to the relationship
3. Giving, supporting, and caring for each other
4. Independence/Separate interests and friends
5. Sharing common interests
6. Communication

Leo Tolstoy observed, "Happy families are all alike." He was right. All these couples think, feel, and act the same way when it comes to making their marriages work. So now I shall get on with this chapter, explaining what each of these qualities means to the couples who take their marriage vows quite seriously.

BEST FRIENDS

"There isn't anyone else I would want to spend my time with as much as I want to be with her," said John Mayer, an architect for a big construction company. "It's not that I don't have other friends. I do and they are important to me. But Veronica is my best friend."

"What makes your spouse your best friend?" I asked each couple. Many had not thought about it until I asked. They just "knew" it was so. But as we explored this together they told me how important liking and trusting their mate was to them.

"I like Veronica," John continued. "She's spontaneous, fun, and so interesting. We have been together almost twenty-six years and I don't ever remember being bored. Even if she were married to someone else, I would pick her for a friend. Our friendship is different from the love and chemistry we feel for one another. It is a very special part of our relationship.

"But here's another point that is extremely important. There are other people I like, and, perhaps, as much. But there isn't anyone else I trust like I trust Veronica. She doesn't spend her time judging or criticizing me. I can tell her something and I know that she will never use it against me. I also know she would never betray a confidence. And the best part is you never have to tell her what you've just said shouldn't be repeated."

John paused for a moment, looking around the room while playing with the paperweight on his desk. Finally he looked at me and began, "I hadn't quite thought about it that way. Trust, I mean. It's why we would never have an affair. It's why we never discuss things when we are mad. We don't ever want to destroy the trust it has taken years to build."

And then John said, "Excuse me, I have to call Veronica and let her know how much I appreciate that about her. I want to know if she had thought about it in the same terms."

I knew what she'd say because that morning Veronica had expressed similar feelings to me. Veronica is a tall, elegant redhead who used to model for Eileen Ford. Now she runs her own company, producing fashion shows for charities, department stores, and "anyone who will pay me."

When we met at her office, Veronica defined their relationship for me, "We are best friends. Two of my best girlfriends have been in my life since I was knee high. Even though I have known them longer and we are incredibly close, I hold back some of my feelings with them. But with John, I am never embarrassed about how I feel. We trust one another with our heart and soul."

She paused before adding, "But don't get me wrong. John is not everything to me and I don't expect him to be. That's why I need my women friends Gina and Lois. John is there for me in the most important ways."

When John hung up the phone, he was beaming with pleasure. He recounted for me what I had already heard that morning. It came as no surprise. Continually, as I spoke with happily married couples, separately and together, they would tell me the same stories, express the same feelings, and delight in knowing that they shared a very special relationship.

And that specialness comes from having a genuine interest in and concern for the person you are married to. It means constantly making yourself interesting and sharing that with your mate. But most of all it means liking, accepting, and trusting the person you have chosen to spend your life with.

MAKING A COMMITMENT

"I didn't want to *not* be with her," Charles Loewenberg said to me as I sat in his sunny dining room, looking out at San Francisco's Golden Gate Bridge.

Charles's comment was prompted by my question, "Why did you get married?"

Charles and his wife, Nancy, have been married twenty years— the second marriage for Charles and the first for Nancy. They had been dating for quite some time. Nancy was ready to get married but Charles wasn't. Yet when the prospect of losing her presented itself, he decided that was the worst option.

As Nancy tells it, "Chuck had just gotten out of a marriage. He resisted getting into another one. But I wanted our relationship to go somewhere. So I pushed the issue."

Charles chimed in, "I didn't wear my ring. Of course I used the excuse that I didn't like jewelry. The truth was I didn't want to commit to being married."

After the first five years, Charles resigned himself to the fact that he was married. By their tenth anniversary, he started wearing the ring. And now he is committed to the marriage more than 100 percent.

They recently celebrated their twentieth wedding anniversary at a chateau they bought in France. Seventy-five friends from around the world flew in to help them celebrate. The anniversary party began Saturday at noon and ended Sunday morning when the sun rose. Every one of their friends so admire their marriage and each of them. People didn't want to leave. They didn't want the party to end.

As I saw how happy everyone was being around the Loewenbergs, I recalled how Charles had explained to me, "So many of our friends ask us what makes our marriage work. They tell us we are the happiest couple they know, with the best marriage they have ever seen. Nancy and I have spoken about this. We've thought about doing a workshop for other couples. We've explored the components of our relationship.

"One striking difference," he continued, "is so many of our friends express the thought 'This is not going to last forever,' about their marriages or relationships. Now, how can you expect a marriage to last if you're not committed?"

Nancy sat there nodding her head. As I looked her way, she started to speak. "We are in this together. Divorce is not an option for us. When you decide to commit to another person you have to be willing to work things out."

Charles and Nancy epitomize two common aspects of the committed relationship. First, they never considered "getting out" as an option for dealing with their conflicts and problems. And second, couples must realize that weathering rough times is necessary and important if they want their marriage to last.

"We get beyond issues quickly," Charles told me. "I have a high tolerance level for anything. Nancy often reacts a little stronger. She has more likes and dislikes. But I wasn't always able to handle Nancy blowing up. Now I think of it as Nancy being Nancy."

And then Nancy proceeded to tell me a story Charles had told me weeks before. "One day I blew up at Chuck," she started in, "and he said to me, 'Stop yelling at me.' I told him I wasn't yelling. After that he was more accepting of my 'emotional way' of reacting."

Charles added, "As I mentioned to you a few weeks ago when I told you the story, I realized Nancy thought she wasn't yelling. That was her way of just being. So when I realized that was Nancy being Nancy and I stopped judging her, I didn't take it personally anymore."

Charles frequently used the expression, "Nancy being Nancy." In talking with these couples, they all had found ways of coming to terms with their differences, and it always boiled down to accepting the other person. Acceptance is the key ingredient to a committed relationship.

Take Charles and Nancy's advice, "We don't allow judgments

to get in the way of being together. We help one another through our individual difficulties. For instance, if Nancy doesn't move on [through her personal problem], *we* don't move on. And vice versa. We are virtually always in a state of harmony. But that's because when problems arise, we handle them. And that's why no one questions the strength and endurance of our relationship.''

GIVING, SUPPORTING, AND CARING

"I just came back from Japan a few hours ago," Ed Fogelman started to explain to me, "and whenever Mikey puts on one of her parties, I always go no matter how tired I am."

Mikey, his wife, otherwise known as Michelle Kelly, was a publicist at the time. And we were all at the opening of her client's restaurant. A friend of mine introduced me to her husband, Ed, because his company was considering using my services.

Instead of discussing business, Ed and I had a conversation about his marriage.

A few weeks later I called the friend who had introduced us and suggested that we have dinner with the Kelly/Fogelman clan. As I watched this adoring couple, I knew they had to be profiled.

There have been times I have wanted to put Ed and Michelle on videotape to show others what it means to be supportive and caring of your spouse. They are dedicated to one another's well-being. They adore one another. They each think the other is the best thing that happened to their life.

Michelle and Ed were both married before. When Michelle met Ed, he had a bad case of psoriasis; a nervous reaction to the stress of separating from a bad marriage.

As I sat at their kitchen counter, Ed preparing the food for the barbecue we were about to have, he began to tell me the story. "When I met Mikey, she would rub my medication on my arms. My ex-wife treated me like a leper whenever I had a breakout."

Michelle, sitting on the stool next to me, chimed in, "It was awful. He was in so much pain. And she [the ex-wife] was so mean to him. I wanted to make him feel like he mattered and I didn't want him to feel rejected."

I could go on with countless examples of things Ed and Michelle constantly say that reflect how they are always thinking about the other person.

What people learn from watching Ed and Michelle together is that caring, giving, and supporting your spouse is demonstrated in many little intangible ways. Being supportive means being excited or interested in things that normally would not get your attention. For instance, Ed is not a social animal as is Michelle. Michelle is highly adept at conversing with anyone and everyone. While other husbands refuse to socialize, Ed knows in the whole scheme of things this isn't an issue worth taking a stand on. Doing it because it gives Mikey pleasure is the reason Ed goes along for the ride.

And giving is not buying things. I found that when wealthy men bragged about buying their wife jewelry, a mink coat, taking her on an expensive trip, it was done more to say to everyone else, "See, I can afford this. Look at how successful I am." And those marriages weren't bound together with the qualities I'm outlining here.

Giving means giving of yourself, your time, your energy, your concern. Like Ed, who was jet lagged and tired, but nevertheless went to his wife's event. It's acts like this that make two people feel secure with one another.

INDEPENDENCE

Charles Loewenberg told me, "For some reason I've always had trouble asking permission. I don't like asking, 'May I do this or that?' I used to find it difficult calling Nancy and saying 'I'm staying someplace another hour.' I just assumed she would be mad at me, so to avoid the confrontation, sometimes I wouldn't call. That of course simply made things worse."

And Nancy added, "He would put off calling because he knew I'd be irrational." After pausing for a moment, she continued, "You see, my parents never did anything with anyone else. It was one person with the other person. I always thought of spending time with others as 'taking away' from our relationship. But once I started accepting Chuck being Chuck, I stopped being so insecure."

"Nancy's independence has been the most major positive impact on our relationship," Charles interjected. "She didn't drive the first seven and one-half years of our marriage."

I looked over to see Nancy's response. She was nodding her head in agreement. "I had this insecurity about sharing him. And he fed that insecurity by not changing. But as our relationship grew and became stronger, I was able to be more separate. I have learned to have my own friends."

Nancy is an incredibly independent person. I would have never believed that she was as clingy as they both made her out to be. It seems that Nancy was able to realize her own strength based on Chuck's *unwillingness* to become a willing victim and foster her insecurity. In the relationship Nancy was able to discover herself, a characteristic uncommon for so many women. Frequently women feel they must leave the relationship to find and be themselves.

But not all men are as secure as Charles. In fact, they frequently are threatened by their spouse's independence. Charles felt the more he encouraged Nancy to have her freedom, the more he could have his. And Charles has worked through the fear that his freedom would be taken away or never given to him. He is more able to ask Nancy how she feels about his doing something and less afraid to call if he'll be late or wants to spend more time with the boys after softball.

Different people have different needs to be close and to be separate. There isn't one right way or a correct proportion in a relationship. The degree of independence and the need for separateness must be worked out over time, through trial and error.

Each couple in the study found this quality to be important, but how they incorporated it into their marriage varied. For instance, one couple loved to travel, but they liked different activities for the most part. So more often than not, they took separate vacations. Another couple, in which the wife had a greater need for freedom than her husband, made sure they were together on the weekends, but during the week she used the time to do things with friends.

Most of all, the couples interviewed agreed with the statement, "The fact that we have separate interests and friends helps to keep the relationship interesting and it makes us appreciate each other even more."

COMMON INTERESTS

"He's my companion," stated Tara Jacobs. "He is so much fun to be with. We laugh all the time, over the silliest things. When

be communicative. I found that as I taught them the language of feelings and the skills of communicating, men became quite adept and open.

Whether happily married or not, 87 percent of the men interviewed claimed communication is the most important quality if one wants a good relationship with his employees, customers, and family. It was unanimously agreed upon by the happily married couples.

"If we didn't talk with one another, we wouldn't get through the rough times," Warren Jacobs said.

Men deserve far more credit than they get for their efforts at communicating. Sixty-three percent of the men told me their wife or lover taught them how to express their feelings. Women need to stop expecting men to learn how to walk and run at the same time. I know some women are fed up with having to be the teacher, the mother, the caretaker. Men, however, have taught us many things, and I think it is time we passed on the knowledge and ability of something we do well.

What men do need to learn is how to listen. They have been socially conditioned to be interrupters rather than listeners. To understand others you have to listen to them.

The men who have good marriages know this. Again and again, these men told me stories about how they realized it was only through paying attention to what their wife was saying that they developed a greater understanding of her. And they feel they are listened to in return.

Warren told me how Tara taught him to listen. "At the end of each day we take turns talking about what transpired. The way we do it evolved without our thinking about it. One day we were both in Miami on business. When I got back to the hotel, Tara asked about my day. I told her it went well and then courteously asked how hers went. She stopped me and said, 'I want to hear how your day really went. Give me the blow-by-blow. Then I'll tell you about mine.' From that day on, we really started listening to one another. And it's become a good habit."

Communication is not always what is said; it frequently is what is not said. It is understanding a sigh and knowing that the other person might need you to encourage him or her to talk. It's knowing when your wife asks for a martini, a rare occurrence, that you might ask about her day. It's knowing that you can say whatever you are thinking without fear of retribution.

The president of a major film company told me one day, "Women think they want us to be vulnerable, but when we are they run from us." One of the most common complaints I heard from the men who were unhappy with their marriage and were tempted to or did have affairs was, "I can't talk to her. I want her to listen, to understand me. She doesn't have to fix things for me. Only listen to me and discuss what's on my mind."

Finally, in all of these relationships, none of the women wanted their men to be strong and silent. They were emotionally strong themselves and didn't need to play the helpless female game. If there was something bothering their husband, they wanted to hear it. And none of the men felt they had to live up to the John Wayne image.

HOW DO YOU FEEL ABOUT ONE ANOTHER?

I have compiled a list of questions for you to ask yourself and to use as a means of discussion with your mate. Take some time, first by yourself, to carefully think about your answers. Perhaps you might want your mate to do the same. I recommend giving the questions careful thought before you discuss your answers together. They will reveal how you feel about one another, your commitment to your marriage, and the needs that are being met. They will also provide insights into the areas in which improvement is needed.

ASSESSING YOUR MARRIAGE

1. Do you like one another? What is it about your partner that you like? How often do you mention the things you appreciate about one another?
2. Have you ever thought, I can get out of this if it doesn't work? or, Divorce is not an option, I'll find a way to make this work?
3. Are you proud of your mate? In what ways?
4. Are you accepting of your mate's faults? How so? What do you find difficult to accept about your mate?
5. How do you show each other that you care?
6. How important is having separate friends and interests to both of you? Do you feel the same or does one have a greater need for dependency or independence?

7. Do you have fun together? In what ways? Anything else you want to do together but haven't done?
8. When was the last time you laughed together? What was the situation?
9. What interests do you share?
10. Do you constantly have things to talk about or do you find yourselves spending silent hours together?

PART VI

TAKING OFF THE MASK:
MEN IN TRANSITION

Rather than love, than money, than fame, give me truth.
                                    —Henry David Thoreau

CONCLUSION

For more than ten years, this study has been a major part of my professional life. As I have traveled around the country listening to men talk about their inner worlds, I have come to believe that the myths we use to describe and define men are, for the most part, invalid. When men wear their masks, they are wearing the masks of male mythology. When these same men take their masks off, they show us who they really are: searching, vulnerable, excited, thoughtful, growing human beings.

Men have made great strides and changes over the past decade. If I were writing this conclusion five years ago, I would not be writing with such hope and optimism. The changes men are making in their personal and professional lives surpass anything I ever imagined possible. Contrary to Shere Hite's diatribe against men, I find many willing to talk about what they think and how they feel. I see men reaching out in the hope of understanding others and themselves better.

Five years ago, for men to succeed they had to play by the rules, surrendering freedom and control over their work life. Today, many corporations encourage entrepreneurial traits in their executives. Five years ago, executives ran from their work and personal problems for they felt it was a sign of weakness to admit they had a problem. Today, I am often asked to consult with companies where the executives realize they need to change but don't know how.

I would have never imagined senior executives hiring me to determine what they were doing wrong in managing and leading their divisions or companies. Now they want that feedback. They want to know how to improve. And they are receptive to my comments as well as those of their employees. In some respects, they are asking me and their employees to help them take off their masks, to expose flaws previously concealed behind armors of positional power and title.

And when they hear the truth, they respond quite favorably. That doesn't mean they don't feel hurt and embarrassed when certain weaknesses are exposed. But they accept them as part of their humanness, which, in turn, makes their employees feel accepted for who they are. It is impossible for these executives to be accepting of others' mistakes if they can't accept their own. The ones who have no idea what their inner world is all about are the ones who project their own confusion and discontentment onto others. On the other hand, I have found those executives who have developed a respect and love for themselves are able to genuinely respect and love others. These are the men capable of leading others to achieve both personal and professional success.

It is important to note that my thinking is contrary to the assumption underlying the thinking of Luther and Calvin and also that of Kant and Freud, which is: Selfishness is identical with self-love. To love others is a virtue, to love oneself is a sin. Furthermore, love for others and love for oneself are mutually exclusive.

And I mention this for a very specific reason: many men I interviewed have been indoctrinated with thoughts along the same lines. I think there has always been a parenthetical statement following one of the Ten Commandments: Love thy neighbor (instead of thyself).

I am more inclined to agree with Erich Fromm, the noted psychoanalyst, who, in his book *Escape from Freedom*, states, "if he can only 'love' others, he cannot love at all."[1]

The men who will lead us through the next decade and into the next century are men who live balanced lives. They are men who value marriage and relationships, handling interpersonal situations with ease and confidence. They are men who have worked through their need to be liked by learning to like themselves. They are men who enjoy watching others explore and grow. As leaders, they are concerned about creating an environment where others feel comfortable to reach their own decisions, to take risks, to experiment, to learn and to change.

The men who speak out in this book have resolved their own quiet desperation by facing their inner truth. For most of these men, contentment and self-esteem did not come easily. It took time, and often longer than they desired. But the results were worth every second of pain and conflict they experienced. These men have tried out new ways of being, and in doing so serve as role models for other men. They have created possibilities that many men would never have dreamed about.

By taking off their masks and divulging their inner world, these men offer comfort to others that they are not alone with their feeling. My hope is that the men whose stories are told in *Quiet Desperation* inspire you, the reader, to reflect on your own values, behavior and needs. I hope this helps you to find your own answers and to define what is important to you and you alone.